Live Well in
IRELAND

HOW TO RELOCATE, RETIRE, AND INCREASE YOUR STANDARD OF LIVING

STEENIE HARVEY

John Muir Publications
Santa Fe, New Mexico

Acknowledgments

I wish to thank the many people who gave me their time and helped in providing such a wealth of information. Too many to mention individually, but a special tribute to Finn's of Claremorris for the guided tour of Mayo properties; John Kerr for the trip around Clonakilty; the ever-helpful Mary Heaslip in Galway; and Vincent and all his staff at Egan's in Boyle.

Thanks also to all the government departments and tourist offices in Ireland. And to Brenda Weir of *Inside Ireland* magazine, Barbara Periello and the gang at Discovery Tours, and Joan of the Irish-American Society.

A huge bouquet to everybody at John Muir and especially my editor, Jill Metzler, who always managed to light up the crooked path. Jill, you're a star!

Finally, heartfelt thanks to my husband Michael. Not just for your wonderful photographs and stalwart encouragement, but for always being there.

John Muir Publications, P.O. Box 613, Santa Fe, New Mexico 87504

Printed in the United States of America.
First edition. First printing September 1999.

ISSN 1523-0732
ISBN 1-56261-427-4

Editors: Ellen Cavalli, Jill Metzler
Graphics Editor: Heather Pool
Production: Marie J.T. Vigil
Cover Design: Marie J.T. Vigil
Design: Marie J.T. Vigil
Typesetting: Laurel Avery
Map Style Development: Mike Hermann—Purple Lizard Maps
Printing: Publishers Press
All interior photos ©Michael Harvey
Front cover photo: ©Michael Harvey (Schull, county Cork))
Back cover photos: *vertical*—©Michael Harvey (Grafton St., Dublin)
　　　　　　　　　horizontal—©Michael Harvey (Killary Harbor)

Distributed to the book trade by
Publishers Group West
Berkeley, California

While the author and publisher have made every effort to provide accurate, up-to-date information, they accept no responsibility for loss, injury, or inconvenience sustained by any person using this book.

Contents

Welcome to Ireland

Wrapped in a soft green cloak of ancient memories, Ireland is one of the most beautiful and fascinating small countries in the world. Cast adrift in the Atlantic Ocean to the west of Britain, this jewel of an island has become one of Europe's most desirable addresses for those wishing to swap the stresses of city life for old-fashioned rural bliss.

The renowned Irish welcome has never depended on the size of a person's bank balance, and whether you hope to rent or buy a property, it's easy to acquire residency here. Maybe your idea of heaven is a little white-washed cottage; maybe it's a thatched farmhouse or even an ivy-clad Georgian mansion. A pretty bungalow with ocean views? A centuries-old castle? Somewhere there's a dream home waiting.

But why does Ireland exert such a pull on the imagination? After all, most people realize it's a divided island, and that the easy-going south—the Republic of Ireland—has a grim-faced neighbor called Northern Ireland. And here's another puzzle—anyplace that's called "the Emerald Isle" certainly didn't get all those lush green meadows through baking blue skies and unlimited sunshine. So what *does* make Ireland so special?

Most expatriates are enticed here for many of the same reasons as holidaymakers—Ireland's unique amalgam of storybook scenery coupled with space, safe streets, and a far more gentle way of life. Along with an absorbing tangle of history, it also offers up colorful festivals and curious traditions. What's more, its vibrant culture of music, dance, and poetry remains wonderfully intact and accessible to everybody. The country is so proud of its literary and cultural heritage that resident writers, artists, and musicians are allowed generous tax breaks to promote creativity. Here you're never considered too young or too old to learn to play the fiddle, take up painting, or write a masterpiece.

In our polluted world, the notion of a clean, green environment is hard to resist. Europe's industrial revolution hardly touched provincial Ireland. Between the bright lights of Dublin and the Atlantic's fossil shores, much of the country remains pleasingly rural, a pastoral haven of small farmsteads, quiet lanes, and rolling pasturelands. Particularly in the wilder reaches of the west, old-fashioned ways stubbornly survive, with many communities clinging like limpets to the patterns that departed from neighboring European countries generations ago.

Here you're never considered too young or too old to learn to play the fiddle, take up painting, or write a masterpiece.

Tradition is part and parcel of everyday life, not a tourist sideshow laid on by the heritage industry. Turf, the brown slabs of winter fuel, is still hand-cut from the bogs in many parts of Connemara. Some fishermen continue to put to sea in currachs, fragile hide-bound rowing boats that have been used since Celtic times. Visit a horse-fair such as Ballinasloe and you'll see deals conducted in old-fashioned style—with spits, handshakes, and the return of "luck money."

Yet the great paradox is that Ireland is also part of the new Europe, a modern country with good hospitals and top-class restaurants. Its capital, Dublin, is no stuffy museum-piece city but a place where you'll now find cybercafés and a club scene, as well as all that renowned Georgian architecture, traditional theater, and legendary pub crawls. And, if you enjoy outdoor pursuits, there's plenty to keep you busy. The enviable array of activities includes sailing, hill-walking, fishing, and riding to hounds (fox hunting), not to mention golfing at more than 350 superb courses. And although many of you may take a dim view of blasting our furry and feathered friends to kingdom come, shooting is also a tremendously popular country pursuit.

Most Irish people enjoy good living standards; the economy is in great shape, combining high growth with low inflation. Rather than laboring in smokestack industries, many of the country's young and educated workforce are employed in pharmaceuticals, telecommunications, and computers. Your new Irish neighbors are just as likely to be working at the cutting edge of technology as tending sheep and cattle!

In contrast to many Irish home-buyers, foreigners tend to want to escape the cityscape world of the workplace. Cities are fine for shopping trips, but most newcomers have a craving for nostalgia, preferring to seek out the quintessential Ireland of small towns and villages where everybody knows their neighbors. What they yearn for is a kind of Gaelic version of paradise, a picture-postcard country where the traffic is only a faint hum in the distance and timeless villages huddle below a backdrop of misty blue mountains. Thankfully that paradise is still pretty much intact.

It's impossible to pinpoint any one county as being *the* place to head for. The western seaboard is a rugged patchwork of loughs, mountains, and offshore islands that's just as spine-tingling and heart-wrenchingly beautiful as imagination always promised. Alternatively you may prefer the lesser-known coastal villages of Ireland's sunnier southeast corner or the lush river valleys of an inland county such as Kilkenny.

Color is splashed everywhere: Donegal's village cottages sparkle white, while those in West Cork are as bright and varied as a child's paintbox. Flowers refuse to be confined tidily to gardens, and Kerry's seasonal colorfest ranges from the pink springtime blaze of wild rhododendrons to summertime's hedgerows of crimson fuchsia flowers, charmingly known in the old Irish language as *Deora Dé* (the tears of God). You don't need a botany degree to appreciate a stroll along the crooked trackways of Clare's Burren region, a stony wilderness that blooms into a rock garden of orchids, gentians, and

Foreign residents often seek quiet, small-town homesteads.

other rare wildflowers each spring. Just as beguiling for ramblers are the crescent-moon coves of the far west, solitary golden-sand beaches where you're far more likely to encounter families of seals and otters than regiments of sunbathers armed with noisy boom-boxes and mobile phones.

Complementing all the attractions for the eye is balm for the soul. The rich layer-cake of Irish myth and tradition is just one feast that awaits. The call of the past is another. Laced with pilgrim paths, waymarked with

Quiz: Twenty Teasers

1. **The Republic of Ireland's flag is** a) A gold harp on a green background. b) A gold shamrock on a green background. c) A tricolor of green, white, and orange bands.
2. **What should you do with a crubeen?** a) Eat it. b) Wear it. c) Show it to your doctor.
3. **Which figure appears on an IR£10 banknote?** a) St. Patrick. b) W.B. Yeats. c) James Joyce.
4. **What's a pishogue?** a) A month-old piglet. b) A spade for digging turf. c) A fairy spell.
5. **Size-wise, which is Ireland's largest county?** a) Dublin. b) Cork. c) Galway.
6. **What can be heard in Dáil Éireann?** a) Political debate. b) Opera music. c) Silence.
7. **Roddy Doyle and Maeve Binchy are** a) Novelists. b) Musicians. c) Politicians.
8. **What's a sheila-na-gig?** a) A spinning wheel. b) A pagan fertility symbol. c) A pony trap.
9. **Which American directed _The Quiet Man_?** a) Steven Spielberg. b) Francis Ford Coppola. c) John Huston.
10. **Who is Ireland's president?** a) Mary McAleese. b) Mary Robinson. c) Bertie Ahern.
11. **What color are Irish mailboxes?** a) Red. b) Yellow. c) Green.

countless historical remains, Ireland once shimmered at the very edge of medieval Christendom. This remote island outpost of saints and scholars was where the maps ran out and the known world ended.

For anyone with even a smidgen of romance in the soul, the allure of long ago is thoroughly irresistible. The early Irish bequeathed an incomparably rich legacy—not just of ornately carved crosses and high round towers, but a huge trove of folklore, manuscript illumination, and gold and

12. **What's a Ban Garda?** a) A sticky tea-bread. b) A female police officer. c) A blanket ban on immoral publications.
13. **Which animal appears on a five-pence coin?** a) A stag. b) A bull. c) A cat.
14. **Where are the Cliffs of Moher?** a) Clare. b) Kerry. c) Donegal.
15. **The Irish place name cnoc means** a) Fortress. b) Church. c) Hill.
16. **How do you pronounce "lough," the usual word for an Irish lake?** a) Luff. b) Low. c) Lock.
17. **Why would you go into a turf accountant's office?** a) To buy turf. b) To place a bet. c) To buy a horse.
18. **When was the Battle of the Boyne?** a) 1690. b) 1916. c) 1140.
19. **The Romans called Ireland "Hibernia." Hibernia means** a) Land of Winter. b) Land of Water. c) Land of Dreams.
20. **In Irish, what's a Meiriceánach?** a) A mercenary. b) An American. c) A missionary.

Answers:
1-c; 2-a; 3-c; 4-c; 5-b; 6-a; 7-a; 8-b; 9-c; 10-a; 11-c; 12-b; 13-b; 14-a; 15-c; 16-c; 17-b; 18-a; 19-a; 20-b.

Score:
16–20 Clever clogs! You've been here before, haven't you? 10–16 Well done! You obviously have a love for all things Irish. 5–10 Ah well, everyone admires a trier! Under 5 Hmm. I'd like to be in the doctor's surgery whe you show him your crubeen. (It's a pig's trotter!)

**Small ports like this one in Schull, county Cork,
prove to be great places to retire.**

silver craftsmanship. Celtic metalsmiths produced sumptuous treasures,
often decorated with enamel-stylized animals and studded with amber and
rock crystal. Masterpieces such as the Tara Brooch and Ardagh Chalice
have never been equaled, let alone surpassed.

Ever yearned to slip through a crack in time and connect with the
long-gone world of myth and magic? Countless localities resonate with
even older messages than those left by the scholarly Celtic monks who
darkened the Druidic balefires with the beacon of Christianity. Ireland is a
land with a thoroughly pagan past, a twilight realm of mysterious stone
circles, hollow hills, and prehistoric earthen burial mounds known as "fairy
raths." Every mirror-bright lough and green-cloaked mountain seems
spellbound by enchantments; listen hard and the westerly winds still carry
the fading whisper of otherworldly voices.

The midsummer bonfires of St. John's Eve are but a continuation of
the ancient fires lit in honor of the goddess Danu. Hallowe'en originates
from the great feast of *Samhain*, when the door to the Celtic otherworld
was said to creak fully open. The Garland Sunday pilgrimage to Croagh
Patrick (now a holy mountain but once a pagan sun sanctuary) takes place
around *Lughnasa*, a Celtic feast that celebrated the onset of the harvest. So
does Kerry's Puck Fair, an age-old festival where a goat is hoisted aloft on

a platform to oversee the shenanigans. You never have to dig very far below the surface to find the pulse of Ireland's ever-present Celtic past.

The famous (or infamous) laid-back lifestyle of the Irish people is another good reason to bid farewell to the rat race. A cliché it may be, but Ireland really is one of the friendliest, safest, and most relaxing countries in which to live. It's a caring society where people are more important than profits. Hospital treatment is free; and, if you need medical attention, you'll find family doctors make house calls—even in the middle of the night.

Whether you're looking for a retirement destination, a holiday home, or a place to raise a family, it's easy to fall in love with Ireland. The clouds do sometimes leak, but contrary to rumors, we often enjoy dry days and sunshine, too. Although it remains a divided island, immense progress has been made in trying to solve the problems of Northern Ireland.

The drawbacks? Well, Ireland isn't an especially inexpensive place to live, and the cost of running a car is higher than it may be at home. And although it's still possible to buy homes for $60,000 or less, nowadays much depends upon location. Be warned that a huge prosperity gap exists between Ireland's eastern seaboard and many western communities. Dublin and its surrounding counties have benefited most from the booming economy and this translates into increased property values. House prices in these areas are now on par with other major European cities, so if you're looking for bargains it's necessary to look to rural areas.

But wherever you choose to live, you won't pay property taxes. Many of you will be able to travel around for absolutely nothing—all retirees travel free on the country's public transport systems. Seniors entitled to Irish citizenship or those receiving social-security pensions may also be able to benefit from an additional number of free health and welfare plans for older people. Who says that age doesn't have its advantages?

Although relocating to another country is always going to be a bold move, it's a blessing to know that here you won't have the constant frustration of trying to communicate in a foreign language. Well, not unless you go to live in one of the *Gaeltacht* areas where the ancient Irish language is still spoken. OK, it may take you a while to decipher the different Irish accents, but folks here *do* speak English.

Some Americans come here to enjoy new adventures. For others it often feels more like coming home. Largely due to the tragic famine years of the last century and the resulting Irish diaspora, it's estimated that around 70 million people throughout the world have what you might call emerald-green blood coursing through their veins. But that doesn't mean you need Irish ancestry to make friends and appreciate the quality of life here. Whatever your own ancestral background, you'll certainly find the phrase *Céad Míle Fáilte* (a hundred thousand welcomes) applies to you, too.

An Emerald Overview

What makes Ireland tick? This chapter aims to tell you something about the places and faces—the land, its climate, its people, and their civil structures and social lifestyle.

The Land

Comprising a total area of 84,421 square kilometers (52,763 miles), Ireland lies in the Atlantic Ocean at the extreme edge of northwestern Europe. If numbers mean nothing to you, imagine the island as being a little larger than West Virginia. A highland fringe of hills and mountains hems the interior of fertile rolling plains, loughs, and river valleys: The western Atlantic Coast is especially inviting with sandy coves tucked away between cliffs and rocky headlands. Hills march in an almost continuous chain from Donegal to West Cork with the highest pinnacles clustering in the southwest. County Kerry's dramatic landscapes include Carrantuohill, at 1,038 meters Ireland's highest mountain.

Ireland's longest river is the Shannon, a 259-kilometer water highway that forms a glittering necklace of loughs as it meanders in a southwesterly direction from its source (the Shannon Pot) in county Cavan. Other notable rivers include the Liffey, which runs through Dublin, and the Lee, in Cork. In the northeast, the banks of the Boyne River witnessed a bloody battle between Catholic and Protestant forces in 1690.

Almost 17 percent of the country is covered by peat bogs, located mainly in the west and midlands. Peat bogs are made up of water and decayed vegetation and were formed around eight thousand to 10 thousand years ago. Two types of bogs—raised bogs and blanket bogs—provide fuel for domestic and industrial usage. Peat (or turf as it is usually called in Ireland) is mostly harvested by machine nowadays, but in some communities it continues to be cut by hand.

From its limpid loughs to its encircling seas, Ireland is a world of water. Rivers and loughs are the habitats of wild salmon, brown trout, char, eel, pike, and bream—and also the haunt of the reclusive otter that feasts upon them. Seals bask along rocky coasts and Dingle has a famous resident wild dolphin. Of Ireland's 31 species of mammals, the ones you're most likely to spot are rabbits, foxes, and badgers. Hares, stoats, and squirrels are also common; smaller species include hedgehogs, field mice, and shrews. Elusive pine martens are found in forests and the country also supports herds of red deer, notably in Kerry and Donegal. And the legend is true—there are no snakes. Ireland's amphibians are a solitary species each of toad, frog, and newt; its only reptile is the common lizard.

Some 380 species of wild birds have been recorded, with 135 breeding here. Year-round residents that feed in gardens include various types of finches and tits, blackbirds, songthrushes, and red-breasted robins. Walk by a lough and you'll often glimpse the turquoise flash of a kingfisher or a solitary gray heron flapping toward its reed-bed hideaway. Summer migrants include

Water surrounds and runs through the Emerald Isle.

swallows, swifts, and various kinds of woodland warblers; winter visitors include fieldfares from Scandinavia and white-fronted geese from Greenland (around half the world's population overwinters around Wexford). The thousands of miles of unspoiled coastline offer excellent opportunities for viewing seabirds such as cormorants, storm petrels, and puffins.

The Weather

As far as the weather is concerned, Ireland knows little about typhoons, ice storms, or killer heat waves. Influenced by the Gulf Stream, the mild maritime climate is remarkably consistent, with few extremes. Seasonal temperatures hardly vary throughout the entire country; April in Dublin feels much the same as April in Galway. Although it occasionally gets hot, it's never too hot. Winter sometimes results in a few chilly days but heavy snowfalls are rare except in mountainous areas.

The coldest months are usually January and February with mean daily air temperatures hovering between four and seven degrees Celsius (39 and 45 degrees Fahrenheit; see Appendix for metric conversion table). July and August tend to be warmest: 14 to 16 degrees Celsius on average, though the mercury has risen to 30 degrees on rare occasions. May and June usually produce the most sunshine, averaging five to seven hours of cloudless skies per day.

The driest months are April, May, and June, but rainfall levels should not be underestimated. The west's picture-postcard landscapes get it in bucketfuls, and you may find yourself opening an umbrella on as many as 270 days of the year. The likeliest place to escape a drenching is the southeast, where cloudbursts may only produce an annual 750 millimeters (30 inches; see appendix for metric conversion table). In low-lying midland areas, average rainfall usually amounts to between 800 and 1,200 millimeters. Parts of the west regularly receive an annual 1,500 millimeters, while the mountainous southwest often experiences a monsoon-like 2,000 millimeters or more.

The People

The Republic's population stands at 3.62 million with 41 percent under the age of 25. Over a third live in the Greater Dublin area, the boundaries of which encroach further into the countryside with each passing year. Census figures (1998) for principal cities break down as follows: Dublin: 953,000; Cork: 180,000; Limerick: 79,000; Galway: 57,000; and Waterford: 44,000. Urban households account for 56 percent of the population; the remaining 44 percent are rural households, of which 16 percent are family farms.

The last census delivered some curious additional statistics. If you're seeking a partner for instance, head to Maynooth in county Kildare where 53 percent of the adult population are singletons. In the country as a whole, only 49 percent of citizens of marriageable age have actually tied the knot. Galway City is another place where over half the population remains in unwedded bliss. Although Ireland has long tended toward late marriages, it's a sign of changing times that around a quarter of all births are now to single mothers. The birth rate, which has been falling since the 1980s, also indicates a rebellion against traditional values: The average number of children per family is now only 1.8.

Steeped in ancient values, this truly is a land of holy wells, visions, moving statues, and pilgrim paths.

Ninety-three percent of citizens residing in the Republic were born in Ireland and three out of every four still live in the county of their birth. The remaining seven percent were mostly born in European Union (EU) member states, and only 42,000 people originate from elsewhere. People aged 65 and over account for 11 percent of the total population, with a slight majority of seniors living in rural areas. The town with the most senior citizens is Kanturk in county Cork where they constitute 22 percent of the population.

Approximately 92 percent of the Republic's population is Roman Catholic. Steeped in ancient values, this truly is a land of holy wells, visions, moving statues, and pilgrim paths. Thousands of people annually climb to the summit of Croagh Patrick, Ireland's "holy mountain" on the shores of county Mayo. Another famous and popular pilgrimage is to St. Patrick's Purgatory in county Donegal where the ritual involves fasting, sleeplessness, and going barefoot.

Although church attendance remains high in rural areas, recent scandals have meant that the Catholic hierarchy no longer commands the same unquestioning respect and political influence as in past decades. And although the Church remains closely involved in the health and education services, Ireland's latest generation is less awed by authority.

Of Ireland's minority faiths, the largest grouping is the Protestant religion, which numbers around 3 percent. Church of Ireland members account for 2.35 percent of the population, Presbyterians .37 percent, and Methodists .14 percent. There are also small communities of Muslims (.11 percent), Jehovah's Witnesses (.1 percent), and Jews (.04 percent). In Northern Ireland, the religious breakdown is approximately 60-percent Protestant and 40-percent Catholic.

Ireland's biggest export used to be its people. That's no longer true: The

**These pilgrims to St. Patrick's Purgatory in county
Donegal are an example of Ireland's ancient faith.**

recent economic boom has meant more people are immigrating to Ireland
rather than leaving its shores. Even so, Ireland remains one of the EU's
most homogenous countries with a 99-percent white populace. Some older
people in rural areas have never met anyone with a different colored skin.

Despite the Irish reputation for friendliness, racial prejudice occasionally surfaces. In recent years, certain marginalized peoples from throughout
the world have targeted Ireland as a country with fairly lax asylum laws.
Often arriving hidden in container lorries, around seven thousand refugees
have managed to reach Ireland on ferries from France. Most originate from
Eastern Europe, Turkey, and sub-Saharan Africa.

This has led to resentments, particularly against Romanian gypsies, who
are regarded as economic migrants rather than genuine refugees. Some critics
feel it's wrong that such migrants are readily found accommodation while little is done for homeless Irish people. African refugees have also reported
incidents of racial abuse, especially in inner-city Dublin. For refugees who do
encounter racism, it must seem ironic that so many past generations of Irish
people emigrated themselves to create better lives overseas.

Ireland also has its own marginalized section of society—the tinkers, or
traveling people, as they prefer to be called. There are around 10,800 travelers within the country, and very few "settled" Irish people have a good

word to say about them. Prejudice runs high, and whether justified or not, any outbreak of petty crime is invariably put down to tinkers. Journeying between halting sites and litter-strewn roadside rest stops, few tinkers wander the roads in horse-drawn caravans any longer. The barrel-shaped Romany *vado* wagons have long since been replaced by modern, unromantic trailer homes.

Some say the tinkers are descended from orphans cast out on the roads during the nineteenth century's Great Famine; others claim they share distant kinship with European gypsies. Living in close knit communities who still produce large families, the travelers' average life span is shockingly low: Census figures suggest only 1 percent of such travelers can expect to live longer than the age of 65. Tinkers once made a living by tinsmithing and horse-dealing, yet while they still congregate at horse fairs, they no longer find much business mending the pots and pans of housewives. Most menfolk now deal in scrap metal and used car parts, and it's not uncommon to see traveler children begging. At festivals, some women make money by telling fortunes.

Education

Education within the Republic of Ireland is compulsory between the ages of 6 and 15. While schooling is free, the cost of books and most extracurricular activities is not, though poorer families do receive book grants and allowances for school uniforms. Until around the age of 12, most children attend National Schools. Serving about 500,000 children, the primary system incorporates 3,200 mainstream schools staffed by around 20,000 teachers. In Gaeltacht areas, the entire curriculum (excluding English and foreign language lessons) is conducted in Irish.

Second-level education consists of a three-year Junior Cycle followed by a two or three-year Senior Cycle. Most post-primary schools are run by religious organizations or are vocational schools with boards of governors. Over 95 percent of funding is met by the State, but again, students' families pay for books and extras. There are currently 370,000 students being educated at a total of 775 publicly aided schools.

Going to college or university depends on how well students do in the Leaving Certificate exam, which they take at the age of 17 or 18. College placements are allocated on a points system and competition is fierce, particularly for openings at prestigious universities such as Dublin's Trinity College. With tuition fees having recently been abolished, college has become a lot more accessible: around 90,000 students are now enrolled. However, putting your kids through college is still an expensive business as student maintenance grants are means-tested against parental income.

Culinary Delights

Herb-encrusted Connemara lamb and wild asparagus; *goujons* of monkfish served in olives and oranges; a fricassée of clams, shrimps, scallops, and mussels along with organic artichokes in a herb sauce. All sound delicious, but so do venison pate and roast Barberry duck with turnip buttons and sautéed foie gras in a raspberry-vinegar *jus.* Or should you go for baked rock oysters with crunchy samphire followed by turbot garnished with shrimp and leeks in a wine and lobster butter sauce?

Irish cuisine has emerged from the Dark Ages with top restaurants and country house hotels now producing a mouthwatering range of innovative dishes based on fresh local produce. Even in simpler seaside restaurants, seafood is almost always guaranteed to be a joy. Between sea fish and shellfish, the number of edible species netted off Ireland's coast amounts to well over 60. Although the country is renowned for salmon, the annual fishing catch of 340,000 tons also includes cod, haddock, plaice, and sole, as well as unusual fish such as gurnard and John Dory. For a simple lunch, nothing beats a salad with a serving of smoked mackerel or rollmopp herrings—coiled silvery slivers of pickled herring fillets that soak up their vinegary juices like a mop soaks up water. Follow up your fishy lunchtime treat with a plate of scrumptiously fresh Wexford strawberries.

Or with, perhaps, some treacly brown soda bread with farmhouse goat's cheese. The country larder delivers tasty meat, poultry, vegetables, and dairy produce—what's created from the original ingredients is up to you. At least in rural areas, most Irish families still prefer good plain cooking of the meat-and-two-veg variety with the pig, potato, and cabbage being staple items. One popular family dish is Irish stew in which neck of lamb, onions, carrots, and potatoes are gently simmered together. At Christmastime, butcher shops are unusually aromatic with the scent of cloves, nutmeg, and other spices that accompany joints of spiced beef. This traditional meal is often complemented by roast potatoes and a dish of apples and red cabbage.

Most Irish food items will be familiar to you, but even those that aren't, such as ice cream flavored with *dulsk* (seaweed), often are better than they sound. However, if you have a queasy stomach, avoid the following: *crubeens* are pigs' trotters, often jokingly tagged as "low-mileage"; black pudding appears on breakfast menus and isn't a delicious concoction of black currants and chocolate (this pudding is made from congealed pig's blood, studded with fat and encased in a sausage), *drisheen*, a similar sausage, is made from sheep's blood. Other foods with curious names are rather more tempting: *Boxty* is a potato pancake, usually fried with bacon, eggs, and sausage; *colcannon* is a tasty winter supper dish of mashed potatoes, onions, and leftover cabbage, cooked in butter and milk; and *barm brack* is a chewy, spiced tea-bread, traditionally baked on Hallowe'en.

Irish beers and whiskeys are afforded a status that other countries usually reserve for wine. Creamy-topped stout is a black beer—in addition to the famous Guinness brand, try weighing the merits of Murphy's and Beamish. Harp lager is sold in most pubs as is a British-style bitter called Smithwicks (pronounced "Smithicks" without the "w"). Popular brands of Irish whiskey are Jameson's, Paddy, Powers, and Blackbush. The notorious *poitín* is illicitly distilled moonshine liquor, often made from potatoes. Because production is illegal, *poitín* is only likely to be available from "a man who knows the cousin of a man who knows."

Crime and Safety

Crime and personal-safety issues are important considerations when contemplating relocation. How many murders were there in your own hometown or city last year? In 1998 there were only 39 murders committed in the entire Irish Republic. But although Ireland's crime rate is one of the lowest in the European Union, Dublin does have drug problems. Addicts require funds—and aren't too fussy about who provides them. Just as you would in any city, lock your car and keep an eye open for pickpockets, bag snatchers, and other shady characters.

In rural areas, the crime problem is minimal. Leaf through the provincial papers and you'll see that the "criminals" who've appeared in court are likely to be speeding motorists, the odd feuding neighbors, and pub landlords who've been caught serving drinks at three o'clock in the morning (or, indeed, their customers—it is actually an offense to be "found" on licensed premises after closing time).

Politics

In 1920, Britain's Government of Ireland Act partitioned Ireland. Understanding how to refer to the two different parts of the island can be baffling. Over 75 percent (70,282 square kilometers) of the landmass forms the Republic of Ireland (southern Ireland). *Live Well in Ireland* focuses on the Republic, and its residents usually call it "Ireland." Official documents often refer to the Republic as "the State." You've probably also seen the word *Éire*. This, the Irish-language title for the island of Ireland, is rarely used in everyday speech. Éire is normally restricted to texts in the Irish language.

Before plunging into the morass of the Republic's politics, it's worth clarifying the situation in neighboring Northern Ireland. Often referred to by its citizens as "the Province," it's part of the UK (United Kingdom of Great Britain and Northern Ireland). Although many people regard its problems as solely sectarian, recent struggles have been about political power. The majority of Northern Ireland Protestants vote the Unionist ticket and both David Trimble's Ulster Unionist Party (UUP) and Ian Paisley's Democratic Unionist Party (DUP) want to maintain strong links with Britain and its monarchy. Most Catholics vote for Nationalist or Republican parties such as John Hume's SDLP or Sinn Féin, which both support the concept of a united Ireland.

Until the formation of the new Northern Ireland Assembly in 1998, which devolved greater power to local politicians, the Province came under Westminster's jurisdiction. Its legal and political framework is separate from that of the Irish Republic, and Queen Elizabeth II is head of state. Although Northern Ireland's "Troubles" have never really affected the economy or day-to-day lives of Irish people in the south, happenings across the border have always been headline news. When the Irish Republic's constitution was drawn up, it laid claim to the entire island of Ireland—that didn't help to foster good relations with the North's Unionist majority. However, in a referendum following 1998's Good Friday Agreement between Northern Ireland's Unionists and Nationalists, the Republic's citizens voted by an overwhelming majority to rescind constitutional claims to their neighbors' territory. Sadly the bombing of the Northern Ireland town of Omagh in August 1998 indicated the peace process still has a way to go.

To further muddy the waters, the island of Ireland is divided into the same four provinces as before Partition. Roughly corresponding to north, south, east, and west, these provinces are called Ulster, Munster, Leinster, and Connacht. Although Ulster is often used as a synonym for Northern Ireland, parts of this province, such as counties Donegal, Cavan, and Monaghan, lie within the Republic's territory.

The four provinces are subdivided into 32 counties: 26 in the Republic of Ireland and 6 in Northern Ireland. The Republic's largest county is Cork; the smallest is Louth. The capital of the Irish Republic is Dublin, which is also the country's main commercial port. Northern Ireland's principal city is Belfast.

With a legal system based on the Constitution of 1937, the Republic of Ireland is a parliamentary democracy. The Oireachtas, or national parliament, consists of the office of the president along with a House of Representatives (Dáil Éireann) and Senate (Seanad Éireann). The main political power rests with Dáil Éireann, whose 166 members are elected by the people for a maximum term of five years. Elected members to the Dáil are called Teachtaí Dála (TDs). The prime minister holds the title An Taoiseach.

The Republic's 26 counties are divided into 41 Dáil constituencies, each returning between three and five TDs. Known as proportional representation by single transferable vote (PRSTV), the voting method is fairly complicated and based on a quota system.

The electoral system invariably returns coalition governments. Under Taoiseach Bertie Ahern, the present government is a power-sharing arrangement between the centrist Fianna Fáil party, the smaller but more right-wing Progressive Democrats, and various Independents. Led by John Bruton, the previous administration (the Rainbow Coalition) consisted of some curious bedfellows: the right-of-center Fine Gael party, the soft-left Labour Party, and the solidly socialistic Democratic Left. As Fianna Fáil or Fine Gael always make up the largest party in whatever coalition is formed, the governance of the country remains on a fairly even keel with few major policy swings. Other political parties attracting limited amounts of support within the Republic include Sinn Féin, the Workers' Party, and the Green Party.

The Seanad's 60 senators are either nominated directly by the Taoiseach or indirectly from within five panels with particular expertise. More a talking-shop than a body with political clout, the Seanad can, however, petition the president to refuse to sign a bill until the matter is put before the people in a referendum. No bill can become law without the president's signature.

Like TDs, the president (an Uachtarán) is elected by popular vote. The current incumbent is Mary McAleese, who followed on from Mary Robinson. The president's term of office is seven years and he or she can only stand for reelection once. Although the office is largely ceremonial, the president takes on the role of guardian of the constitution, which lays down the fundamental rights of citizens.

Guaranteeing a swathe of rights, the constitution covers personal rights, the family, education, private property, and religion. Amendments can only take place if the people give their say-so in a referendum. Social change recently resulted in one important amendment: that of allowing divorce through the Irish courts. And while the rights of the unborn child were designed to be protected by the constitution, abortion remains a thorny issue. In the early 1990s, a case in which a young rape victim was prevented by the courts from traveling to Britain for an abortion resulted in a hotly contested public debate. Were Irish women to be subjected to pregnancy tests at ports and airports before being given leave to travel? In the subsequent 1992 referendum, the people voted to clarify the matter by allowing all citizens freedom of movement. Even so, abortion for any reason whatsoever (including rape, incest, or evidence of a severely malformed fetus) remains outlawed.

On the defense front, Ireland isn't a member of NATO and, like Switzerland, maintains a neutral stance. Recruitment to the defense forces is on a voluntary basis. Of the 11,500 members of the permanent defense force, around 9,500 men and women serve in the army, 1,000 in the air corps, and 1,000 in the naval service.

It's not unusual to see soldiers guarding bank premises when large amounts of cash are being transferred. As well as defending the State against any foreign aggression, another of the army's duties is to aid the civil powers. The Gardaí (police) are a mainly unarmed force and bank security was increased following a number of IRA bank raids during the 1970s.

Around eight hundred army personnel are also active in UN peace-keeping missions. Their involvement ranges from monitoring and observation duties to a humanitarian role. The air corps' brief includes search-and-rescue operations, air ambulance missions, and fishery protection patrols. The naval service is also involved in fishery protection.

Money

Now that you've got your head around the island's political geography, a word about the currency. Until 2002, when the new Euro currency takes over, you'll be using the punt: the Irish pound. Each punt is divided into 100 pence and, like the British pound sterling, carries the £ sign. The largest coin is worth one punt; smaller coins come in values of 50p (pence), 20p, 10p, 5p, 2p and 1p. Irish banknotes come in denominations of IR£100, IR£50, IR£20, IR£10, and IR£5. However, if you travel across the border you'll need to change your punts into pounds sterling.

Although the setting of interest rates is now decided by the European Central Bank, any plans for European federalism still have a long way to go. Despite Europe's monetary marriage, Irish politicians aren't entirely toothless when it comes to fiscal policies. For example, the finance minister still juggles the country's budget.

Ireland's History

I reland's history has been shaped by invasions. Has any other country been battled over so fiercely or so long? Headhunting Celts were followed by marauding Vikings; land-hungry Anglo-Norman knights by armies of the British Crown. For good or ill, each successive wave of invaders left its mark.

Celtic Ireland

One of Ireland's most fascinating historical chapters is that of those early invaders, the Celts. Evoking dreams of a glorious heritage, their legacy never fails to kindle the imagination. Yet much of what we *think* we know about the Celts is based on guesswork. Theirs was an oral tradition and they left no written records.

It's generally presumed they were Iron Age warrior tribes from central Europe who migrated northwest, reaching Ireland around 500 B.C. However, folklore clouds the issue with some tales having the Celts originating from Spain. Wackier myths moot the theory that Ireland's Celtic forebears sprang from doomed Atlantis whose people had migrated to Mediterranean and Middle Eastern regions several millennia before.

Like their origins, the customs of Ireland's early Celts are also shrouded in historical mist. Their stories weren't recorded until centuries later, when Christianity had eclipsed the old pagan beliefs. What is indisputable is that they brought with them a new language, a tremendous appetite for feasting and drinking, and an ability to fashion native gold into highly decorative jewelry and weapons. Their bloodthirsty Earth gods took their place in the existing pantheon of Irish deities, becoming part of the mysterious "Otherworld."

Tantalizing glimpses of that Otherworld appear in folklore, place names, and symbolic carvings such as the lasciviously grinning fertility figures known as *sheila-na-gigs.* The Celts had a great veneration for the forces of nature, and other stone figures may portray the guardian spirits of wells, rivers, and sacred trees. One winter afternoon, in an overgrown graveyard on Fermanagh's Boa Island, I gazed upon the implacable features of a two-faced January God. Definitely no Christian figure, his exaggerated eyes stared both forward into the realm of men and backward into some unknown twilight. It was an uncanny sensation, realizing that this cross-limbed idol had watched the sun go down long before St. Patrick ever reached these shores.

> *Despite Christian teachings, Celtic magic and mystery hadn't fled Ireland's landscape.*

Although the observations of classical writers relate only to mainland Europe, Ireland's Celts probably had customs similar to their Continental

IRELAND'S PREHISTORY

Ireland's turbulent tale begins soon after the Ice Age, some 10 thousand years ago. The first inhabitants, who may have come via Scotland, were hunter-gatherers who left little evidence of their lifestyle. Only small communities developed with the arrival of neolithic tribes around 5000 B.C. Raising cattle in stonewalled fields and building hill-forts, Ireland's Stone Age farmers also practiced elaborate funerary rites. The island's thousands of neolithic sites include the chambered passage tombs at Newgrange (county Meath), mysteriously decorated with cosmic symbols.

One of Europe's most famous prehistoric centers, Newgrange existed long before the Celts invaded. When dawn breaks on the morning of the winter solstice (December 21), a pencil-thin ray of sunlight creeps along the passageway and illuminates the lightless inner chamber. On the shortest day of the northern year, was this perhaps a symbol of rebirth? Nobody knows the real explanation why Newgrange was built, but it remains a remarkable feat of Stone Age engineering.

cousins. According to Julius Caesar, their druid priests taught that souls were immortal and passed after death into another body. They also believed that all men were descended from the god of the underworld. To Irish Celts this was Donn, "the Dark One."

Common to the entire Celtic world was the Cult of the Head. Much as crucifixes represent Christianity, the Celts' foremost religious symbol was the human head. In Irish myths, heads—even when parted from the body—possessed numerous mystical powers, including the ability to sing, prophesy, tell stories, and preside over warriors' banquets. Most important of all, these grisly trophies also protected against the dangerous forces of the Otherworld. It's not only literature that suggests Celtic Ireland enthusiastically collected human heads—skulls excavated from hill-forts have shown the marks of nails where they were suspended from gateways.

The Christians and the Vikings

Ireland's Celts escaped the acquisitive clutches of the Roman Empire, but their animistic world began to disintegrate once Christianity arrived. This was a bloodless invasion and conversion came slowly. By the time St. Patrick was brought to Ireland as a slave (circa 405), most inhabitants

Dancing at Lughnasa? Stone Circle, Drombeg, county Cork

The Celtic Calendar

The Celts dated the beginning of their year from **Samhain**. Pronounced "Sow-an," this was the most important of the annual festivals. Not only did it mark the passing of the old year and the end of the grazing season, it was also a symbolic occasion of death and rebirth. Surplus livestock were brought down from mountain pastures to be slaughtered; hearth fires died and didn't blaze again until the great ritual balefires of the druids had been lit. Samhain wasn't a time to be far from home, for this was when the invisible veil between the mortal world and the Otherworld got torn asunder. Who could say what supernatural dangers lurked in the lengthening shadows? The Christian Church rechristened the feast as All Hallows, and All Hallows' Eve (October 31) lives on today as Hallowe'en.

Imbolc corresponded to February 1, St. Brigid's Day. A pastoral festival, it marked the start of the lambing season and the first lactation of the ewes. It was dedicated to the pagan fire-goddess Brigid who was associated with fertility and crafts. Made from straw, the St. Brigid's crosses often seen in Irish homes may have more of a heathen than a Christian origin.

Beltaine (pronounced Beltanny) fell on May Day. May 1 heralded the advent of summer in the Celtic lands and was a frolicsome festival of regeneration. May bushes were decorated with spring flowers to appease the spirits of the land; cattle were driven through the charmed smoke of the Beltaine bonfires to give them protection in their summer pastures.

August 1 was **Lughnasa** (pronounced Loo-nasa) and harvest home. The day was dedicated to the god Lugh, and a symbolic loaf was baked for him from the first corn. The Christian calendar transformed Lughnasa into Lammas, but it remains an auspicious day for digging up the first potatoes.

remained under the sway of pagan religions. To help foster the new faith, the early monks of what became known as the Celtic Church built places of worship on sites sacred to the druids: in woodland groves or beside healing springs and wells. One pagan goddess, Brigid, even found herself Christianized and elevated to sainthood.

By 563, monastic settlements had grown sufficiently in size and numbers to export missionaries. Columba's Hebridean foundation on Iona is well known, but other Irish monks also established centers in mainland Europe. Within Ireland itself, monastic communities at sites such as Clonmacnoise, Kildare, and Clonard became major seats of learning in a period tagged "the Golden Age." It was in such monasteries that gospels were illuminated and tales about the old heroes and gods recorded.

Despite Christian teachings, Celtic magic and mystery hadn't fled Ireland's landscape. News from the annals has showers of honey and blood raining down in the year 717. In 752, a whale came ashore bearing three teeth of solid gold, each weighing 50 ounces. The fiery ships seen in the air in 784 were perhaps a dire portent of a new invasion force. Many of the fledgling abbeys and churches were soon to be rededicated into temples to Odin; prayers and plainsong replaced by lusty drinking bouts and sagas about Valhalla and its shield-maidens.

Reminiscent of an upturned stone boat, the Gallarus Oratory in county Kerry is a beautifully preserved relic of an early Christian church.

"The wind is fierce tonight, it tosses the sea's white hair. I fear no wild Vikings sailing the main," penned one optimistic monk. But come the mighty dragon ships did. From 795, Ireland was subjected to sporadic Viking attacks and by 823 the Norsemen had rounded the coastline. Vikings craved booty like vampires crave blood, and Ireland's great rivers served as watery highways to fabulous prizes: the wealthy inland monasteries. In 842, Clonmacnoise was burnt and pillaged by a Viking named Turgesius. His wife apparently used one of the altars to give out oracles.

The Viking Age lasted until the eleventh century. Although early raiders returned to Scandinavia with their treasures, later, Norsemen began settling in Ireland, first in winter quarters and then more permanently. Alliances with local chiefs and intermarriages gave the invaders a secure position from which to establish trading posts: Dublin, Limerick, Waterford, and Wexford all have Viking origins.

Along with European trade, Ireland inherited its first coinage from the Vikings. Who knows—one day you may dig up a thousand-year-old King Sitric silver penny. And although the Celtic Church was never to recapture its glory days, many of the invaders eventually embraced Christianity; evidence of this acceptance can still be seen today. The ancient cathedral in the Shannonside town of Killaloe, for example, is home to Thorgrim's cross, which carries a blessing in Norse runic script.

The Middle Ages

For centuries, Ireland's petty kingdoms (some eighty to one hundred) had battled over territory, cattle, and women. Now control of trade meant control of wealth, and a powerful dynasty under the kingship of Brian Boru emerged. Boru set out to win high kingship and by 1011 had achieved his goal. However, "the Emperor of the Irish" didn't enjoy his lofty position for long. A Viking-aided revolt against the king ended with the Battle of Clontarf in 1014. Boru's side won, but he was killed.

With Boru's death, Ireland returned to tribal squabblings. In 1166 control of Dublin was wrested from a very aggrieved Dermot MacMurrough. MacMurrough fled to Britain in search of mercenaries to help him gain back his kingdom—a move that was to have far-reaching consequences.

Ireland's next invaders entered with the clink of chain mail and clash of broadswords. The first Anglo-Norman knights arrived in 1169 and, after recapturing MacMurrough's territories, they quickly began invading adjoining kingdoms. This was Ireland's first taste of English rule. Although nobody could have guessed it at the time, it was to endure for more than seven centuries.

As the thirteenth century progressed, the Anglo-Normans imposed themselves on about three-quarters of the land, building castles and fortified towns such as those at Limerick, Trim, and Waterford. Like the Vikings before them, many secured their position by marrying into Irish clans. But by the mid-1300s, both natives and newcomers were being terrorized by a new and very sinister invasion: bubonic plague. Carried by rats, the "Black Death" decimated around half the population—some 750,000 people. England's writ of authority shrank to a small area around Dublin that became known as "the Pale." (In case you've ever wondered, that's how the term "beyond the pale" originated.)

The Early Modern Period

Ireland's fortunes plummeted when England's Henry VIII (the one with the six wives) broke with the Catholic Church. He also declared himself king of Ireland, a title resolutely embraced by successive monarchs. Under the Tudor and Stuart dynasties of the sixteenth and seventeenth centuries, Ireland was subjected to a new kind of "invasion": colonization. These were confusing times with a dizzying array of Protestant monarchs succeeding Catholic monarchs and vice versa. Religion became a major factor in Ireland's colonization process, and previous generations of English settlers were often uprooted to make way for new royal favorites.

The seeds of Ulster's troubles were sown in 1607, when it was opened up for expansion by England's new Protestant king, James I. In an episode known as the Plantation of Ulster, it was decreed that settlers should outnumber the Irish, who mostly remained loyal to the Roman Catholic religion.

"Undertakers," new arrivals from England and Scotland who guaranteed to bring 10 Protestant families with them, were given land completely cleared of natives. "Servitors," who had served the Crown in some fashion, were allowed to retain some native labor for an increase of 50 percent on rent. Finally, any "deserving Irish" were allowed to rent land for double the normal rate. Areas remained segregated: Scots here, English there, Irish somewhere else. Around 100 thousand Protestant settlers arrived between 1610 and 1640. Unlike the Celts, Vikings, and Normans, this new batch of invaders rarely integrated.

In 1641, as the English parliament vied with its monarchy for absolute power, Ulster's native Irish took up arms. Nearly 2,000 Protestant settlers were murdered, but civil war raging in England prevented any large-scale measures against the rebels. It was 1649 before action could be taken against Ireland's unruly dispossessed.

Cromwell and the Penal Times

Retribution came courtesy of England's "Lord Protector," Oliver Cromwell, the villainous bogeyman of Irish history. With England's civil war over, his victorious Parliamentary Army set sail for Ireland. Heading an invasion force 20 thousand strong, Cromwell quickly crushed the rebellion, butchering the citizens of Drogheda and Wexford in the process. Widespread confiscation of estates was accompanied by the banishment of thousands of Irish citizens to the country's poorest lands. Like Cromwell himself, the infamous diktat of "to hell or Connacht" still arouses bitterness.

Catholicism in the form of public worship became illegal as Cromwell considered demands for the right to celebrate Mass as "abominable." Yet the Mass continued in secret, often being held in places sacred to the old Celtic religion: remote woodland glades or mountain areas where large boulders made for improvised altars. In memory of those times, annual outdoor Masses are still celebrated at many such sites today.

In 1685, after more than a century of unbroken Protestant rule, Britain and Ireland found themselves with a new Catholic king, James II. Although the contrary-minded James had quite lawfully succeeded his brother (Charles II), who died without legitimate offspring, the English establishment were strongly opposed to "Popery." They decided the best way to keep the Protestant flag flying was by deposing James and depriving his son of any succession rights. The throne was offered to a Dutchman, William of Orange. Backing his claim with force, William's troops inflicted rapid defeats on the King's loyal forces in England. The conflict moved to Ireland where the deposed monarch again lost crucial battles including the decisive Battle of the Boyne in 1690. That victory by Protestant King Billy (William of Orange) over Catholic James Stuart is still celebrated by many Ulstermen every July 12.

Even though he died nigh on 300 years ago, William of Orange's name still echoes down the centuries. An icon within Northern Ireland's Unionist culture, Dutch William appears on countless banners during the Easter-to-July marching season. It explains why Ulster Protestants are known as Orangemen and their meeting places as Orange lodges.

Penal laws for the governance of Ireland were quickly enacted. Catholics couldn't enter parliament, buy land, nor own a horse worth more than £5—nor could they marry Protestants without first converting. The purpose of the draconian legislation was to ensure a Protestant ascendancy within Ireland. It succeeded, but the Irish parliament remained subordinate to its English counterpart at Westminster: any bill of law for the governance of Ireland had to first receive approval from English politicians, much to the chagrin of the new ruling class, who were mostly descended

St. Patrick

Ireland's patron saint is popularly credited with copper-fastening Christianity in fifth-century Ireland. But although St. Patrick is a worldwide symbol of Irish identity, you may be surprised to learn that he wasn't Irish at all. In his *Confessio* (a spiritual autobiography), the saint tells us he was born in Britain, in a Roman settlement called Bannavem Taburniae. Where exactly this village was is a bit of an unsolved mystery. What is clear is that Patrick came from a wealthy family of priests and minor officials; his father, the deacon Calpurnicus, owned a villa.

Imagine coming from such a background and then finding yourself kidnapped and sold to an uncouth Irish chieftain. That's what happened to 16-year-old Patrick, who was snatched from his home by marauding pirates. Instead of continuing his studies, he was forced to tend his new master's pigs and sheep in the bitter winds of a northern winter. Patrick lived as a slave in Ireland until escaping to France, and thence home, on another pagan ship. He later returned to France and entered the priesthood. Believed to have been ordained as a bishop by the pope, he returned to Ireland as a missionary in 423, landing at Saul in Northern Ireland's County Down. There he made his first convert—a local chieftain named Díchú.

Numerous places, north and south, have links with St. Patrick. Legend tells us that he lit a paschal (Easter) fire on the Hill of Slane in county Meath as a challenge to the pagan king of Tara. He also apparently visited the Rock of Cashel in county Tipperary for a conversion ceremony where he accidentally pierced the local king's foot with his crosier. Thinking this was an important part of Christian ritual, the king suffered his pain in silence!

Both Slane and Cashel claim to be the place where St. Patrick plucked a shamrock leaf to explain the concept of the Holy Trinity. As most people know, St. Patrick's Day is March 17.

from Norman knights and Protestant settlers who had arrived in Tudor and Cromwellian times.

Toward the end of the eighteenth century, rebellion simmered once again. America's War of Independence and the French Revolution had engendered radical ideas of establishing an Irish Republic. In 1791, two years after the storming of the Bastille, the Society of United Irishmen was formed. The Society's most illustrious member was Wolfe Tone, but (somewhat ironically) the founding fathers were predominately Belfast Presbyterians—today probably the staunchest opponents of a united Ireland and Republican aims.

Wolfe Tone managed to enlist French support for his fellow Republicans and an invasion force was sent to Ireland in 1796. Yet despite all the patriot games, Ireland never experienced any glorious revolution and no aristocratic necks bowed to Madame Guillotine's kiss. Ireland's weather conspired against the plotters: Severe storms broke up the French fleet, preventing the landing.

When rebellion finally erupted in 1798, it was badly organized and speedily suppressed. Following this revolt, the London government decided the troublesome Irish were best dealt with through the union of both parliaments. Although many of Dublin's ruling class trenchantly opposed the idea, bribery won the day. Ireland's parliament voted itself out of existence and the Union came into force on January 1, 1801.

Ireland and the Union

Few Irish towns lack a street named after Daniel O'Connell, a Kerry lawyer and an important figure in Ireland's long struggle against sectarianism. In the opening decades of the nineteenth century, Irish Catholics remained in a political wilderness. Attempts to introduce Catholic emancipation were continuously blocked in London's Westminster Parliament where all Irish matters were now decided. However O'Connell's arrival on the scene gave Catholics hope of gaining some form of political representation.

O'Connell began the Catholic Association in 1823 "to further the interests of Catholics in all areas of life." Fearing a mass political party had been born, the authorities unsuccessfully attempted to indict him for incitement to rebellion. Despite the association's suppression, O'Connell was elected a member of parliament for Clare in 1828.

Because of his Catholicism, the law forbade O'Connell from taking his Westminster seat. However, the government was alarmed at the possibility of numerous democratically elected Irish Catholics seceding. Forced to counter this, the Catholic Emancipation Act was passed in 1829. The victory was not without cost. Freehold property ownership was the deciding factor as to whether citizens were entitled to a vote. Known as "the franchise qualification," the entry level of property value was immediately increased five-fold from 40 shillings to £10. As most Irish Catholics were impoverished tenant farmers who didn't own property anyway, ordinary people were consequently still denied voting rights. It was only the Catholic owners of grander properties who retained the franchise.

Even so, O'Connell was hailed as "the Liberator" and began campaigning for the repeal of the Act of Union. Huge crowds attended his rallies, which were often held on famous Irish sites. In 1843 a vast gathering took place on the Hill of Tara, the centuries-old seat of Ireland's high kings. The satirical magazine *Punch* nicknamed O'Connell "King of the Beggars," but an agitated British government made it plain the Union would be defended. When another "monster rally" was planned for Clontarf (site of Brian Boru's famous victory in 1014), the government banned the meeting, threatening to send in troops if it proceeded. Not wanting to subject his countrymen to a full-scale military invasion, O'Connell accepted the ban and the Repeal Association's campaign petered out.

Famine and the Push for Home Rule

In 1845 an old invader returned to haunt Ireland: Famine. Throughout the centuries the country had experienced disastrous harvests and widespread starvation. Crop failure in the 1740s may have killed an equivalent proportion of Ireland's populace but the Great Hunger of the 1840s was better documented and thus had a greater historical impact. The potato crop failed again in '46, '47, and '48 with horrific and devastating consequences: A million people died from hunger. Another million people were lost to disease or by emigration on the coffin ships that carried them away from their homeland forever. By 1851, Ireland's population had fallen from more than 8 million (in 1841) to a little over 6 million. The crazy thing is that Ireland continued to export food during the famine years, which may have given rise to rumors that mass starvation never happened or was greatly exaggerated. Certainly there were abundant harvests of wheat and oats, but grain crops do not thrive in Ireland's rock-strewn west, the part of the country that suffered an almost apocalyptic devastation. Here the potato really was the staple foodstuff—if the poor wanted grain then somehow they had to find the wherewithal to pay the market price for it. Very few could. Nor was there much in the way of charitable handouts, though some landlords did set up soup kitchens. However, for the people of Mayo's Achill Island, accepting famine aid brought with it the risk of excommunication and thus eternal damnation. Under the supervision of the Reverend Edward Nangle, a kind of missionary outpost was established on the island. Catholic families were indeed fed and clothed—providing they worshiped at the Church Mission Society's newly founded Protestant church and the island children attended its school.

Pro-independence activists decided the time for rhetoric alone was past. Despite the very real threat of transportation to Australia's Botany Bay, secret societies proliferated and sectarian violence became commonplace. In 1858 the Irish Republican Brotherhood was established, followed the next year in America by the "Fenian Brotherhood." Both aimed to achieve an independent republic by means of violent revolution.

The Home Government Association, founded in 1870, again signaled that the majority of Irish people yearned to follow a more peaceful route to self-determination. In Britain's (and thus Ireland's) first secret ballot election, in 1874, Alliance of Home Rule candidates won 60 percent of the Irish seats. The Alliance's leader was Charles Stewart Parnell, whose name is also honored by numerous streets within the Republic. A skillful politician, he even persuaded the Fenians to travel the parliamentary road to reform with him.

But Ireland still wasn't about to witness an invasion of democratic ideals. The passing of the Victorian Age saw Ulster's politicians uncompromisingly rejecting the notion of autonomy and a Dublin government. However, British Prime Minister Gladstone did indicate his awareness of

A poignant reminder of the famine years in Skibbereen, West Cork.

Ulster's opposition and hinted that an amendment to exclude the province from any Irish Home Rule bill was a possibility. For the first time, the specter of partition beckoned.

Scandal erupted in 1890 when it became public knowledge that Parnell was living with Kitty O'Shea, a colleague's wife. Gladstone refused to continue negotiations with someone who was "morally tainted," and the disgraced Parnell died the following year. In 1893 Gladstone successfully steered an Irish Home Rule bill through parliament, but the non-elected aristocrats of the House of Lords rejected it. A fact not entirely surprising, considering that many of them owned Irish estates.

The Twentieth Century

After the 1910 general election, the Irish National Party's 84 members held the balance of power at Westminster. However, the Ulster Unionist Party and its leader, Sir Edward Carson, still fiercely opposed any change in the status quo. When a new Irish Home Rule bill was passed by Westminster's parliament, Carson formed what was effectively a private army, the Ulster Volunteer Force (UVF).

Although the Lords again rejected the bill, delaying its implementation, Ulster sensed the times they were a-changing. And from a Unionist standpoint, not for the better. Determined to remain British at all costs, the UVF's early paramilitaries quickly acquired arms from Germany and began drilling. On the Nationalist side, the Irish Republican Brotherhood formed the Irish Volunteers.

Ireland's Home Rule bill received royal assent in 1914 but the outbreak of the First World War resulted in the knotty Irish problem once again being put on the governmental back burner. Continuously thwarted in their attempts to achieve any form of autonomy by parliamentary methods, a number of Nationalists weren't prepared to wait for British agreement any longer.

Why was Britain so reluctant to let Ireland go? Well, it has been suggested that Ireland was seen as the linchpin of that empire on which the sun proverbially never sets. Remember, in those days Dublin was the "second city" of the empire, Britain a major power, and more than a fifth of the global map was colored red. To British eyes, removing the linchpin opened up the horrendous possibility of other colonies demanding independent status.

On Easter Monday 1916, the Irish Volunteers and the smaller Irish Citizen Army finally rebelled against British rule. With a force of less than two thousand, they occupied the General Post Office and other buildings in central Dublin. Patrick Pearse, elected by the IRB as "president," emerged from the post office to declare a republic.

But the Easter Rising generated little public support and after six days of holding out against superior numbers and heavy artillery, the Volunteers surrendered. However, the British government's response soon changed popular opinion when martial law was declared, and rebel leaders were court-martialed. Fourteen faced the firing squad in May that year and many others would be shot before American pressure stopped the executions.

By now the public's general mood had changed, and Sinn Féin, a small group formed in 1905 by Arthur Griffith, began attracting support. In the 1918 general election, Sinn Féin swept the boards. Pledging not to go to Westminster, they formed the first Dáil, or independent parliament, under Eamon De Valera as president. Britain's attempt to suppress the new parliament led to more conflict. The Irish Volunteers became the Irish Republican Army (IRA) and fought a guerrilla war against British troops and police.

In today's Ireland most people shun terrorism. Yet the fact remains that violence and bloodshed served as midwives to the birth of what became known as the Irish Free State. Were the original IRA members bad guys or good guys? Terrorists or patriotic freedom fighters? It's still hotly debated whether the people of southern Ireland would have cast off the shackles of imperialism without the gunmen.

But if nationalist Ireland were to be given autonomy, what was to be done about Ulster, whose majority Protestant community insisted on remaining part of the Union? In agreement with the Ulster Unionists, British Prime Minister Lloyd George came up with new legislation— Ireland was to be divided. The 1920 Government of Ireland Act partitioned the island the following year.

Were the original IRA members bad guys or good guys?
Terrorists or patriotic freedom fighters?

Negotiations to end the war of independence in the south took place later in 1921 with Arthur Griffith and Michael Collins representing the Dáil. Offered much less than hoped for, they nevertheless signed the Anglo-Irish Treaty. An Irish Free State of 26 counties was given dominion status with 6 Ulster counties remaining British and outside the new State authority.

The British parliament's satisfaction with the deal wasn't mirrored in Dublin: Bitter divisions arose in the Dáil. Having to swear allegiance to the British monarch was an especially contentious issue, but in January 1922, the Dáil voted to accept the treaty. De Valera, trenchantly opposed, resigned. Civil war followed within months, with the country splitting into pro- and anti-treaty factions. Friends and neighbors, who had fought as comrades-in-arms against the British, now started slaughtering each other. The brutal conflict finally ended with a truce in May 1923.

Slowly, and by degrees, southern Ireland continued to break with Britain and the monarchy. In 1937 the Irish Free State declared complete independence and changed its name to Éire. Finally, on Easter Monday 1949, Éire became the newly inaugurated Irish Republic and said farewell to the British Commonwealth.

In 1972 the country elected to join the European Community, which effectively resulted in an influx of financial help from wealthier neighbors such as Germany. Not only did this set the scene for today's economic success, it gave Ireland newfound confidence. As a member state on equal terms with its European neighbors, there has been a transformation of the national psyche. Most Irish people fully embrace the European ideal—it could be that the country has at last emerged from the shadows of its ancient struggle with Britain.

People and Culture

Someone once said that the Irish are really a Mediterranean people who got stranded much further north than they should have been. It's true that most of the Irish are extremely convivial with an unflagging appetite for music and chat, but where does the blarney end and reality start? Not every Irishwoman is a red-haired beauty, wrapped in a long green cloak, wandering the hillsides with an Irish wolfhound. Nor is every Irishman a silver-tongued charmer. Hollywood movies such as *The Quiet Man*, made for a mostly American audience, still color foreign ideas about Irish identity.

You'll certainly not encounter the kind of stage Irishman who spends his days making moonshine and gazing out at the ocean muttering "Ah, Begorrah, the shores of Americay . . . ." And you'll get some strange looks if you insist on greeting people with "Top o' the morning to ye." Within Ireland itself, such phrases are mockingly dismissed as "Oirishisms" or "Paddywhackery," so please don't use them unless you want to be laughed at behind your back.

As an American, maybe you're wondering how your countrymen are regarded in Ireland. The answer is pretty favorably, but you'll have to get used to being known as a "Yank," even if you hail from deepest Alabama. Cultural stereotyping cuts both ways and, whether you have $10,000 or $100,000 in the bank, some people will inevitably describe you as "that wealthy Yank."

Although there are occasional grouses about the creeping Americanization of Irish life (the march of McDonald's, TV schedules crammed with ghastly soaps and chat shows), it's almost impossible for anyone to think too harshly of a country that acted so generously to their ancestors. Centuries of emigration mean many Irish families have American relatives somewhere in the background.

That said, Ireland is a highly politicized society and not everyone agrees with American foreign policy. When it comes to global affairs, Ireland instinctively sympathizes with the perceived underdog. President Clinton's 1998 decision to rain down missiles on a Sudanese aspirin factory and a herd of camels attracted vociferous *vox pop* condemnation.

One sure way of offending Irish sensibilities is by whining on about how things are so much bigger/faster/better in America. Do it too long and too loud and someone is likely to tell you to !@#?! off back there. Yes, many Irish people swear at the drop of a hat, and colorful cursing often comes from the most unexpected quarters. It's not usually meant to be offensive, but simply part of the conversation.

It's difficult to package the Irish lifestyle into a neat little box, but do note that most people abhor pretentiousness. Delusions of grandeur and classism do not go down well. The Republic of Ireland's rebirth as a nation-state sounded the death knell for its former masters, the Anglo-Irish Ascendancy. With their demise went any notions of perceived inferiority or forelock-tugging—most people have peasant forebears in their background and don't feel any need to apologize for it. Unlike in neighboring Britain, Irish people aren't categorized into that ludicrous system of working class, lower middle class, upper middle class, etc.

It's always a lovely day for a Guinness!

Nowadays the aristocratic "big houses" with their courtyards, coach houses, and servants' quarters belong to wealthy business people and rock stars rather than lordlings with obscure titles. As regards the other end of the lifestyle scale, the country's fairly recent history of high unemployment means no real social stigma is attached to the jobless or those receiving social-welfare payments. Ireland most definitely doesn't use that cruel American expression, "trailer-park trash."

Not everybody you'll meet will be university educated, but never presume that someone with a modest job will have a stunted intellect. In no other country have I encountered such a thirst for knowledge or interest in the wider world. I once met a housepainter whose favorite author was Dostoevsky—and he was teaching himself to read it in the original Russian.

Of course, people are people the world over, and money always creates its own kind of social gulf. For example, you'll rarely come across professionals such as doctors, lawyers, and accountants socializing with the hoi polloi who live in rented accommodation on local authority-council estates. Nor are the unemployed likely to be found at prestigious golf clubs like Mount Juliet and Druids' Glen.

IRELAND'S FLAG

Sent as a gift by French revolutionaries in 1848, the Republic of Ireland's flag is a tricolor of vertical bands: green, white, and orange. The green and the orange represent the island's Catholic and Protestant traditions. White, the color of peace, symbolizes the unity that should exist between them.

In the heavily populated areas it's patently obvious which are the "posh" sections of suburbia, but in rural areas the neighborhood mix is usually far more diverse. My neighbors include a telephone engineer, a plumber, a schoolteacher, a retired civil servant, a 90-year-old bachelor, three farming families, a florist, and a wildlife warden. Until fairly recently the former Church of Ireland rectory was owned by a German artist, but it has since been bought by two Dublin families as a weekend-holiday home.

Although it's generally agreed that most Irish families enjoy a decent standard of living with over 80 percent of households owning the accommodation in which they live, shopping for what Americans might consider to be vital consumer durables doesn't seem to be a huge priority. According to data from the Central Statistics Office, 76 percent of households have a telephone and 65 percent own a video recorder, but only 16 percent own a home computer. Dishwashers aren't exactly objects of desire either—only 18 percent of households have one. And 53 percent of Irish families feel they can live without the ubiquitous microwave oven.

Ireland is a small country and there is no distinct regional variation regarding attitudes and lifestyles. However, there is indeed something of an urban-rural divide. People tend to be more conservative on the so-called "moral issues" outside the cities and well-known tourist areas. The 1995 referendum to allow divorce was passed by a mere 9,000 votes and a majority of voters in six of Ireland's rural constituencies actually voted "No" by margins of more than 25 percent. There was no obvious regional pattern to this—the six constituencies registering the strongest opposition were scattered throughout the entire country: Cork North-West, Limerick West, Galway East, Mayo East, Cavan-Monaghan, and Longford-Roscommon. If the undiluted family values of "holy Ireland" appeal to you, you'll be cheered to know they still hold sway in these deeply traditional rural strongholds.

Whether you choose to live in urban or rural Ireland, you'll find there's much less urgency regarding time-keeping than you're probably used to. Tradesmen promise to do work on a certain day and then don't appear until a fortnight later. Letters sometimes stay unanswered, phone calls go unreturned. You may even make an appointment with a realtor and then find he's neglected to inform you that he'll be out of the office all afternoon. Of course, it's possible that you'll experience no problems whatsoever, but it's as well to be forewarned.

**Mixing music and Guinness at Cryan's Pub in
Carrick-on-Shannon, county Leitrim.**

People still count, however, and maybe the realtor didn't show because he was at a neighbor's funeral. Provincial Ireland's strong sense of community means that it's not uncommon for hundreds (and sometimes thousands) of people to pay their respects to the surviving family by attending the graveyard ceremony. It doesn't matter if you only knew the person slightly or even if it was a neighbor's mother whom you had never met. Being part of a village community means attending neighborhood funerals, even if that entails closing down your business for an hour or two. What faith you belong to doesn't matter. Most of my own neighbors are Catholic, but almost three thousand people attended the funeral of a young local Protestant boy who tragically died in a house fire.

Many people are teetotalers, but the pub is where they'll gather to play cards, trade gossip, and often meet up with their local political representative.

Although money is important, when it comes to the work ethic there isn't quite the same grab-it-all attitude that's often found elsewhere. Want to do business on Saturday? Tough. Few business people will work weekends for something that can wait until Monday. Nor are employees prepared to give up their social life to work long hours of overtime, let alone take a second job.

The pub undoubtedly plays a major part in Ireland's social life but it's a complete fallacy that the entire country is drink-mad. Many people are teetotalers, but the pub is where they'll gather to play cards, trade gossip, and often meet up with their local political representative. A number of Western Ireland TDs actually hold "surgeries" for their electoral constituents in the pub! (Not to be confused with doctors' surgeries, these are a forum where you can ask what he—and it's usually "he"—plans to do about the state of the roads or improving farm incomes.) It's still common in the West to give up drinking for Lent, but again, neighbors will still meet friends in the pub for conversation oiled with glasses of lemonade rather than pints of the black stuff.

Central to Irish society is "the Family." Older people are treated with tremendous respect and there isn't the same emphasis on youth culture that exists in many other Western countries. Visitors often comment on how Irish youngsters seem so polite and good mannered. It's not unusual to find three generations of an Irish family sharing the same house, especially if "Mammy" or "Daddy" has been left bereaved.

Compared to neighboring Britain, social change has been slow in coming. Only very recently has the country been offered the option for divorce along with legislation to decriminalize homosexuality. The liberal agenda has its strongest support in the Dublin area, but when it comes to the abortion issue, even Dublin lobbyists come up against a brick wall in the shape of the Church-backed Society for the Protection of the Unborn Child (SPUC). Abortion remains outlawed and, even on vital medical grounds, pregnant women still have to travel to England for surgery. Nearly 5,300 Irish women made the journey last year, but those are only the ones who felt confident enough to give Irish addresses.

Mary Robinson's appointment as Ireland's first woman president (since succeeded by Mary McAleese) gave women's self-esteem a big boost, but as yet there aren't many others who've achieved top positions in business or day-to-day politics. Although women make up around 40 percent of the workforce, only 5 percent of Ireland's business executives are female. When it comes to managing directors and departmental heads, the numbers fall to less than 3 percent. There's still a tendency for women to gravitate towards the "caring" professions such as nursing, teaching, and the social services. Until the early 1970s, women had to give up civil-service jobs upon marriage, and even today there's a commonplace attitude within rural Ireland that a woman's place is in the home. For any career-minded Irishwoman, "tradition" sometimes has negative aspects.

Contemporary Culture

Although Ireland's cultural reputation is founded on its Celtic traditions and huge body of Celtic literature, many people in today's arts world have achieved a high international standing. Irish playwrights such as Brian Friel (*Dancing at Lughnasa*) are well known on Broadway, and the Druid Theater Company's production of Martin McDonagh's *The Beauty Queen of Leenane* garnered four Tony Awards. Irish-made movies go from strength to strength and even if you haven't heard of home-grown directors such as Neil Jordan and Jim Sheridan, you'll undoubtedly be familiar with silver-screen celebrities such as Liam Neeson, Gabriel Byrne, Brenda Fricker, and Pierce Brosnan. Irish films of the 1990s that successfully transferred to an international audience include *The Field, The Crying Game, The Snapper, In the Name of the Father,* and *Circle of Friends.*

Contemporary Irish music encompasses everything from the rock-band giant U2 to teen heartthrobs Boyzone and the grannies' favorite crooner, Daniel O'Donnell. Country-and-western bands attract a big following, especially in the midlands. If you're a jazz fan, make for the annual fall festival in Cork; if you're an Enya fan, get yourself to Leo Brennan's Tavern near Crolly in county Donegal (Enya is Leo's daughter and customers are occasionally treated to a free performance when she's back home). By now a musical institution, the Eurovision Song Contest has been won by Ireland more times than anyone cares to remember.

Traditional Culture

Ireland's symbol is the harp, a wonderful motif for a land of music, dance, and storytelling. Nowhere else in Europe does the folk tradition carry quite as much impact, burst with quite so much dynamism. Wherever you settle, you won't be very far away from the tinkle of the pennywhistle, the droning lament of the uilleann pipes, or the unmistakable thump of the *bodhrán*, the Irish drum.

Music and dance have overlapped and woven themselves into the very fabric of society. More than just cultural pastimes, these are art forms that are accessible to everyone. The fellow who comes to fix your plumbing or dig your garden may well be an accomplished fiddle player or flautist who learned his skills in a farmhouse kitchen. And all over the country you'll notice little girls skipping along in what seem to be Celtic party frocks, intricately embroidered with the kind of patterns usually associated with the Book of Kells and other illuminated manuscripts. The youngsters are off to their Irish dancing class, heads filled with dreams of traveling the world as part of the Riverdance troupe.

The bastion of the traditional-music scene is, of course, the pub. Inns in tourist towns such as Killarney have *seisiúns* (sessions) of music scheduled on a nightly basis, usually at regular times. Much of the instrumental music that's played is actually dance music and includes everything from jigs to reels to the hornpipe. *Seisiúns* also often include ballads, rebel songs, and the lone voice of a *sean-nós* singer. Unaccompanied by any instrument and usually sung in Irish, their throbbing songs are the stories of thwarted love, sad farewells, and a heart-wrenching yearning for a faraway homeland.

In quieter areas where tourists rarely go, *seisiúns* are more impromptu. Someone whips out a fiddle, an accordion appears, and before you know it the entire bar is tapping its feet and raising the rafters with a rousing rendition of *The Fields of Athenry*. Once underway, the entertainment can roister on until way past pub closing time.

County Clare is especially good for tuning into traditional melodies that have been passed on like heirlooms down through the generations. Folk-music enthusiasts from all over the world embark on a kind of pilgrimage to the fishing village of Doolin and its three "singing pubs," McGann's, O'Connor's, and McDermott's. Some come to listen, others to join in. Another Clare village, Miltown Malbay, is the venue for the Willie Clancy Summer School, Ireland's largest musical summer school, which attracts beginners and local masters every year. As much social event as musical academy, the school hosts classes for most instruments, and set-dancing and singing, too.

The Irish word for a traditional-music festival is *feis* (pronounced "fesh"). There are dozens of them, but the biggest is the *Fleadh Cheoil* (pro-

Sports of the Emerald Isle

With more horses per head of population than anywhere else in Europe, Ireland is the equine isle. Thanks to generous tax concessions, many top European racehorses are at stud here, and there are pony-trekking facilities and riding stables in every part of the country. Even if you don't ride, one of the most enjoyable events is a day at the races, whether it be at a little local course or one of the major classic meetings at the Curragh in county Kildare.

Ireland's 350-plus golf courses are world-renowned and range from parkland courses to breezy seaside links where the hazards often include dry-stone walls and mad-eyed wandering sheep. Green fees average IR£20 to IR£25, though you can pay as little as IR£10 in the midlands or as much as IR£65 to play the classic course at Portmarnock near Dublin.

Other than skiing, baseball, and American football, most sporting interests are catered for. There are sailing clubs in many maritime counties, loughs and rivers provide tremendous fishing, and almost every community has a gun club. The traditional rural pursuits of fox-hunting and beagling are particularly strong in counties Limerick, Tipperary, and Cork. As regards spectator sports, Ireland's soccer team reached the World Cup finals in 1990 and 1994, and the rugby team takes part in the annual Five Nations Championship along with England, Scotland, Wales, and France. And although rugby can often be violent and bloody, it seems like a game for namby-pambies once you've encountered Gaelic Games.

nounced "flah kol," it means "feast of music"), which takes place in a different Irish town each year at the end of August. Ten days of nonstop competition and entertainment, it's a fantastic chance to see the country's top step-, set-, and *ceili* dancers.

In step-dancing, the dancers' arms and upper bodies stay rigid while the feet perform the mazing magic of slip jigs, triple jigs, and the hornpipe. Step-dancing is as rigorous as it looks and you really need to learn it as a

Gaelic Games are almost exclusive to Ireland and both Gaelic football and hurling have huge followings. Gaelic football is a field game of 15 players who use a round ball that can be played with either hands or feet and a goal similar to that on a rugby pitch. Depending on whether the ball goes over or under the bar, scoring is a mix of points and goals. Dating back to Celtic times and mentioned in epic sagas, hurling has a similar scoring system but in this case the game involves a hurley stick and a smaller ball. And regardless of what you'll see, hurley sticks are intended to whack the ball, not opponents' heads. Teams from the 32 counties, North and South, annually compete in the All-Ireland Championships, during which fans hang their county flags from windows, gateposts, and anywhere else they can proclaim their allegiance. Watched by enthusiastic crowds of around 70,000, hurling and Gaelic football finals take place at Croke Park in Dublin.

child to reach competition standard. *Feis* rules require "authentic Gaelic dress" to be worn, but although today's costumes look fabulous, they're hardly authentic. Not when you consider that these dances used to take place at country crossroads and were performed by peasant villagers dressed in shawls, petticoats, and homespun breeches!

Like *ceili* dancing, which developed from the French quadrille, set-dancing is a form of social dancing bearing some semblance to English and Scottish country dancing. It generally involves four couples who follow the intricate turns, steps, and patterns of a series of figures—the set. It often takes 15 to 20 minutes to dance an entire set, so participants need plenty of stamina.

Competitively danced sets at a *feis* come from an approved repertoire of dances with evocative names such as the Siege of Ennis, the Blackthorn stick, the King of the Fairies, and Hurry the Jug. Some dances are more than 250 years old—a dance known as the Blackbird actually doubled as a secret code for Irish supporters of the ill-fated Bonnie Prince Charlie who tried to wrest back the Scottish throne for the Catholic Stuart dynasty.

Many set dances originated during the eighteenth century, the heyday of the Irish Dance Master. Circuiting a county's villages, he passed on his latest stock of dances to local people, devising new steps and sets with each visit. It was considered a great honor to have a Dance Master boarding with you, even though he was likely to be eating you out of house and home for a period of anything up to six weeks.

Another mainstay of the *feis* is the *seannachie*, or storyteller. The art of storytelling is as old as man himself and was a revered profession during

THE SHAMROCK

Anybody can be Irish on St. Patrick's Day—all you need to do is wear a sprig of shamrock. But although many people imagine that this unofficial symbol of Irishness must be something unique and special, the truth is rather mundane. Shamrock is nothing other than young clover.

Seamróg in the Irish language, it derives its name from seamair (clover) and óg (young). The expression "drowning the shamrock" comes from the custom of dropping a sprig of clover into the last pint you swallow on St. Patrick's Day. Once the glass is drained, toss the soggy shamrock over your shoulder. This should ensure a full year's good luck!

Celtic times. Journeying from fireside to fireside, the ancient bards and poets thrilled their audiences with elaborate creation myths and stories of heroic victories achieved with the aid of magical weapons. They told of doomed love affairs, of lone warriors battling against the shadowy forces of the supernatural, of severed heads that could prophesy and provide wondrous entertainment. Like his or her poetic forebears, the *seannachie*, too, relies on memory alone. Some of the best hail from the kingdom of Kerry, a county where stories are apt to grow very long legs indeed.

For forthcoming events, contact Comhaltas Ceoltoiri Éireann (Belgrave Square, Monkstown, Co. Dublin; tel. +353 0-1 280 0295). Pronounced "Coal-tis Kyol-tory Air-in" and commonly referred to as the CCE, its name loosely translates as "a gathering of Irish musicians," though it exists to promote all aspects of traditional culture. The organization has branches all over Ireland and you don't have to be Irish-born or Irish-speaking to join.

Throughout the country, activities generally mirror what happens in county Cork where a CCE branch meets up for a Monday night *seisiún* in Rosie's Bar at Carrigaline. Other nights are given over to teaching *ceili* and set-dancing—fees are just IR£1 per person per night. And, if you have a basic level of competence in your chosen instrument, they'll teach you traditional tunes and how to play with other musicians. Fees are IR£20 per term. Concerts are regular events with performances given in local churches at Epiphany and on St. Patrick's Day.

Another big day in the Irish social calendar is St. Stephen's Day, December 26. As part of the celebrations, musicians and dancers dress up as Wren Boys and roam Carrigaline's streets and pubs, collecting money for local charities. It's always a colorful occasion with the Wren Boys giving a cheery send-off to the horses and hounds of the South Union Hunt, its riders dressed in hunting pink.

"Hunting the Wran" (the wren) was more common in previous years than it is today, but groups of colorfully disguised revelers still appear on St. Stephen's Day as part of the Christmastime festivities. Although costumes sometimes differ from county to county, most Wren Boys wear white tunics and conical straw hats, and paint their faces black and red. A century ago they would have rambled across open fields to call on neighbors. In return for a monetary donation and some food and drink, the odd-looking visitors entertained the household with music, dancing, poetry, and drama.

Mean householders often got more than they bargained for. Along with their musical instruments, the Wren Boys carried a holly bush or pole decorated with the slain bodies of harmless little birds called wrens. Any house or farm making an inadequate donation could later expect to find a wren buried near the doorstep. As well as being a dire insult, this act supposedly ensured that the stingy family suffered a full year's bad luck.

Today it's illegal to hunt wrens so revelers top their poles with a papier-mâché effigy. And instead of making house calls, most Wren Boys center their activities on pubs and clubs. Besides Carrigaline, two other places where you're certain to see Wren Boys are Woodford in county Galway and Dingle in county Kerry. Led by the colorfully disguised Lord Mayor, Wren Boys also parade through Dublin on December 26.

Language and Literature

The country's incomparable literary traditions are rooted in the ancient language of the Celts. And if the pen really is mightier than the sword, then Ireland's legions of poets, playwrights, and novelists should have conquered the world twice over!

Language

Céad Míle Fáilte. Ceol agus Craic. Sláinte is Saol. If you believe that the Irish language is merely English spoken with a soft brogue, surprises are in store. For starters, we don't have a prime minister, we have a *Taoiseach*. Our biggest political party is called *Fianna Fáil*, the Soldiers of Destiny. Ever received an Irish Christmas card? Look at the special seasonal stamps— they aren't marked "Christmas," they're marked *Nollaig*.

Not everybody realizes that the Republic's first official language is Irish, or, to give it its proper title, *Gaelige*. Often also referred to as Gaelic, it bears little resemblance to English—like Scots Gaelic, Breton, and Welsh, it belongs to the Celtic language group. Until the seventeenth century, nearly all the population spoke Irish, but English rule undermined most aspects of Ireland's traditional culture including teaching of the native language. The situation was further exacerbated by the Great Famine and the long decades of mass emigration that drained the country of countless native speakers. Although Irish has been in slow decline ever since, there has been an enthusiastic revival in recent years. For example, all schoolchildren study Irish as part of the curriculum, and proficiency in the language is a requirement for careers in teaching, banking, and the civil service.

Despite the language's official status, newcomers aren't pressured to learn Irish. Whilst Gaelige is regarded as a cornerstone of the cultural heritage, most people use English as their preferred tongue. The latest census figures show that although around 1.4 million Irish people describe themselves as having an understanding of Irish, nearly two thirds of them either never speak the language at all or use it less than once a week. Even so, you'll soon be using odd Irish words as part of everyday conversation. Many of your new friends will have names like Niamh (pronounced "Neev") or Blaithin (pronounced "Bloheen"). You may want to visit the *Fleadh* (literally "the Feast"), Ireland's biggest traditional-music festival, or even learn how to play the *bodhrán*, the Irish drum.

You'll soon notice that place-names and street signs are invariably given in both Irish and English. Galway is also *Gaillimhe*; Cork doubles as *Corcaigh*; Sligo is *Sligeach. Baile Átha Cliath* isn't so easy to guess—any bus bound for what translates as "the town at the ford of the hurdles" is actually taking passengers to Dublin.

Follow a sign pointing to *An Lár* and it leads you to a town center. You may also see signs for *an Scoil* (a school), *an Leabharlann* (a library), or *an Ospidéal* (a hospital). A stroll down *Sráid Padraig* (Patrick Street) could take you past the *Oifig an Phoist* (post office), and if you get lost you can always ask a *Garda* for directions. Colloquially called "the guards," the *Garda Síochána* is the official title of Ireland's police force.

Which way to Tralee?!

There are a few places in the remoter parts of Ireland where even Dubliners feel like strangers in a strange land. Counties Donegal, Kerry, Cork, Waterford, Mayo, and Galway all possess little enclaves known as Gaeltacht areas. The inhabitants of the Gaeltacht only number around eight thousand, but more than 60 percent of the residents speak Irish within the home and on the street. During summertime, many city kids are sent here to board with local families—they get a thorough immersion course in Gaelige as preparation for forthcoming exams.

Gaeltacht roads aren't for the faint-hearted. When exploring the country's Irish-speaking pockets, it's

Irish Place Names

Many place names are anglicized renderings of original names in the Irish language. Their meanings often describe the landscape, ancient monuments, or important local happenings. Common prefixes are the words *dún* (fort); *cill* (church), which is often written as *kill* or *kil*; *cnoc* (hill), which usually is written as Knock; and Bally, which takes its roots from *baile* (town). Clon derives from *cluain*, meaning "meadow." Signposts pointing to Drum this and Drom that are all linked to the Irish word *druim*—a ridge.

The well-known tourist town of Killarney's original name was Cill Áirne—the Church of the Sloes. Donegal derives its name from Viking times when it became known as Dún na nGall, the fort of the foreigner. Gortahork (Gorta Coirce) initially sounds like an incomprehensible mouthful, but *gort* signifies "field" and *coirce* means "oats." Thus it's fairly reasonable to assume that Gortahork was once renowned for its oat fields. Knockcroghery, a village in county Roscommon, has a darker derivation—that of a place of execution. Although *cnoc* means "hill," *crochaire* is the Irish word for "hangman." Knockcroghery translates as Hangman's Hill.

The word *tobar* within a place name usually signifies a healing well dating back to pre-Christian times. Mapmakers often wrote it as "*tubber*" or "*tober*," and in county Mayo you'll come across Ballintober (Baile-an-tobar), the town of the well. Tubbercurry in county Sligo takes its name from Tobar-an-choire, the well of the cauldron.

One of the most malevolent creatures of the Celtic Otherworld was the *púca*, a shape-changing goblin that haunted lonely places and often appeared to travelers in the form of a black horse. On the boundary of counties Limerick and Cork, the bridge at Ahaphuca, from *ath* and *púca*, translates as "the goblin's ford." *Poll* signifies "hole," "cavern," or a deep pool of water, and in the wild glens of county Wicklow, the river Liffey spills over a ledge into Pollaphuca—the goblin's hole.

well worth understanding a smattering of the language as here direction signs are *not* bilingual. Yes, your map book may read "Carraroe," but the signposts confusingly point to *An Cheathrú Rua*. Although everybody in the Gaeltacht does speak English, few concessions are made to the linguistically challenged visitor. If you're seeking the restroom in some little pub, it's handy to know the difference between the doors that read *Mná* (ladies) and *Fír* or *Fear* (men). It could save your blushes!

Ireland's best-known bilingual town is Dingle, a color-washed harbor town on county Kerry's wild and witchy Dingle Peninsula. East of Dingle town, the language is English; head west and you'll soon be deep into Irish-speaking territory. Stay in town and the place to head for is An Café Litearta, Ireland's first literary coffeeshop where you can puzzle over the Irish menu and also browse for books on *Tír na nÓg*, or the land of everlasting youth. (Rumor has it that this fairytale land lies somewhere off the Dingle Peninsula, out in the Atlantic beyond the misty hummocks of the Blasket Islands. However, if you go to the Irish-speaking Aran Islands off the county Galway coast, you'll probably hear that it lies somewhere in that part of the western ocean!)

> *There are a few places in the remoter parts of Ireland where even Dubliners feel like strangers in a strange land.*

Fairy folklore throws up an interesting example of how many Irish words became anglicized over the centuries. Take the Bean Sidhe, whose name translates as "spirit" or "fairy woman." She is, of course, much better known to the English-speaking world as the fearsome Banshee.

Should you wish to learn Irish, plenty of summer schools and evening classes offer adults the opportunity to get to grips with this intriguing ancient language. Radio programs and an Irish-language television station, Telefis na Gaelige (TnaG), also broadcast into the country's sitting rooms. The majority of TnaG's scheduling is in Irish, but it occasionally carries programs from our Celtic neighbors, too. Just to baffle the novice student of the Irish language, the station's output sometimes includes sessions of Gaelic ballads from the Scottish Hebrides, Welsh dramas such as *Pobol y Cwm* (People of the Valley), and—don't ask me why—Australian Rules football.

Where to Learn the Language

Probably the most enjoyable introduction to the Irish language is to attend a course that combines class work in the morning with activities in the afternoon. Oideas Gael has summer schools in county Donegal's Gaeltacht where you can also take part in workshops ranging from Irish dancing to tapestry weaving, hill-walking, archaeology, and *bodhrán* playing. The morning language classes are designed to give beginners the basics. Alternatively you could give the activities a miss and opt for a more intensive language course. The price for a weeklong language course (45 hours of study) is IR£100; that for a language and culture course is IR£115. A three-day-weekend course is IR£50. Accommodation and board with local families costs an additional IR£120 for the week, or IR£55 for the three-day weekend. Contact Oideas Gael, Gleann Cholm Cille, Dún na nGall; tel. +353 (0)73 30248. (That's how Irish speakers write "Glencolmcille, county Donegal"; postmen know how to recognize both forms of address.)

In the Galway area, contact Áras Mháirtín uí Chadain, (the Irish Language Center of University College Galway), An Cheathrú Rua, Co na Gaillimhe; tel +353 (0)91 595101. Some courses are more intensive (two weeks in length) and often draw foreign students wishing to gain university credits. Fees for these start at IR£560.

Literature

Ireland always seems to have had more writers, poets, and playwrights than there are sheep in the fields, and when you consider the country's size, its

---

COMMON IRISH EXPRESSIONS

- **Dia duit** (jeea ditch)—Good day, hello; its literal meaning is "God be with you."
- **Conas tá tú?** (kunas taw too)—How are you?
- **Fáilte** (fawlcha)—Welcome!
- **Tá go maith, go raibh maith agat** (taw gu mah, gura mah ugut)— I'm fine, thank you.
- **Cad é an t-ainm atá ort?** (kajay in tanyim ataw urt)—What's your name?
- **Atá orm** . . . (ataw orim)—My name is . . . .
- **Slán leat** (slawn lyat)—Goodbye (if *you* are staying).
- **Slán agat** (slawn ugut)—Goodbye (if *you* are leaving).

You may hear these expressions spoken slightly differently as there are three distinct varieties of pronunciation: Ulster Irish, Connacht Irish, and Munster Irish.

literary achievements are tremendous. You could say that it all began with the unknown monks of the Celtic Church. Not only did they create illuminated gospels such as the Book of Kells and Book of Durrow, they recorded the ancient myths and heroic sagas that had been thrilling listeners since pagan times. It is these early Irish monks you can thank for timeless stories such as *The Children of Lir* in which four children were bewitched into swans by a jealous stepmother. The most famous ancient epic is *The Cattle Raid of Cooley* (*Táin Bó Cuailnge*) whose hero Cúchulainn uses a frightening array of otherworldly powers to aid the warriors of Ulster in battle against Queen Maeve of Connacht.

Dublin's streets alone have spawned an incredible number of literary greats—not only James Joyce, but also George Bernard Shaw, William Butler Yeats, and Samuel Beckett, all of whom won the Nobel prize for literature. Sean O'Casey told of a tenement world of poverty and revolution in dramas such as *The Plough and the Stars, Juno and the Paycock*, and *Shadow of a Gunman*, classics that are still performed today. Jonathan Swift, who became Dean of St. Patrick's Cathedral, has delighted generations of youngsters with *Gulliver's Travels*. Then there is the witty Oscar Wilde, who once informed customs officials "I have nothing to declare but my genius." Add Brendan Behan, author of *The Borstal Boy*, and Bram Stoker, master of gothic macabre and author of *Dracula*, and the litany is staggering.

Other acclaimed names include the Wicklow wordsmith John Millington Synge, who wrote of the vagrants who tramped the empty white lanes of county Wicklow and told of village humor and cruelties in the islands of the West. One of Synge's best-known works is *The Playboy of the Western World*, which had the distinction of being greeted with riots when first performed at Dublin's Abbey Theater in 1907. The entire country brims with literary associations: The bleak hills of Monaghan provided Patrick Kavanagh with poetic inspiration; the now-empty Blasket Islands are brought back to life in works such as Maurice O'Sullivan's

The gravestone of the famous poet William Butler Yeats bears an epitaph he penned himself.

Twenty Years A-Growing and Peig Sayers' *Peig*. Sligo will forever be linked to W.B. Yeats; Edgeworthstown in county Longford was the home of Georgian novelist Maria Edgeworth of *Castle Rackrent* fame; county Westmeath is associated with Oliver Goldsmith who lived here during the 1740s.

Dublin now has a Writers' Museum on Parnell Square to go with its literary pub crawls, James Joyce Trail, and Bloomsday (celebrated on June 16), when Joyce's admirers don Edwardian dress and retrace the odyssey of *Ulysses'* Leopold Bloom around the city's landmarks. Yet Irish literature isn't solely devoted to past glories—the country continues to produce an endless stream of talented writers and poets. John McGahern, John Banville, and Edna O'Brien are only a few contemporary novelists whose books are well regarded by critics.

The poet Seamus Heaney scooped another Nobel Prize for Ireland in 1995. His 1997 collection of poems, *The Spirit Level*, encompasses both the hopes and disappointments of the peace process. For an inkling into the trials and tribulations of working-class life on Dublin's sprawling council estates, read Roddy Doyle, whose memorable books include *The Van*, *The Snapper*, *Paddy Clarke Ha Ha Ha*, and *The Woman Who Walked into Doors*. If you like romantic weepies, Maeve Binchy never disappoints—of her numerous novels three of my own favorites are *Light a Penny Candle*, *Circle of Friends*, and *Tara Road*. One of the most unlikely recent bestsellers was *Angela's Ashes* by retired New York schoolteacher Frank McCourt. The grim autobiography, which won the 1997 Pulitzer Prize, recounted McCourt's impoverished Limerick childhood.

Money Matters

A sking how far your money will stretch in Ireland is one of those "how long is a piece of string?" questions. Although there's no escaping the fact that many day-to-day–living costs are higher than they are in the United States, other factors help create some balance. For starters, you won't be paying property taxes or rates (local council taxes). Retirees can take advantage of a valuable free travel concession, and free hospital emergency treatment is there for any resident who needs it. And, if you're on a fixed income, it's reassuring to know that Ireland has a relatively low inflation rate—currently 1.4 percent.

As in any other country, much will depend on where you choose to live, the kind of lifestyle you expect to enjoy, and your hobbies and interests. Theater tickets, for example, are astoundingly cheap, but computer and good-quality photographic equipment is exorbitantly expensive. With greens fees pitched between IR£12 and IR£15, a membership at many of the small midland clubs that form the backbone of Irish golf can often be had for IR£300 annually. On the other hand, founder members of the prestigious new Kinsale course in county Cork were charged IR£10,000, and it costs IR£120 to play a round in high season at Kildare's K Club.

In a nutshell, if you're happy with simple country pleasures—a modest home with all the necessary comforts, a small fuel-efficient car, adequate health coverage, and occasional treats—then IR£1,200 to IR£1,500 ($850 to $1,064) per month should prove ample. Obviously, if you're the type of person who expects to dine out regularly in top-class Dublin restaurants, drive a Mercedes, belong to an exclusive gym, and own a huge Georgian mansion with equally huge heating bills, then you're going to need rather more in the way of funds.

To put the income question into some kind of context, the basic state pension for Irish couples under 80 years of age currently stands at IR£542 per month. Single pensioners receive IR£332. The average monthly wage, a figure that encompasses some extremely varied salary levels, is IR£1,268 for males and IR£845 for females.

To cite a few examples, clothing-factory machinists average IR£560 per month, whereas sales reps in the software industry can command monthly salaries of around IR£3,800. A post for a systems analyst with the Western Health Board was recently advertised at IR£1,775 per month, but the starting pay of a new police recruit is only a little over IR£1,000 per month. An executive clerk with the Department of Defense earns around IR£1,375 per month, but any good Dublin-based bricklayer will expect to be making around IR£2,000 over the same period.

Ireland is one of the 11 participants in Europe's fledgling single currency, the Euro. Although Euro notes and coins won't replace national currencies until January 1, 2002, all shops and restaurants throughout Euroland have been encouraged to display prices in both Euros and the local currency since January 1, 1999. Payment can be made in either currency until July 2002 when the old national currencies will finally disappear.

Banking

Do you find articles on banking and savings accounts a source of endless fascination? Or are you like many people—they make your eyes glaze over? Well, apologies if money matters bore you rigid, but these practicalities need addressing.

Opening a bank account in Ireland is straightforward. There are no exchange controls and thus no limit on the amount of money you can bring into or take out of the country. If you are buying property, it will be important to have funds transferred as soon as possible. Even if you've chosen to rent a home, you'll almost certainly want to have a current account with a bank near the town where you plan to live.

EXCHANGE RATE

At the time of writing, the exchange rate against the U.S. dollar was IR£1=$1.36.

A current account is a checkbook account that you'll probably use for day-to-day expenses or to pay off credit card bills. It can be used in conjunction with a cash card, which acts as a check-guarantee card and allows holders to draw funds from ATMs, sometimes known as hole-in-the-wall machines. Through a current account, you can also arrange standing orders to pay off regular bills such as electricity and telephone.

When opening an account, all banks ask you to show a passport or some other form of identification. This is to comply with government legislation (Criminal Justice Act 1994), which was introduced to prevent criminal organizations and drug dealers from using Irish banks as laundry baskets. Accounts are largely confidential although the Revenue Commissioners, Ireland's tax authorities, can scrutinize certain types of deposit accounts.

Charge cards such as Diner's Club and American Express are accepted in many places where tourists gather, but you rarely see their signs in more out-of-the-way localities.

The two largest retail banks are Allied Irish Bank (AIB) and Bank of Ireland, both of which maintain branches even in the smaller towns. Larger towns usually host branches of National Irish Bank, Ulster Bank, and TSB Bank, too. Irish Permanent and First Active are former building societies (mutuals) that converted to banks and floated their shares on the stock market. Both offer the same kind of financial services as their high-street competitors.

It should come as no surprise to find that banks are out to profit from their customers and most transactions attract charges. If, however, you keep at least IR£100 in your current account throughout the fee period, you won't pay for most normal transactions. All banks apply similar charging structures and their fees shouldn't be a worrying sum for the average spender. Looking at my own recent bank statement, quarterly fees amounted to just over IR£8.

For an annual fee of around IR£10, banks also handle credit-card arrangements. Ireland's two main companies are Visa and Access (the local brand name of MasterCard); their cards are accepted in most large stores, supermarkets, and petrol (gas) stations. Around 30 thousand Irish establishments take credit cards but it's still cash-or-check in most village shops, and definitely cash-only in pubs. If you're traveling around the country, be aware that not all bed-and-breakfasts take credit cards either. As you already know, credit cards can prove an expensive way of borrowing if bills aren't settled on time. In Ireland, the annual percentage rate (APR) on credit card borrowing is typically twice the standard bank overdraft rate of 11.5 percent.

Charge cards such as Diner's Club and American Express are accepted in many places where tourists gather, but you rarely see their signs in more out-of-the-way localities. For Amex cardholders in Ireland, the annual fee is currently IR£37.50. Although this entitles holders to only a limited number of benefits, it does include IR£75,000 worth of travel accident insurance when tickets are charged to a card.

For more information on bank services, call into any local branch or contact the following:

AIB Bank Headquarters, Bankcentre, Ballsbridge, Dublin 4;
  tel. +353 (0)1 660 0311
Bank of Ireland Head Office, Lower Baggot St., Dublin 2;
  tel. +353 (0)1 661 5933
First Active, Skehan House, Booterstown, Co. Dublin;
  tel. +353 (0)1 283 1801
Irish Permanent, 56/59 St. Stephen's Green, Dublin 2;
  tel. +353 (0)1 661 5577
National Irish Bank Head Office, 7/8 Wilton Terrace, Dublin 2; tel. +353
  (0)1 678 5066
Trustee Savings Bank, Frederick House, South Frederick St., Dublin 2;
  tel. +353 (0)1 679 0444
Ulster Bank, 33 College Green, Dublin 2; tel. +353 (0)1 677 7623

Savings

As permanent residents, most people will be seeking a safe Irish home for at least part of their savings. All banks and building societies offer various types of deposit accounts that will certainly give you sleep-easy-at-night security. Unfortunately, Ireland's low interest-rate environment equates with paltry returns for savers, and it would be hard to make our savings rates seem sexy.

Without getting too technical, when a country offers high interest rates on savings deposits, it usually indicates galloping inflation and an unstable economy. Interest rates of 40 percent sound brilliant, but you just don't get them in Ireland. The only way you'll get returns like that is through exchanging your hard-earned dollars for dodgy third-world currencies held in even dodgier third-world banks. When the ruble/peso/ringgit or whatever plunges against the dollar (and it always does) you'll come to the sickening realization that hyperinflation has wiped out the value of your savings. That 40-percent return? It's going to take a lot more than *that* to buy back your original amount of dollars.

Thankfully Irish punts are not Russian rubles. And nor is Ireland one of those "emerging markets" from which it always seems impossible to emerge. So, where to stash your cash if you don't want keep it all Stateside?

Well, fixed-term accounts are the best hedge against inflation, but even if you're willing to tie up ordinary deposit savings for 12 months, current yields only average between 4 and 5 percent. It will be difficult to find better returns because Irish interest rates need to comply with European monetary union criteria. To find which institutions are offering the most attractive rates, buy a financial publication such as *The Sunday Business Post*. Comparative interest-rate tables of all Ireland's banks and building societies are published weekly.

Broadly speaking, most types of savings accounts don't deliver tax-free gains on any interest earned. A tax known as DIRT (Deposit Interest Retention Tax) is deducted at source and the current rate is 24 percent. However, those older than 65 who aren't liable to pay income tax may be able to claim it back from the Revenue Commissioners.

A lower rate of DIRT applies to products known as Special Savings Accounts (SSAs). By holding one of these accounts, individuals may save up to IR£50,000 with interest taxed at 20 percent. Most financial institutions offer SSAs with minimum opening balances varying between IR£1 and IR£3,000. Thirty days withdrawal notice is generally required and the typical interest rate is 5.5 percent.

You can also place your nest egg with An Post, the State-owned postal service. Its savings certificates and bonds deliver totally tax-free returns and are guaranteed by the State. And, if you need to get at your money quickly, only seven days' notice is required. With savings certificates, individuals can invest amounts of between IR£50 and IR£60,000 over varying terms ranging from six months to five and a half years. If held to maturity, savings certificates currently return 30-percent interest over the full term. Bonds pay 14 percent, again tax free, over a three-year period. With these, individuals can invest between IR£100 and IR£60,000. For further information about An Post, contact An Post Investment Services, College House, Townsend St., Dublin 2; tel. +353 (0)1 705 7200.

It's certainly worth stashing a little money in a building society (you may know these as mutuals, or savings and loan institutions). These are mutual societies that are theoretically owned by their members—savers and borrowers. The possibility exists that more will change their status to banks and so deliver windfall shares to account holders. This already happened in the case of First Active (formerly First National) and Irish Permanent when they demutualized and floated on the Irish stock market. Two of the largest remaining mutuals are:

Educational Building Society, 30 Westmoreland St., Dublin 2; tel. +353 (0)1 677 5599

Irish Nationwide, 1 Lower O'Connell St., Dublin 1; tel. +353 (0)1 478 0022

(For equity-based investments, see Chapter 12, "Working and Investing in Ireland.")

Borrowing

Ireland has one of Europe's highest rates of home ownership with over 80 percent of families having a stake in the property market. Their principal source for home financing is, again, the bank or building society. Subject to income, status, and good references from a U.S. bank, American newcomers seeking a mortgage may be able to raise between 50 and 70 percent of a house or business purchase price. Once you've been a resident of Ireland

CURRENT COSTS OF SOME BASIC FOODSTUFFS ARE AS FOLLOWS:

100-gram jar of Nescafe:	IR£2.20
Pound of pork chops:	IR£2
80 good-quality tea bags:	IR£1.70
Medium-size chicken:	IR£4
Six free-range eggs:	IR£.75
Liter of milk:	IR£.64
Liter of orange juice:	IR£.60
225 grams of butter:	IR£.85
Head of lettuce:	IR£.25
Half pound of sausage:	IR£.70
Seven pounds of potatoes:	IR£1.40
Standard brown soda bread:	IR£.80
Kilogram of sugar:	IR£.85
500 grams of cornflakes:	IR£1.30
Pound of apples:	IR£1–1.25
500 grams of strong white flour:	IR£1.12
Pound sirloin steak:	IR£3
500 grams of cheddar cheese:	IR£1.40
1.5 kilograms of porridge oats:	IR£1.65
Pound of marmalade:	IR£.95
341 grams of natural honey:	IR£1.25
Medium can Heinz baked beans:	IR£.37
Pound of frozen haddock fillets:	IR£3.29

for a while, you may be able to obtain a 90-percent loan if you've established a sound financial relationship with the prospective lender. This 90-percent maximum criterion applies to Irish citizens, too.

Ireland doesn't seem to have heard of the "gray power" movement, and age plays a big part in whether you'll be considered a suitable borrower. Unless seeking a short-term mortgage (5 to 10 years), those over 50 years of age may find it difficult to get finance. And there is no point in me giving you any blarney about arranging a mortgage Stateside. When it comes to foreign-home ownership, American banks are just as timid as their Irish counterparts.

According to the Home Owners Finance Center, "American lenders have no interest in funding loans where the security is foreign property." Gloomy confirmation came from Chase Manhattan, which "does not finance homes located outside of the United States." Older readers needing to raise capital to fund the purchase of an Irish home may find the only solution lies in selling or remortgaging any property they own Stateside.

In general, Irish lenders take income into consideration when determining the amount you can borrow. Working individuals can typically borrow two and a half times their annual income; thus someone on IR£30,000 could borrow IR£75,000. This sum can be upped if your spouse also has an income, generally by the equivalent of that spouse's income. For example, a couple earning IR£25,000 and IR£15,000 should be able to borrow IR£77,500.

Mortgage repayments can either be at a fixed rate for a given number of years or fluctuate with prevailing interest rates. There are dozens of packages on the market; as a ballpark figure, a one-year fix on a 20-year term annuity mortgage with the Educational Building Society is set at 5.7-percent interest; a 10-year fix is set at 6.95 percent. Assuming you've borrowed IR£50,000 over 20 years, a variable rate of 7.1 percent (7.3-percent APR) means monthly repayments of IR£390.50. If interest rates increase by 1 percent, an additional IR£31 would be payable monthly.

Inflation

Money loses its purchasing power if inflation is running above the after-tax rate of savings interest. The good news in recent years is that inflation has not decimated the value of Irish savings and investments—the average rate has been under 2.5 percent throughout the 1990s.

Even so, the country doesn't have the greatest record of inflation-proofing people's wealth if you go back a little further in time. Within the 30-year time span, some damagingly high levels have been scaled, particularly between 1969 and 1983. The nadir was 1975 when inflation soared to the astonishing level of almost 21 percent.

As indicated by the savers' deposit rates currently available with financial institutions, interest rates are historically low. Once tax has been deducted, savers are only just keeping a step or two ahead of inflation. For those trying to make gains in Ireland's present low interest rate environment, the only real solution has been to have part of their portfolios in property and equities. Obviously this requires a willingness to expose your capital to risk factors such as a collapse in house prices or sharp downturns on the stock markets.

Comparing the Cost of Living

Throughout the world, countless analysts devote their entire working lives to gleaning cost data from numerous cities. Most recent surveys show that Dublin scores better than New York for home services, utilities, entertainment, and, somewhat surprisingly, groceries.

Whether that's correct or not, shopping-basket items usually provide worthwhile cost comparisons. Supermarket prices within Ireland tend to be on par with those in the United States, although bargain hunters can often snap up special deals: two chickens for the price of one, a pound of sausage free with a pound of bacon rashers, etc. Figures released by the Central Statistics Office show that an average household (two adults, two children) with a weekly income of IR£328 spends IR£70 of that on food.

Buying a modest farmhouse to refurbish could stretch your borrowed cash.

Smokers may decide to quit when they discover a pack of 20 cigarettes costs between IR£3 and IR£3.10. A bottle of white Australian chardonnay wine costs IR£4.99 minimum in most stores, while a decent French red like Crozes Hermitage will set you back around IR£7. A six-pack of beer (Heineken lager) costs around IR£7.80.

Sharp-eyed readers will have noticed that the shopping list on page 59 indicates weights by both the imperial and metric standards. Although Ireland theoretically went metric over 20 years ago, a dual system still operates. In most butcher shops and greengrocers, foodstuffs continue to be priced by the pound. And although milk is now sold in liters, bartenders continue to measure out beer in pint and half-pint glasses.

Value Added Tax (VAT)

While sales tax isn't charged on groceries, Ireland does have a general sales tax that applies to numerous goods and services. Known as VAT (Value Added Tax), it's not generally itemized separately except for on utility bills. In all shops, restaurants, and other consumer outlets, the amount you see on price tags and menus is the price you'll pay. Aside from groceries, certain other items are VAT-free: These include books and children's footwear and clothing.

Varying rates of VAT apply to different services and sales. The standard 21-percent rate is charged on things such as telephone bills, new vehicles, petrol, beer, spirits, most household goods, adult's footwear and clothing, and many professional bills including lawyers' fees. A reduced 12.5-percent rate applies to electricity, fuel for the home, restaurant meals, newspapers, and cinema tickets. A rate of 3.6 percent covers the sale of livestock, greyhounds, and the hire of horses. VAT isn't a talking point for most consumers as it's an invisible tax—it is only if you intend to *provide* any services that it need concern you. (Entrepreneurs will find more VAT information in Chapter 12, "Working and Investing in Ireland.")

Household Goods

Many electrical and other household goods are quite expensive, particularly when it comes to good-quality furniture. Furthermore, items such as cookers (ovens) and iceboxes (refrigerators) are like dinky dollhouse pieces compared to what's available in North America. You'll just have to keep telling yourself "small is beautiful."

Even if you plan to rent rather than buy a property, the cost of furnishings is something you may need to budget for. Although holiday lets and student accommodations almost always have the basics, not all Irish

FAQ about the Euro

Q. What is the Euro and where can I use it?

A. Europe's new single currency, the Euro, is to be legal tender in Ireland, Austria, Belgium, Finland, France, Germany, Italy, Luxembourg, the Netherlands, Portugal, and Spain. The four remaining EU states (Britain, Denmark, Greece, and Sweden) are keeping their own currencies for the time being.

Q What is the timetable for this changeover to a single currency?

A E-Day was January 1, 1999, but the actual transition period is quite lengthy. Although member countries have permanently locked the exchange rates of their old currencies against the Euro, at present the new single currency is only useable for noncash transactions such as checks, direct debits, and credit transfers. However, shops and restaurants throughout the participating member states are being encouraged to display prices in Euros alongside their national currency.

Q. When will Euro notes and coins go into circulation?

A. Irish banknotes and coins will begin to be withdrawn on January 1, 2002 and, by July 1, 2002 at the latest, the changeover to the Euro will be complete.

Q. What will happen in the meantime?

A. In a nutshell, cash transactions will continue to be made in Irish punts; noncash transactions can be carried out in either Irish punts or Euros.

Q. How will I recognize Euro money?

A. Coins will range in value from one cent to two Euros with larger coins being white and yellow and carrying a national symbol on one face—in Ireland's case, the harp. Bearing bridge designs, notes will be standard and in denominations of 5, 10, 20, 50, 100, 200, and 500 Euros.

Q. Where can I get more information?

A. From the Euro Changeover Board of Ireland, Department of Finance, Merrion Street, Dublin 2; tel. +353 (0)1 676 7571 (the local number is 1890 201050).

houses up for long-term rental are let as furnished. It isn't possible to rent furniture, though many newer properties will have fitted kitchens and built-in wardrobes. Those on tight budgets should check out local auctions where often it is possible to find some great furniture bargains.

It's not worth bringing electrical items with you as the voltage system here is different: 230 volt AC 50 Hz. Plugs are normally of the flat three-pin variety. For the moment, TVs operate on the 625 line PAL system, although the expected digital explosion will bring myriad changes. Don't bring VCR tapes as they will be incompatible with Ireland's VHS system.

Light and Heat

Electricity bills are sent every two months and include a standing charge of IR£6.75. The general domestic charge for electricity is IR£.0743 per

---

**A SELECTION OF BRAND-NAME ITEMS
TAKEN FROM LARGER STORES
(all prices are for new items and include VAT):**

Beko five-cubic-foot fridge:	IR£145
Novum eight-cubic-foot freezer:	IR£219
Bosch dishwasher:	IR£330
Servis washing machine:	IR£240
Sharp microwave:	IR£90
Ferguson 21" TV:	IR£279
Krups vacuum cleaner:	IR£95
Kenwood toaster:	IR£20
Astral shower unit:	IR£170
Five-foot divan bed:	IR£195
Triple wardrobe:	IR£399
Natural wool carpeting:	IR£15 per square yard
Ferguson video recorder:	IR£169
Creda Cadenza cooker:	IR£199
Creda tumble dryer:	IR£159
Moulinex food processor:	IR£85
Pentium personal computer (16 MB RAM):	IR£899

unit. Costs obviously depend upon usage: Including VAT, my own bill for the March/April billing period was IR£101.33. This covered lighting, the usual electrical items, and bedroom radiators.

Natural gas is only available in Dublin and along parts of the east and southern coasts. The rest of the country uses bottled gas, which is sold by most supermarkets, village shops, and hardware stores. If you plan to use a gas cooker, a bottle of gas should cost around IR£11.50 and last around five weeks with normal usage.

If you want a peat (turf) fire, there are two methods. The easy way is to buy bales of peat briquettes, which are again sold by most general stores. They cost around IR£1.50 per bale, which should be sufficient for a roaring blaze in the sitting room all evening. The alternative is to rent a patch of bog from a farmer during summer and cut, foot, and dry your own turf. Believe me, it's filthy, backbreaking work, and you'll probably only try it once. Costs depend upon the quality of the turf: I paid IR£100 for a supply that lasted most of the winter.

Coal is mostly Texan or Polish. Ireland's coal mines have closed down, for they yielded low-grade "brown" coal suitable only for industrial use. A 25-kilogram sack of smokeless coal for domestic fires costs between IR£4 and IR£4.50. Like peat, coal can also be used in old-fashioned kitchen ranges, many of which provide hot water as well as cooking facilities.

Hiring Help

You shouldn't come here expecting to find legions of maids, cooks, and gardeners looking for live-in positions. Nor are people prepared to work for a pittance. Although it's common to find Dublin's professional classes employing cleaning ladies, this isn't really the case in the rest of the country. And although nearly every parish priest still has a housekeeper, ordinary mortals would be considered very odd if they advertised for home-help nowadays. Most people in rural areas are fiercely independent and it's only the very elderly or housebound who require assistance, in which case it's classed as a social need and provided by the health authorities.

That's not to say you won't be able to get paid help, though it will come at a price. High living costs apply to Irish people, too, and a daily "treasure" will expect between IR£3.50 and IR£4 an hour. Persuading someone to come and dig the garden or paint the house will cost at least IR£25 per day, plus materials. If it's a case of occasional help to mow the lawn or weed the flowerbeds, you'll almost certainly find plenty of willing schoolboys available for weekend and holiday work at around IR£2.50 per hour.

Entertainment Costs

Culture is wonderfully accessible with ticket prices for most forms of entertainment very inexpensive. Art exhibitions are generally free. The price of listening to traditional pub music is merely the cost of your drinks—a pint of Guinness costs between IR£1.90 and IR£2 in most country pubs; around IR£2.20 in Dublin. Most tickets for classical-music concerts cost between IR£4 and IR£12. Sometimes you don't even have to pay that. Dublin's Hugh Lane Gallery recently celebrated the centenary of the poet Lorca with a free concert of Spanish classical music.

Irish theater tickets are very well priced, and you don't necessarily have to take a trip to Dublin to catch a good play—especially during the summer months, theater companies regularly tour the provinces. Two of Dublin's top theaters are the Abbey and the Gaiety; ticket prices are IR£10.50 to IR£22.50 and IR£8 to IR£15 respectively. Tickets for Cork's Opera House are IR£10 to IR£14 and, for plays at its Triskel Arts Center, IR£8. Galway's Town Hall Theatre charges IR£9 per ticket.

Cinema tickets are a real steal with prices in most Dublin multiplexes starting at IR£6. Provincial prices average IR£4.75, though the manager of the Diamond Screen Cinema in Monaghan Town quoted IR£2 for the early show and IR£3.50 for the main evening screening. All the big films

In Sligo, these entertainers share their song for free.

from the United States are shown here, though they do seem to have later release dates.

Eating-out costs vary and choice will depend upon population size and whether you're living in a touristy area. Wherever you live, there's never any problem in finding old-fashioned cafés serving tea and scones for IR£1.20 or tucking into a hearty pub lunch for IR£5. Away from larger towns and the better-known tourist routes, things can get a bit more difficult in the evenings. Small-town Ireland does not really have a dining-out culture, and choice is often limited to a hotel dining room, a burger or pizza place, or the local Chinese restaurant. Although a three-course meal will only cost between IR£7 and IR£10, the chef is more likely to have trained in Sligo's catering college than in Hong Kong.

Country house hotels usually have some very innovative menus and are often open to nonguests. However, a meal at such a place is generally in the "treat" category as prices come in at the IR£20- to IR£25-per-head level, with wine extra. On the other hand, Dublin never need prove an expensive place to visit: It has some wonderful ethnic restaurants in the Temple Bar quarter where three-course meals cost less than IR£10 per head.

Personal Taxation

Taxation is horrendously complicated and much will depend on your personal circumstances. For instance, are you planning to become a permanent resident or just spend the summers in Ireland? Are you contemplating self-employment or simply planning to enjoy a well-earned retirement? Do you intend to trade on the Irish stock market? The list of financial activities that can result in having to take care of a tax liability is extensive, but the basic rule is that *all* income arising from Irish sources is subject to Irish income tax. That's unless you are an artist or writer—Ireland can be a wonderful financial haven for creative types, as royalties and sales of works considered worthy of artistic or literary merit are tax-exempt.

As regards income from sources outside Ireland, the State has a double taxation agreement with a number of countries including the United States. In essence, this ensures that you'll not be taxed twice on the same income such as moneys from a company or social-security pension (which can be paid to you in Ireland). You'll receive a credit to cover the tax that's already been paid in your country of origin, which you must produce when submitting tax returns within Ireland. U.S. citizens will obviously have to obtain this proof from the IRS. To ensure no delay in receiving your social-security pension, contact the authorities before you move to Ireland. You can write to the Social Security Administration Office of International Policy, P.O. Box 17741, Baltimore, MD 21235.

To be classified as a resident for tax purposes within Ireland, you need to spend 183 days in the State during the tax year that runs from April 6 to April 5. Spend less than 183 days in Ireland and the Revenue Commissioners deem you to be a visitor and no part of your income from non-Irish sources is subject to personal taxation. If a visit falls across two separate tax years, the number of days for tax residency purposes is 280.

For more extensive information on the tax residency laws, contact the Revenue Commissioners, Dublin Castle, Dublin 2; tel. +353 (0)1 878 0000. A useful free booklet available here is "RES 1." It details the tax liabilities of foreigners residing in Ireland.

Income tax provides around 38 percent of the Government's total tax revenues. The system covers PAYE (pay as you earn), which employers are obliged to deduct from workers' salaries, as well as self-assessment. In both cases, everyone is entitled to certain allowances and reliefs and persons whose income falls below a certain level aren't taxed at all. Current income-tax exemption rates for individuals are IR£4,100 for those under the age of 65; IR£5,000 for those between the ages of 65 and 74; IR£5,500 if over 74. For married couples the exemption rate is doubled. Thus a couple with both members aged 66 are allowed an income of IR£10,000 before they start paying tax.

If income is above these amounts, an individual receives a personal allowance of IR£3,150 on which no tax is levied. (A lower allowance of IR£1,040 applies to the self-employed.) After this allowance has been deducted, the rates on taxable income are 24 percent for the first IR£10,000 and 46 percent on the remainder. A 46-percent top rate of tax may seem shocking, but it has come down from the 65-percent levels of the 1980s.

If applicable, you can also claim relief on things such as mortgage-interest repayments, health-insurance premiums, charitable donations, and, if in employment, contributions to pension schemes. Mortgage-interest relief is two-tiered: First-time buyers are allowed to claim IR£2,500; others IR£1,900. Private health-insurance premiums are eligible for tax relief of 24 percent, regardless of whether you fall into the 46-percent tax bracket. Pension plans allow eligible individuals to invest up to 15 percent of their income every year. These qualify for full tax relief and the returns also grow tax-free.

Unless you find paid employment within Ireland, PRSI (Pay Related Social Insurance) contributions won't apply. PRSI is an additional tax on wage-earners, which goes toward State contributory pensions, unemployment benefits, disability allowances, etc. The PSRI system is complex with differing levy rates, but most workers pay 4.5 percent on weekly incomes above IR£100. Again, you can obtain more information from the Revenue Commissioners.

The rate of capital gains tax (CGT) stands at 20 percent with an annual exemption of IR£1,000 per individual. Investments that may attract capital gains tax include directly held equities, bonds, and certain types of property. The sale of the principal family home is exempt from CGT, as are lottery winnings and bets. A higher rate of 40 percent applies to disposals of development land.

Capital acquisitions tax (CAT), probate tax, and inheritance planning are a minefield for the layperson. If you have substantial assets, it's vital to discuss the subject with a solicitor or a financial adviser who specializes in inheritance laws. While the Revenue Commissioners do produce guidance on these taxes, the language is arcane and blood relationships are subject to all kinds of provisos. The situation is especially tricky for cohabitants who are deemed "strangers in law" in the matter of inheritance rights.

Key points are that spouses are exempt from CAT and probate tax, as is the family home. Children can inherit up to IR£185,550 each before becoming liable to pay CAT. If you die intestate (without making a will), your estate gets divided up according to guidelines in what's termed the Succession Act. Although not everybody feels comfortable about making a will, it's the only way of ensuring your wishes will be carried out. A straightforward will costs in the region of IR£75; details of solicitors in your own locality can be had from Citizens Advice Bureaus, Law Centers, or the Law Society of Ireland, Blackhall Place, Dublin 7; tel. +353 (0)1 671 0711.

Health and Medicine

One of the central issues of moving to a new country is the standards and costs of its health care services. Ireland's are of a high quality for such a small country, though it must be pointed out that the range of services is nowhere near as high-tech or extensive as in the United States.

While most county towns have a good general hospital, patients needing procedures such as specialized heart surgery invariably have to travel to Dublin. However, be assured that general health care within rural communities is fairly well served by family doctors, health centers, and public-health nurses.

For administrative purposes, Ireland's national health service is divided into a regional system of health boards. Residents of counties Galway and Roscommon, for instance, come under the Western Health Board. They will provide information on local doctors, dentists, and public-health centers. To obtain the address of a relevant board, contact the Department of Health, Hawkins House, Hawkins Street, Dublin 2; tel. +353 (0)1 671 4711.

Whether you're arriving as a visitor or hoping to establish residency in Ireland, there are no strange and worrying diseases to be aware of. You certainly won't need shots, though if you're of a very cautious nature you may wish to get inoculated against tetanus.

Those working on farms and in the building trade are always advised to have inoculations as the Irish countryside delivers hazards in the shape of barbed-wire fencing and rusty nails. Keen gardeners won't need reminding that a thorny rosebush can also occasionally yield a nasty surprise and an unwelcome stay in a hospital. Tetanus shots are generally effective for a 10-year period.

You are not going to tread on snakes, encounter any other poisonous reptiles, or meet up with marauding packs of rabid dogs. Rabies is unknown within Ireland, largely thanks to the country's strict quarantine laws. The bug-life is pretty harmless, too: Midge bites are just an irritant, and the stings of wasps and bees are only life-threatening if you're really unlucky and suffer from a rare allergy. In rural areas the nastiest bite you're likely to receive is from a horsefly, colloquially known as a *cleg*. Bites result in angry-looking red lumps, which can be quickly soothed with antihistamine cream and shouldn't require a visit to the doctor.

An obvious concern to some people will be Ireland's damp climate, particularly during winter. If you suffer from respiratory ailments or asthma, there's no avoiding the fact that long sojourns in Ireland are unlikely to improve your condition.

On broader health issues, Ireland is a modern country with modern problems. Like everywhere else we have AIDS and HIV sufferers, with the highest infection rates among young heroin addicts in inner-city Dublin. In the period between 1986 and 1997, 593 cases of AIDS were reported. Sexually transmitted diseases aren't unknown either, but at least the problem is recognized and condoms are readily available in both pharmacies and public restrooms.

One frequently asked question is whether it's safe to drink the water. Yes, it's perfectly safe whether from taps or spring wells. In parts of the midlands and Western Ireland you may notice the water sometimes has a brownish tinge, a bit like very watered-down whiskey, but this doesn't indicate contamination. The color results from the high peat content of the ground through which it flows.

Another issue is BSE, better known as "mad cow disease." There *were* cases in Ireland, though nothing like the numbers in neighboring Britain. Animal screening measures have been brought in and farm management procedures are now subject to rigorous scrutiny by the Department of Agriculture. Nobody wants to take any chances as the country depends heavily on beef export markets.

Costs of Medical Care

Illness isn't something that most people want to dwell on, but it's vital you take precautions against it happening. You may have heard mention that Irish residents enjoy free medical care. So they do—up to a point. Qualification for the entire raft of free services largely depends on status, income level, and exactly what level of medical attention is required.

To begin with, those who are coming to Ireland as holidaymakers or on a short fact-finding mission will need private medical insurance. Free or reciprocal emergency care only applies to EU citizens who can produce what's known as an E11 form. As an American citizen you will undoubtedly be familiar with the concept of private health insurance—you will of course need to check if yours covers foreign travel or whether you need to take out a separate policy.

Irrespective of nationality, once you become resident in Ireland the picture changes. Should you need emergency treatment, you are now entitled to free medical attention in all hospitals and it isn't dependent on income levels. If, however, you and your broken finger simply turn up at a hospital casualty department without a doctor's referral, you'll be liable for a charge of IR£12 for the initial visit. Common sense should dictate what constitutes an emergency requiring immediate attention.

As an Irish resident, again irrespective of nationality or income, you'll also be entitled to free inpatient and outpatient services in public hospitals. This includes such things as consultation services and surgeons' fees, but does not cover the cost of hospital meals and accommodation. The rate charged is IR£25 per day, up to a maximum of IR£250 in any one year. People on very low incomes who hold what are called "medical cards" don't have to pay this accommodation levy.

As free hospital care for residents seems such an attractive proposition, you may well wonder why more than 1.5 million people here belong to private health-insurance plans. The answer can be summed up in three short words: hospital waiting lists. Treatment and operations for what are classified as non-emergencies can sometimes mean very lengthy waits. It isn't unknown for some patients to have spent three years or more waiting for hip replacements.

Private Health Care

Joining an independent health-insurance plan means you can effectively leapfrog the waiting list and obtain treatment as required. Furthermore, health care premiums can be offset against standard-rate income tax. Depending on the level of coverage chosen, subscriptions allow for anything from semiprivate accommodation in a local public hospital to care in your own room in one of Dublin's private institutions such as the Mater Hospital or the Blackrock Clinic.

You can generally assume that premium-priced plans deliver premium-priced hospital accommodations. On the treatment side, all price bands within these plans cover general medical costs; fees for anesthetists, radiologists, surgeons, and consultants; and most outpatient charges. Private health plans are regulated under the government's Health Insurance Act of 1994.

Within Ireland, you'll often see health-insurance plans referred to as health-insurance schemes. Here the word "scheme" does not have the same kind of negative connotation as it does in the United States.

Ireland's largest independent provider is the Voluntary Health Insurance Board (VHI). Founded as a nonprofit mutual organization in 1957, it has around 1.4 million members throughout the country. Irrespective of your age, if you are already a plan-holder with Blue Cross, Blue Shield, or any other member of the International Federation of Voluntary Health Service Funds, you'll be able to transfer it to the VHI. Those under the age of 65 may join the VHI directly; if you're older than 65 you will not be taken on as a member.

Five different plans are offered; depending on the coverage selected, annual adult premiums range from IR£200.85 to IR£811.15. Costs are not age-dependent; a 30-year-old pays exactly the same as a 60-year-old with the same plan. Although you don't have to undergo any medical examination, there are some initial limitations on coverage if you're joining independently and not transferring a current plan. While benefit is immediately available for treatment due to accidents, for other illnesses and conditions there is a waiting period: 26 weeks for those under 55, and a full year for those over 55.

Health care in Ireland is readily available for most procedures.

Preexisting medical conditions are subject to a very lengthy restriction period: five years for those under 55, seven years for those between the ages of 55 and 59, and 10 years for those over 60. Note too that routine dental and ophthalmic treatment isn't covered. For further information contact the Voluntary Health Insurance Board, Lower Abbey Street, Dublin 1; tel. +353 (0)1 872 449.

Competition offering very similar coverage has recently come to the Irish marketplace in the shape of BUPA (British United Provident Association), an international health-insurance provider. It has a choice

---

Should you need emergency treatment, you are now entitled to free medical attention in all hospitals and it isn't dependent on income levels.

---

of three plans called Essential, Essential Plus, and Essential Gold. Annual premiums are IR£187.87, IR£260, and IR£933.33 respectively.

The main difference with BUPA as opposed to the VHI is that it also allows cover for alternative therapies such as acupuncture and homeopathy. Additionally, patients needing very specialized attention can receive treatment at an appropriate hospital in Britain. But as with VHI, unless you already hold current medical insurance, BUPA won't take you on if you're older than 65. Contact BUPA Ireland, Mill Island, Fermoy, Co. Cork; tel. +353 (0)25 42121.

Critical-illness Insurance

For a real belt-and-braces approach, pre-retirees could also take out critical-illness insurance. Although it's not designed to replace health insurance such as that offered by BUPA and VHI, critical-illness policies pay out a tax-free cash benefit if you or another named party gets a serious illness or requires surgery. Unlike medical insurance, however, critical-illness premiums cannot be offset against a tax bill.

The list of illnesses covered by insurers usually includes such things as heart disease, cancer, kidney failure, etc. Most policies also include a hospital cash plan. This pays an agreed sum per night spent in a hospital, regardless of any other claims made on your ordinary medical insurance. Under these type of policies the cost of coverage *is* linked to age and rises sharply as you become older.

Founded in 1762 and holding offices all over Ireland, Equitable Life is the oldest mutual life-insurance society in the world. On its menu of critical-illness coverage, payments range from IR£1,400 for an appendectomy up to IR£14,000 for a coronary artery bypass. For 59-year-old males requiring lifetime coverage, monthly premiums are IR£45; 59-year-old females can expect to pay IR£31 per month. After 10 years of coverage, monthly premiums drop to IR£37 and IR£27 respectively for men and women 59 years of age. Contact Equitable Life at Odeon House, Eyre Square, Galway; tel. +353 (0)91 565755.

Personal accident plans provide protection against permanent disability arising from an accident. Again, they usually pay out cash sums in the event of hospitalization. Bank of Ireland customers can avail of special policies with Royal & Sun Alliance with monthly premiums for standard coverage starting at IR£4.50 for individuals, IR£7.30 for couples. Ask in any bank branch or contact Royal & Sun Alliance, 13-17 Dawson Street, Dublin 2; tel. +353 (0)1 677 1851.

For information on other Irish brokers offering similar policies contact The Irish Brokers Association, 87 Merrion Square, Dublin 2; tel. +353 (0)1 661 3061.

Family Doctors

Wherever you choose to live, you won't be very far away from the services of a GP (general practitioner), the family doctor. It may come as a surprise to find that Irish GPs are quite prepared to make home visits, even in the middle of the night if necessary. Naturally, if you're simply suffering from general aches and pains, he or she will expect you to visit the surgery (office). This may be in the doctor's own home or at a health center.

Most GPs charge between IR£15 and IR£20 per consultation. If you belong to a private health-insurance plan, part of the cost of GP consultations can be reclaimed under your outpatient coverage. This isn't quite as generous as it sounds as the first IR£250 of fees in any one year has to be met by the individual. Insurance companies only refund anything in excess of that amount, normally up to an annual limit of IR£2,500. Medical card-holders don't have to pay for GP visits or prescribed medicines.

Medical Cards

What are medical cards and are you eligible for one? In general, the answer is only if you have acquired Irish or other EU citizenship. You would also have to have a very low income. Current qualifying rates are a weekly income below IR£89 for individuals under 66, IR£97 for those between

Irish Herb Lore

Camphor plant (*Balsamita vulgaris*): Its dried leaves can be used to keep pesky moths out of wardrobes and linen cupboards.

Feverfew (*Chrysanthemum parthenium*): This daisy-like garden plant was once widely grown to treat fevers, migraines, and headaches.

Fleabane (*Pulicaria dysenterica*): As the name indicates, the burnt foliage can serve to drive away fleas. It was also once employed medicinally against dysentery.

Heartsease (*Viola tricolour*): An attractive flower with multicolored white, yellow, and purple petals, it's commonly associated with love potions.

Horehound (*Marrubium vulgare*): Commonly used by herbalists in syrups for coughs, colds, and lung ailments, before the introduction of hops it was one of the bitter herbs used in making beer. Black horehound was also once used to treat the bite of mad dogs.

Houseleek (*Sempervivum tectorum*): Fleshy and rosette-like, its juice is still sometimes used for skin ailments such as sties on the eyelid. Superstition says that if growing on a roof, the houseleek provides protection against fires.

Mugwort (*Artemisia vulgaris*): Traditionally associated with magic and the ability to ward off evil spirits on St. John's Eve, its feathery fronds can serve as an insect repellent.

Speedwell (*Veronica chamaedrys*): Low-growing with tiny blue flowers, this creeping plant was once used to treat coughs, asthma, and catarrh.

Valerian (*Valerina officinalis*): A tall, red-flowered plant that's pretty enough for the garden, its roots yield a strong sedative.

Vervain (*Verbena officinalis*): Apparently an important plant in Druidic times and later used as a charm against witchcraft, today it treats nervous disorders, staunches blood, and eases the pangs of childbirth.

the ages of 66 and 79, and IR£101.50 for those over 80 years. For couples in the same age brackets, qualifying weekly income rates are IR£129, IR£144, and IR£151.50 respectively. If you think you may qualify for a medical card (perhaps through holding dual citizenship), the scheme is administered through regional health boards.

Medicines and Pharmacies

Unfortunately, private health insurers don't cover the cost of medicines prescribed by your GP. To cite one example, it costs around IR£22.50 for a short course of antibiotics for a chest infection. There is a safety net, however, to help residents avoid running up massive bills.

Persons who, in the view of their doctor or consultant, suffer from a long-term condition that requires ongoing treatment can reduce their expenditure under the Drug Cost Subsidization Scheme. Eligible persons only have to pay IR£32 per month to their local pharmacy, even if the real cost of monthly prescriptions amounts to hundreds of punts. Epilepsy, diabetes, and Parkinson's disease are just a few of the conditions that qualify.

Another way to reduce costs is with the Drug Refund Scheme. No matter what the illness, if you spend more than IR£90 on prescribed medicines within a three-month period, you may reclaim anything in excess of this amount. Claim forms are available from pharmacies and should be submitted to the relevant regional health board along with receipts.

Every small town has at least one pharmacy, better known in Ireland as "the chemist." They are generally open during normal retail hours but within larger towns a rota system allows for late-night services, too. Along with prescription drugs, cosmetic items, and toiletries, they also stock a range of over-the-counter medicines such as painkillers, cough syrups, and the like, many of which are manufactured by international drug companies.

Plenty of medicines that you'll be familiar with are to be found in Ireland, too. In more rural districts, chemists are also the purveyors of animal-husbandry products and it's not uncommon to see remedies for cattle fluke sitting above a shelf stocked with such items as shampoos and hair colorants!

Dental Costs

The costs of routine dental care will also have to come out of your own pocket unless you hold a medical card. Fees vary considerably: Expect to pay between IR£20 and IR£40 for an initial check-up, IR£20 and IR£50 for a filling or extraction, and IR£200 and IR£400 for a capping. A course of treatment for gum disease could cost around IR£800, while a full set of dentures averages IR£375.

It's possible to take some of the pain out of paying for dental treatment by traveling across the border to Northern Ireland. Fees charged by Belfast dentists are substantially lower (around 20 percent). You'll see their advertisements in newspapers such as the *Irish Times* and *Irish Independent*.

Senior Health

Specifically on retirement health issues, there's a commitment to develop a national program to promote "healthy aging" among older people. In Ireland's family-oriented society, it's not uncommon to still find three generations living under the same roof: Less than 5 percent of seniors reside in nursing homes or other long-stay institutions. Most seniors are completely independent. According to the National Council on Aging and Older People, four out of five of those living in private households were reported as needing no physical help or care.

Even so, geriatric medicine has developed to become the largest subspecialty of internal medicine with consultants based in most of the country's general hospitals. At present, seniors represent only 11.5 percent of the population, but demographic trends indicate numbers rising to 26 percent by the year 2011.

Volunteers Always Welcome

If you're interested in getting involved as a volunteer with health-education projects, there are quite a few opportunities in these areas, particularly if you're a retiree yourself. For details of projects currently seeking volunteers, contact Age & Opportunity, St. Joseph's Building, Marino Institute of Education, Griffith Avenue, Dublin 9; tel. +353 (0)1 837 0570.

For example, Sonas is a charity helping people with communication difficulties. (*Sonas* is an Irish word meaning joy, contentment, or well-being.) It organizes training workshops for volunteers who then guide individuals or small groups through the Sonas program. Their methods involve gentle exercise, sing-alongs, dancing, and massage, as well as aromatherapy and poetry readings. Contact Sister Mary Threadgold, Sonas aPc, 38 Belvedere Road, Dublin 1; tel. +353 (0)1 836 6874.

In the northeast, people over 65 are being trained to run Lifewise, a health-education program for their peer group of retirees. Its basic priorities are health education, exercise, relaxation, and stress management.

Taking a walk in the country is one way to keep in shape.

Contact Dr. Declan Bedford, Specialist in Public Health Medicine, North Eastern Health Board, Navan Road, Kells, Co. Meath; tel. +353 (0)46 71872.

Keeping Fit

Ireland spends more than IR£67 million annually on leisure and recreation with sales of fitness equipment alone put at IR£20 million. If treadmills, rowing machines, and cardiovascular workouts are your idea of bliss, you may want to join a gym. Nowadays you'll find private gyms and fitness clubs in most cities but the cost of keeping fit can be quite expensive. Furthermore, demand is so high that prospective members may have to join a waiting list.

Before you sign up for a pricey annual membership, ask yourself if you really intend to make good use of all the state-of-the-art equipment. Would you be better off with a weekly aerobics class in the village hall (IR£2 to IR£4 per session) or a free workout on the public tennis courts? The dropout rate of gym members is estimated to be as high as 60 percent, and few clubs give refunds. To help you make your mind up, always ring up to see if any of the local gyms or health clubs offers free trials to prospective members.

In Dublin, one of the largest and best-equipped gyms is the Westwood (Westwood Gym, Leopardstown Racecourse, Foxrock, Dublin 18; tel. +353 0-1 289 3208) near Leopardstown Racecourse. Individual membership costs IR£676, which includes a joining fee of IR£160. Couples pay IR£1,084. The Shelbourne Club (Shelbourne Hotel, St. Stephen's Green, Dublin 2; tel. +353 0-1 676 6471) is even more expensive at IR£1,300 for individuals and IR£2,420 for couples. But this price buys five-star exclusivity—the club has fewer than five hundred members as opposed to the Westwood's five thousand.

In Galway, the Ryan Hotel leisure club (Galway Ryan Hotel, Dublin Road, Galway; tel. +353 0-91 753181) has around six hundred members and charges an annual fee of IR£650 for individuals and IR£1,000 for couples. Facilities include two swimming pools. Cork's Leeside Center

Folk Remedies

Like all societies, Ireland has its folk cures and reputed healers with special powers. Although few people would dream of carrying around a haddock's jawbone in their pocket as a charm against toothaches, it's still widely believed that the seventh son of a seventh son holds "the cure."

Another long-standing tradition is that the waters of holy wells can relieve anything from sprains to skin diseases. Wells dedicated to St. Brigid are commonly credited with an ability to cure eye complaints. That people still believe in their curative powers is evidenced by votive offerings left behind on nearby trees and bushes.

Most country youngsters grow up knowing that dock leaves soothe nettle stings and that a cold iron key pressed against the back usually stops a nosebleed. And, despite the fact that every pharmacy stocks chilblain relief cream, countless older folk swear by the home remedy of bathing cold, swollen toes or fingers in a bowl of fresh urine. Another commonly cited home cure is the treatment of piles (hemorrhoids) with a poultice of boiled onions.

Remedies range from mundane doings with butter and cabbage leaves to some very bizarre notions indeed. One old cure for whooping cough started by giving a meal to a ferret—the portion that the ferret left was then presented to the patient. Another strange idea required any would-be healer of burns to first capture a frog or water newt. The main part of what is undoubtedly an ancient magic ritual was to lick the amphibian's back nine times, an act that needed to be repeated on nine successive days. Apparently the licker was thought to acquire *some* substance from the animal's back that afforded the power to heal burns.

Although science often confirms the value of certain folk remedies, it's hard to explain how smearing a fox's blood on the groin can dissolve kidney stones, or how goose dung boiled in milk is a sovereign remedy against jaundice. In her book *Ancient Legends, Mystic Charms and Superstitions of Ireland*, Lady Wilde even unearthed a recipe for an Elixir of Potency, perhaps a nineteenth-century version of Viagra. The ingredients included cochineal, gentian root, saffron, snakeroot, salts of wormwood, and the rind of 10 oranges, the whole lot of which was steeped in brandy.

Ireland's search for a cure for baldness dates back to at least the twelfth century. In one example of medieval quackery, the follicly-challenged were urged to fill an earthen pipkin—a kind of pot—with live mice. The pipkin's opening was stoppered with clay and, along with its squeaking mice, buried near the hearth. After twelve months had passed, the eager patient could dig up the pipkin and massage the gruesome contents into his scalp. The leech-doctor who devised this practice recommended wearing gloves—so powerful was the mixture that hair was likely to sprout from the fingertips, too.

An equally disgusting remedy suggested the use of earthworms. In this scenario a stoppered jar of worms was buried in a manure heap—only a month needed to elapse before the contents could be rubbed into shiny pates. Sounds unbelievable? After writing about these baldness "cures" in the early 1980s, the Irish author Dr. Patrick Logan was astounded to find readers writing in for the actual preparations. One man even looked up the retired doctor's address and turned up on his doorstep, presumably in the belief that he'd be given pipkins full of rotten mice and worms!

(St. Patrick's Quay, Cork; tel. +353 0-21 551444) has 1,600 members and charges IR£430 for individuals and IR£630 for couples.

In Limerick you could join the six hundred members of the Limerick Inn's hotel club (tel. +353 0-61 326666) for IR£250 per individual or IR£450 per couple.

Keeping in Touch

Forget all those old jokes about the pony express and pigeon post. Ireland now has a modern and efficient communications system.

Mail

Ireland's state-owned postal service is run by An Post. According to their own figures, more than 560 million letters are delivered annually with over 90 percent achieving next-day delivery. Main post offices generally open from 8:30 a.m. to 5:30 p.m. on weekdays, 9:00 a.m. to noon on Saturday. Along with handling mail, they pay out State pensions and unemployment benefits; sell TV licenses, lottery tickets, and prize bonds; stock travel pass and passport application forms; and operate currency exchange facilities and various savings schemes.

Village post offices don't offer as extensive a range of services and most close for lunch. However, as the local post office is often also the village grocery store, it's usually possible to buy stamps after the mail counter has officially closed. To catch the last post you'll need to check locally as every postbox has its own particular collection time.

Within Ireland itself, postcards and standard letters of less than 25 grams cost IR£.30 to mail. Heavier items are charged by weight. A flat package weighing between 250 and 500 grams costs IR£1.15; a two-kilogram package IR£5.

Airmail deliveries to the United States generally take between five and seven days. Letters weighing less than 25 grams cost IR£.45 and are then scaled by weight. A 300-gram package costs IR£4.80; a 900-gram package IR£14.40. Economy surface rates are far cheaper than airmail; that same 900-gram package only costs IR£5 by surface. The major drawback is that it could take as long as 15 weeks to reach its destination.

If posting important documents or valuables within Ireland, you can send them by registered mail for a small additional fee. There are three rates: IR£1.70, IR£2.20, and IR£2.70. Should a package get lost, you can claim compensation of up to IR£100, IR£500, or IR£1,000, depending on the registration coverage chosen. It's also possible to register mail destined for the United States, but the maximum compensation allowed falls to a paltry IR£20.

A Poste Restante service lets visitors have mail sent to a local post office. It's free of charge and can be availed of for up to three months. You can also rent a private box number at head post offices, delivery depots, and certain post offices around the country. In towns, An Post charges IR£70 per annum for letters, IR£140 to include parcels as well. In rural districts the IR£70 fee includes both parcels and letters.

The raft of options for business customers includes prepaid response mail, on-site collection services, and direct mail. Should you wish to shower a locality with leaflets, rates per thousand items start at IR£60 and fall to IR£40 per thousand for a target market of 500,000 householders. For more information contact An Post Customer Services,

The local post office in Killaloe, county Clare.

GPO, FREEPOST, Dublin 1. (Unless you send it from outside Ireland, you won't need a stamp on the letter.) Within Ireland you can ring a special callsave number: 1850 262362. (A callsave number is charged at the local rate from anywhere in the country.)

Most major international courier services are represented in Ireland and have collection depots around the country. Quotes for sending a 50-gram document package to the States are IR£32.50 with FedEx and IR£35 with DHL. For local offices look under "Courier Services" in the telephone directory's Golden Pages. Most have toll-free numbers connecting to a call center. For Fedex, ring 1800 725725; for DHL ring 1800 535800.

Telephone

A telephone will be indispensable to most homeowners. The Republic's domestic service is provided by Telecom Éireann, a partially State-owned company with one of the world's most up-to-date digital systems. Like most monopolies, it's fairly expensive but deregulation in the telecommunications industry should soon open up the market to competition.

Nowadays it rarely takes longer than 10 days to get a telephone installed. Costs of connection depend upon whether it's a first-time installation or if the line is already in place. If reconnection is within 12 months of a line's previous usage, the service is free. Outside of that time period, reconnection costs IR£36. A first-time connection is charged at IR£99—this includes both line connection and a telephone set with features such as call-waiting and three-way calling. Prices include sales tax.

There are 18 telesales centers around the country—simply dial 1901 within Ireland for more information about getting connected. Or contact the head office: Telecom Éireann, St. Stephen's Green, Dublin 2; tel. +353 (0)1 671 4444.

Bills arrive every two months, each one carrying a line charge of IR£20. That's IR£120 per year before you've even made a single call. And I'm afraid there's some more unwelcome news—Ireland doesn't have any such thing as a free local call. Unlike in the States, gossiping to new friends and neighbors down the road will come at a cost. The number of units used determines actual cost of calls. Each unit buys a certain amount of time—how much depends upon the time of day, whether it's a weekday or a weekend, and the destination of the call. Each unit is charged at 11.5p and includes a VAT of 21 percent. Calls at different times of the day are charged by the following method:

Times to Call
• **Standard rates** apply from 8 a.m. to 6 p.m. Monday through Friday.
• **Reduced rates** apply from 6 p.m. to 8 a.m. Monday through Friday and all day on weekends and public holidays.
• **Weekend trunk rates** (long distance within Ireland) apply from midnight Friday to midnight Sunday and all day on weekends and public holidays.

Local and Trunk Rates
• **Local calls** at the standard rate cost 11.5p for three minutes.
• **Local calls** at the reduced rate cost 11.5p for 15 minutes.
• **Trunk calls** (long distance within Ireland) to destinations within 56 kilometers cost 11.5p for 66.7 seconds at the standard rate, and 11.5p for 100 seconds at the reduced rate. To destinations beyond 56 kilometers, the cost is 11.5p for 31.7 seconds at the standard rate, and 11.5p for 47.6 seconds at the reduced rate. Weekend trunk rates are 11.5p for 10 minutes to anywhere in Ireland.

International Calls
To call the United States or Canada, charges from private phones are .36p per minute standard rate; .34p per minute reduced rate, and .31p per minute economy rate. Time bands are calculated differently for domestic calls and are as follows:
• **Standard rates** apply from noon to 6 p.m. weekdays.
• **Reduced rates** apply from 8 a.m. to noon and 6 p.m. to 10 p.m. weekdays.
• **Economy rates** apply from 10 p.m. to 8 a.m. weekdays and all day Saturday, Sunday, and public holidays.

Making international calls from a public payphone is very costly. Charges (per minute) are IR£1.45 standard, IR£1.24 reduced, and IR£1.11 economy to the United States and Canada. To call the Middle East or South Africa costs a staggering IR£3.03 per minute.

How to Make Calls
Within Ireland, telephone numbers are quoted with subscriber trunk dialing (STD) codes given first in brackets. These are the equivalent of area codes. For example, the STD code for Dublin is 01; for Galway it's 091. Say you were in Dublin and wished to call Galway's tourist office (tel. 091 563081). The digits given are those you would dial. If, however, you were calling from within Galway itself, simply ring 563081.

When phoning from the States, you first need to dial the international access code (011) followed by the country code for Ireland (353). And although Galway's STD code is 091, that initial "0" is dropped when phoning from abroad. Thus, to reach Galway's tourist office, dial 011 353 91 563081.

As another example, say you want to call the Revenue Commissioners at Dublin Castle (tel. 01 878 0000). That's the number you call if phoning on an Irish phone from outside Dublin. Within Dublin you ring 878 0000. If calling from the United States, you dial 011 353 1 878 0000.

To call the United States from Ireland, dial the access code (00), the country code (1), the area code, then the local number. The Irish Embassy's number in Washington, D.C., is 202/462-3939. To call from Ireland dial 00 1 202 462 3939.

Public Phone Boxes

Public payphones accept either coins or calling cards, which are sold at post offices, petrol stations, newsagents, and most grocery stores. Calling cards are available in units of 10 (IR£2), 20 (IR£3.50), 50 (IR£8), and 100 (IR£16). Units are charged at different rates depending on whether a coin-operated or card-operated phone is used. A .20p coin buys a three-minute local call, but the cost drops to .17p if you're using a 50-unit calling card. Operator-assisted calls cost .70p minimum. To call the operator dial 10.

Emergency Calls

In an emergency, dial either 999 or 112. Calls are free and you must ask the operator for the service you want: fire brigade, gardái (police), ambulance, lifeboat, or mountain rescue. When the emergency service answers, state the address or location where help is required.

Directory Inquiries

Can't find the number you're seeking? Call 1190 for numbers within Ireland and Northern Ireland, 1197 for numbers in Britain, and 1198 for all other international inquiries. Customers are allowed four free directory-inquiry calls per two-monthly bill. Otherwise the charge is 34.5p per call for a maximum of three inquiries. If you're a real penny-pincher, inquiries from public payphones are free of charge.

Mobile Phones

Mobile phones are not a very common sight in rural Ireland, although business is certainly booming within Dublin. At present, two companies within Ireland provide access to mobile-phone technology. Eircell, part of the Telecom Éircann network, offers both analogue and digital service. Esat Digifone is a private-sector operator whose network is entirely digital.

Ireland on the Web

For those who already have computers with an Internet connection, there's an amazing amount of information available on all things Irish. For example, ask a search engine to come up with details on Irish travel and you'll be overwhelmed with a choice of thousands of sites ranging from corporate golfing holidays to cottages for rent in county Clare. Many Irish-interest Web sites are actually based in the United States, but there are some interesting homegrown ones, too. Have a browse around some of these:

www.irlgov.ie
The Irish government's official Web site with links to various departments such as Foreign Affairs, Health, Justice, the Revenue Commissioners, etc. Although visiting the taxman isn't exactly an entertaining experience, you can download comprehensive files on everything from vehicle-registration tax to self-employment requirements.

www.luminarium.org/mythology/ireland
An absolutely fascinating site of myth, folklore, and stories containing heaps of esoteric material. Did you know that *caisean uchad* was a kind of Celtic pass-the-parcel game in which a burning sheep's head was passed around a group of revelers?

www.mayo-ireland.ie
Where you'll find Comhaltas Ceoltori Éireann, Ireland's main organization for keeping the flame of traditional culture alight. Plenty of information on festivals, music teaching, music publications, and local branches.

www.ceolas.org/ceolas.html
Another Irish music site with sound clips and a wealth of information on traditional music and dance.

www.failte.com/macnas
All about Galway's community-based arts and street-theater group with clips of the annual madcap parade during Arts Week.

www.avery.med.virginia.edu/~eas5e/irish/famine.html
A long way in, but one of the best sites for anyone seeking information on the Great Famine. Along with photos, prints, and drawings, the site contains reportage and commentary from the time.

www.iavi.ie
Real estate through members of the Irish Auctioneers and Valuers Institute. Some members are better than others at keeping their listings up-to-date, but it's a good indication of the availability of countrywide property and the prices those properties go for. You'll find everything from cottages to farmhouses, pubs to hotels, Georgian mansions to urban apartments.

www.ireland.travel.ie
The official site of Bord Fáilte, the Irish Tourist Board. All the basic need-to-know information about hotels, restaurants, sights to see, and things to do. Plus, if you're seeking a special-interest vacation, check out its searchable database. It came up with 148 suggestions for an equestrian holiday.

www.irish-times.com
All the daily news and views from one of Ireland's top broadsheet newspapers. The site includes a genealogical gateway where you can discover the history behind many Irish surnames or embark upon a search for your own Irish ancestors.

www.finfacts.ie
Extremely useful site for current information on economic indicators, savings options, best airfares, etc.

Mobile phones can be bought for as little as IR£10, but calls are far more expensive than on a fixed phone. With Esat's Digilite service it costs 41.3p per minute to call a fixed phone number at peak time. Then there is a connection fee of IR£35 with both companies and also monthly rental costs. The minimum is IR£12.40 with Esat and IR£20 with Eircell. Alternatively, Eircell has a ready-to-go package: mobile phone, IR£20 "Go" card, and a charger. You can top out the credit on your "Go" card as you wish, and thus avoid monthly bills.

The differing networks claim to cover between 92 and 96 percent of the population. Sounds good, but population isn't *territory* and mountains tend to have an unfortunate effect on transmissions. Technology meets its match in west Kerry, Connemara, most parts of Donegal, and sometimes even around Dublin due to the Wicklow Mountains.

Another drawback is that Eircell's system isn't yet capable of connecting customers to mobile-phone numbers in the United States or vice versa. Esat's Digifone network will put you through to "69" numbers in the United States, but again, its roaming service doesn't yet work in the reverse direction. However, you can have two-way dialing with most other European countries. Contact Eircell at Eircell House, 6-8 College Green, Dublin 2. Within Ireland call their toll-free phone number: 1800 225588. Esat Digifone can be reached at tel. +353 (0)61 203501. Once in Ireland call their toll-free number: 1800 222086.

E-mail and the Internet

Ireland has a number of Internet service providers if you're keen on traveling the information superhighway. The average yearly subscription fee is IR£120; installation software is between IR£5 and IR£12.50. Costs of telephone calls connecting you to the Internet or your POP e-mail service are charged according to the local rate. Thus it will cost 11.5p per three minutes during peak weekday hours; 11.5p per 15 minutes during the evenings and weekends.

Telecom Internet (Tinet) is Telecom Éireann's service provider. Contact your local Telecom sales center or ring their special callsave number: 1850 203204. Ireland On-Line is another big player. They can be reached at Alexandra House, Earlsfort Terrace, Dublin 2; tel. +353 (0)1 604 6800. Business users may find it worthwhile to contact the Irish Internet Association, P.O. Box 6118, Dublin 2; tel. +353 (0)1 668 8108.

If you don't yet own a computer, but have a burning desire to read about the latest White House scandals on the Drudge Report, you can log on to the Internet at some public libraries or in one of the growing number of cybercafés. Charges are around IR£5 per hour.

Dublin's many bookstores make it easy to keep up with international news.

Newspapers and the Media

The Republic's two main broadsheet dailies are the *Irish Times* and the *Irish Independent*; both currently cost 85p. The *Irish Times* has quite a serious outlook while the *Irish Independent* carries more gossipy lifestyle features. Both have good business coverage and special weekly property supplements. (Thursdays for the *Times*, Fridays for the *Independent*.)

Published in Cork, the *Examiner* is another daily but its sale is not that widespread outside the southern half of the Republic. If your taste runs to tabloids, there are special Irish versions of British dailies such as the *Sun*, *Mirror*, and *Star*. All carry a relentless cavalcade of celebrity gossip and scandal and not very much in the way of news.

On Sundays you can choose from the *Sunday Independent*, *Sunday Business Post*, *Tribune*, and an Irish edition of Britain's *Sunday Times*. The *Sunday World* is rather more down-market and celebrity oriented but it's undeniably popular. There are also a substantial number of provincial newspapers that are published on a weekly basis and concentrate mainly on local issues and events.

As far as U.S. publications are concerned, *Time*, *Newsweek*, and the *International Herald Tribune* are usually on sale in larger newsagents. If you want regular copies your local newsagent will be able to order them for you. Don't, however, expect to get any papers or magazines through your letterbox—Ireland doesn't have newspaper-delivery boys and girls.

Many of Ireland's local newspapers are flown out to U.S. cities with sizable populations of Irish-Americans. You'll certainly be able to buy the *Sligo Champion* or the *Longford Leader* in New York and Boston. It's also worth looking at magazines such as *World of Hibernia* or *Ireland of the Welcomes*, both of which carry plenty of travel and general-interest features.

One of the best reads for potential new residents is a quarterly subscription magazine, *Inside Ireland*. Most of its readership is American and it contains lots of valuable practical advice along with quirky features and lifestyle articles by folks who have already bought a home here. You can obtain a free sample copy by sending a $2 contribution for postage ($4 airmail) to Inside Ireland, P.O. Box 1886, Dublin 16; tel. +353 (0)1 493 1906.

The public-television service currently consists of RTE 1, RTE 2, and an Irish-language station, TnaG. An independent station, TV 3, is due to join them soon. Home-produced programs that are very popular include *Glenroe*, a soap opera about farming families; and *The Late, Late Show*, claimed to be the world's longest-running chat show. Many other programs (around 60 percent of output) are imported from Britain, Australia, and the United States, so if you're pining for familiar fare, you'll be able to keep up with what's happening in *NYPD Blue* and *The X-Files*. Sports coverage is good: Although you'll rarely catch baseball, there's more than enough Gaelic games, soccer, golf, tennis, snooker, horseracing, and carracing to keep even the most fanatical sports addict satisfied. If you want more, well, there's cable TV and satellite channels such as BskyB and Eurosport.

An important point to note is that you need a license to watch TV. It costs IR£70 annually and you obtain one from the post office. If a detector van comes around and you cannot produce a license, you will be taken to court and fined as much as IR£500 for a first offense. The money garnered from license payers goes to fund the making of RTE programs.

Ireland's three national radio stations are supplemented by a plethora of independent regional stations. Like everywhere else in the Western world, some offer wall-to-wall pop; others a mix of music, chat, and phone-ins. One of the most entertaining phone-in programs where everything and anything is up for discussion is the *Gerry Ryan Show*. It's broadcast on weekdays between 9 a.m. and noon on RTE 2FM (FM 90.4–97 MHz; MW 612, 1278 kHz). Opera and classical music can be found on RTE 3FM (FM 92.6–102.7 MHz).

Getting Around

You'll have to drive on the other side of the road, and you may have to hop a ferry to get where you're going, but you'll soon find getting around in Ireland is no hassle at all.

Air Travel

Deregulation in the air travel business has brought much-needed competition to the skies above Ireland. Scheduled airlines now fly direct to 19 different countries, and every year bring increasing numbers of holiday charter flights to North America, the Caribbean, and Mediterranean hotspots.

With 77 percent of the market share, the country's main international gateway is Dublin Airport, tel. +353 (0)1 844 4900. Shannon Airport, tel. +353 (0)61 471444, 10 miles from Limerick, lost much of its business with the abolition of the so-called Shannon stopover, a ruling that all incoming and outgoing transatlantic flights had to touch down there. Although Shannon still offers limited flights to the United States, its only other links are to Dublin and two UK cities, London and Manchester.

Overseas flights from Cork, tel. +353 (0)21 313131, are confined to the UK, Paris, Amsterdam, and the Channel Islands. However, Belfast's airport, tel. +440 1849 422888, provides another overseas gateway. It's worth considering if you're seeking budget charter fares to Canada: returns (round-trips) to Toronto can usually be had for less than £280 sterling.

Ireland's network of small domestic airports connects Dublin to the provinces and provides limited flights to the UK. Most of these airports are served by the national carrier, Aer Lingus, which flies between Dublin and Cork, Galway, Kerry, Shannon, Sligo, and Belfast. Flight times are under 40 minutes but fares are astonishingly expensive for the relatively short distances covered. For example, return flights between Dublin and Sligo currently cost IR£79. Domestic services are mainly used by business people whose companies pick up the tab. Note, too, that it isn't possible to fly direct between provincial airports—all journeys necessitate a changeover in Dublin.

County Mayo's Knock Airport, tel. +353 (0)94 67222, is served by Ryanair flights from Dublin and the UK. It gets quite busy in summer with charter flights of pilgrims bound for the Marian shrine in Knock village. Out in the Atlantic, the Aran Islands are served by Aer Arann from Connemara Regional Airport, tel. +353 (0)91 75569, with four daily flights during winter and every half hour in peak holiday season. Return fares are currently IR£35.

On the transatlantic route, Aer Lingus flies direct to four U.S. destinations: New York, Newark, Chicago, and Boston. Its North American flying partner is Delta Airlines, which connects Ireland with over 240 U.S. cities through its two gateway airports, New York and Atlanta. As part of its expansion program, Continental Airlines plans to enter the Irish marketplace, providing onward connections to a range of U.S. cities through its gateway airport, Newark. Flight times between Ireland and the U.S. eastern seaboard cities average eight hours.

Transatlantic fare structures are in a constant state of flux and invariably subject to seasonal differences. In general, high summer and the Christmas/New Year holiday periods are the most expensive times to book flights to the States as there's always increased demand from visiting friends and relatives. Much depends on how flexible you can be and how far in advance you can book. Although economy returns to New York are advertised from IR£299, the reality is likely to be in the region of IR£380 for a two-week return in May or June.

At the time of writing, Aer Lingus's best available deal was an economy return from either Dublin or Shannon to Newark for IR£329. Tickets needed to be booked at least seven days in advance and required a Saturday-night stay. And although return flights to Atlanta with Delta could be had for IR£375 in early March, that price had risen to IR£518 by mid-season.

Just as in the States, it pays to shop around and keep your eyes peeled for special promotional offers in the media or travel agents' windows. Again, if you can be flexible, some good bargains can be had with package-tour companies who offer an option of "seat only" deals to independent travelers. Tour America, an Irish-owned company specializing in North American holidays, has flight-only deals to Boston and New York from

IR£275, Chicago from IR£294, and Los Angeles and San Francisco from IR£339. Contact them at 62 Middle Abbey Street, Dublin 1; tel. +353 (0)1 878 0400.

Another way of shaving costs is by booking through a consolidator or independent flight specialist such as Trailfinders. On their North American menu, return tickets from Dublin to Washington, DC, start from IR£263; Las Vegas from IR£339; and New Orleans from IR£357. As always, low-priced seats are subject to availability and fares may be substantially higher if you need to travel at short notice or during the main holiday season. Contact Trailfinders at 4/5 Dawson Street, Dublin 2; tel. +353 (0)1 677 7888.

The real bonanza for Ireland's air passengers is on the Dublin–Britain routes where competition ensures numerous rock-bottom return fares starting at as little as IR£40. It's a great opportunity for you to travel further afield—not just to London, but also to cities like historic Edinburgh, the Scottish capital. Fly to Leeds/Bradford and you're at the gateway to medieval York and the Yorkshire Moors—remember *Wuthering Heights* and the Brontë sisters? Or, for an authentic insight into blue-collar English culture, join the legions of Irish fans who regularly fly to northwest England to watch soccer teams like Liverpool and Manchester United!

Looking at other European destinations, the most affordable cities to reach are Paris, Amsterdam, and Brussels—economy returns can be had for IR£79 to IR£99. As regards other European cities, a sample of the lowest-

FREE TRAVEL FOR RETIREES

Regardless of citizenship or income, all residents over the age of 66 are entitled to free travel on the road and rail services of Dublin Bus, Bus Éireann, Irish Rail, the DART (Dublin Area Rapid Transport), and certain other private bus and local ferry services. There's no limit to the amount of free travel that you can enjoy, although some restrictions apply to city bus services during peak travel times.

The free travel pass can also be used for cross-border journeys to and from Northern Ireland. In addition, Aran Islands' residents can claim up to 12 free return flights to the mainland every year. Another benefit is that your spouse doesn't have to pay when traveling with you, even though he or she may be a pre-retiree. Applications for travel passes can be picked up at post offices or your local Social Welfare office.

priced returns with Aer Lingus include Copenhagen (IR£199), Frankfurt (IR£205), Rome (IR£259), Madrid (IR£252), and Geneva (IR£300). However, you may be able to find better offers with competing airlines such as Air France, Lufthansa, and Scandinavian Airlines, all of which have Dublin offices.

Ferries

Apart from the Aran Islands, which have their own airstrips, the only way to reach the 18 inhabited islands off Ireland's coastline is by ferry. They are mostly run by small, private concerns with some boats only able to take 12 passengers. Larger vessels are equipped to carry cars, but these aren't super-ferries—the Arranmore ferry, for example, only takes eight cars at a time. Sailing schedules vary and there are always more crossings between Easter and late September to cater for tourists.

Ferries are the traditional way to reach Inishmore, Inishmaan, and Inisheer, the three Aran Islands. Depending on your embarkation point (Galway, Rossaveal, or Doolin in county Clare) and eventual destination, journey times take between 30 and 90 minutes. A number of ferry companies serve the islands, though some only operate during summer. Aran Island Ferries runs an all-year service to each island with return fares of between IR£15 and IR£22. Contact them at Victoria Place, Galway; tel. +353 (0)91 561767.

A Gaelic-speaking island nine kilometers from Donegal's coast, Tory

---

THE EMERALD SKIES

Aer Arann (flights to the Aran Islands), Connemara Regional Airport, Inverin, Galway; tel. +353 (0)91 593034.

Aer Lingus (domestic, European, and transatlantic), Dublin Airport, Dublin; tel. +353 (0)1 705 3333.

Delta Airlines (transatlantic), 24 Merrion Square, Dublin 2; tel. +353 (0)1 661 1880.

Ryanair (domestic and European), Dublin Airport, Dublin; tel. +353 (0)1 609 7800.

All travel agents also sell air tickets. The Irish government travel tax of IR£5 is generally included in quotes for scheduled flights, but with charter flights it may be billed separately.

Island endures the full fury of the Atlantic winter gales—it's not unknown for its 140 inhabitants to be cut off from the mainland for days at a time. Weather permitting, daily boats are operated by Tory Island Ferry (tel. +353 0-75 31991) from Bunbeg Pier. In good weather, the crossing time is 75 minutes; return tickets cost IR£12.

Donegal's other major inhabited island is Arranmore, a 25-minute crossing from Burtonport village on the mainland. During summer, the resident population swells from 900 to around 1,500. For sailing times contact the Arranmore Ferry at tel. +353 (0)75 20532. Return fares are IR£6 for foot passengers, IR£18 for car and driver.

Ferries are the traditional way to reach Inishmore, Inishmaan, and Inisheer, the three Aran Islands.

At the opposite end of the country, in county Cork, Cape Clear Island copes with an estimated 20,000 annual visitors. Many come for the birding, for this is one of the main passageways for summer migrants. Sailing time from Baltimore village on the mainland is 45 minutes; contact Coiste Naomh Ciaran for schedules on tel. +353 (0)28 39119. Return fares are IR£8.

In county Mayo, Clare Island was the old stamping ground of Ireland's infamous pirate queen, *Grainne Uaille*. About 150 permanent residents live on the island, which can be reached from Roonagh Quay, 12 miles from Westport town. Return fares are IR£10; contact Westport tourist office for schedules at tel. +353 (0)98 25711. Another island worth exploring is Inishbofin, the "Island of the White Cow" in county Galway. Boats set sail from Cleggan village; fares are IR£12 return (tel. +353 0-95 44642).

Should you want to cross the Irish Sea to Britain, there is a reasonable number of day and nighttime ferries. Services to Holyhead in North Wales are operated by Stena Line, +353 (0)1 204 7700, from Dun Laoghaire and Dublin ports, and by Irish Ferries, +353 (0)1 661 0511, from Dublin port. Prices are similar but tend to rise dramatically in high season. With Stena, a five-day return for car, driver, and up to four passengers costs IR£149 in low season but IR£259 in July. Depending on whether travel is by high-speed catamaran or traditional ferry, crossing time takes between one hour and forty minutes and three and a half hours.

The main crossing point for ferries to South Wales is Rosslare in county Wexford. Again, Stena and Irish Ferries share the route. With Irish Ferries, returns for foot passengers cost IR£30; if taking a car, prices vary from IR£108 to IR£298, depending on season. Four friends or relatives can travel with you for this price and the crossing time averages four hours.

If you have the stamina for a 16-hour-minimum sea crossing, bowls of milky coffee and fresh buttery croissants await in France. Irish Ferries sails to both Roscoff and Cherbourg; tickets cost between IR£35 and IR£70 for foot passengers and there is a range of deals if you want to take the car and stock up the trunk with inexpensive wine. Nine-day spring and fall specials start at IR£155 return.

Buses

In general, all towns of any size are on a bus route with regular links to Dublin or the nearest city. It's possible to travel between most places, though not always by the direct route. Journeys may involve changes and sometimes a lengthy wait in midland transport hubs such as Mullingar and Athlone.

Villages, especially those west of the river Shannon, are not particularly well served. Some rural communities only have a once-a-week service; many don't even have that. There are numerous localities where catching the bus means first having to undertake an 8- or 10-mile trek to the nearest main road.

Dublin Bus provides one type of public transportation in the capital.

The country's national bus service is Bus Éireann, +353 (0)1 836 6111, its logo a friendly looking Irish setter. Fares are less expensive than with the train, though purchasing a one-way ticket isn't substantially cheaper than buying a return. If you're planning just a one-day trip, ask about special day-return offers as these are usually a good value. Ordinary weekday return fares to selected destinations are as follows: Dublin–Cork IR£13, Dublin–Tralee IR£15.50, Dublin–Galway IR£9, Dublin–Ballina IR£9. Services are quite frequent—five buses travel daily to Tralee, for example.

Competition is provided by numerous local operators whose coaches usually provide services to destinations that Bus Éireann does not. Depending on local need, services generally vary between twice a day to once a week. In the little county Leitrim town of Drumshanbo for instance, there's one early-morning bus every weekday taking workers to Sligo. Shoppers can use the service, but it means spending all day in Sligo town as the coach doesn't return until after 6 p.m. and all the regulars are on board.

Most buses leaving for the provinces depart from Dublin's central bus station, Busaras. On the north side of the river Liffey, it's less than a five-minute walk from the Connolly railway station. Within the capital itself, a fairly comprehensive service is provided by Dublin Bus, +353 (0)1 873 4222. As well as linking the city to suburbia and the greater Dublin area, they run frequent services to the airport, ferry ports, and the two main railway stations. The fare to the airport, 10 kilometers north of the city, is IR£2.50 from Busaras, IR£3.50 from Heuston Station. In other cities, Bus Éireann provides the city-to-suburbs service.

Rail

The Republic's rail service is called Iarnród Éireann, Irish Rail, 35 Lower Abbey St., Dublin 1; tel. +353 (0)1 836 6222. Although trains are faster than long-distance buses, the network is by no means extensive—for example, you cannot reach anywhere in counties Donegal, Cavan, and Monaghan. Nor can you travel to the seaside towns of West Cork, Kerry's Dingle Peninsula, or the far western corners of county Clare.

For journeys originating in Dublin, Connolly Station is the departure point for trains north to Belfast, northwest to Sligo, and down the east-coast route passing through Wicklow to Rosslare Harbor. Heuston Station is where to board for Cork City, Limerick, Galway, Tralee, and a number of other towns in the south, southwest, and west. (The two stations are connected by the No. 90 Dublin Bus service.) As with buses, day-return tickets represent the best value in what is rather a complex fare structure of off-peak returns, weekend specials, midweek returns, etc. Staff are normally very helpful in advising what would be the best-priced ticket to suit your plans. Traveling second-class, some sample midweek return fares are as follows: Dublin–Athlone IR£9.50, Dublin–Belfast IR£26, Dublin–Carrick-on-Shannon IR£16, and Dublin–Killarney IR£33.50, Dublin–Westport IR£21.

Dublin also has the DART, an acronym for Dublin Area Rapid Transport. An electric rail system with several stations within the capital, it plies between Howth on the north county Dublin coast and Bray in county Wicklow. For those catching ferries to Britain, a one-way DART ticket from Pearse Street Station in central Dublin to the port at Dun Laoghaire costs IR£1.10.

THE AGE OF STEAM

Steam-engine buffs should make tracks for the Shannonside village of Dromod where enthusiastic volunteers are gradually rebuilding the **Cavan & Leitrim Railway**. First opened in 1887, it was built to the Irish narrow gauge of three feet. In those early years, transportation of livestock was the backbone of the service as the sparsely populated countryside delivered few human passengers. The line's later traffic mostly consisted of coal from the mines of the Arigna Mountains.

By the time the last trains ran in 1959, the line's locomotives were virtual museum pieces. Happily a lifted track was relaid and a project to restore the railway started in 1993. If you have a taste for nostalgia, short-haul passenger services now run on Saturday and Sunday afternoons between May and October. Contact the Cavan & Leitrim Railway, Dromod, Co. Leitrim; tel. +353 (0)78 38599.

Driving in Ireland

Driving in Ireland can be both a pleasure and a penance. Yes, it's true that many roads are blessedly quiet and free of other motorists. It's also true that it's perfectly safe to stop and ask locals for directions if you get lost. Alas, the typical country road is likely to be pitted with potholes, awash in winter floodwater, and—just when you want to use it—being used as a private gathering place by beasts of the field.

Not that us country folk envy city motorists. Peak time in Dublin is an abysmal snarl-up—this was a city built for the horse and carriage trade, not juggernauts, buses, and commuter traffic. Even the brand-new motorway link to the West is subject to frequent tailbacks and delays. Just to add insult to injury, the price of petrol is enough to make you weep. Although all the major oil companies are represented here there is little variation on prices. The average is IR£2.79 per gallon (IR£.60 per liter) for leaded petrol, a few pence less for unleaded and diesel.

Rules of the Road

For first-time visitors from North America, the golden rule to remember is that in Ireland one drives on the *left* side of the road. Other things to get used to are overtaking on the right and giving way to traffic approaching on your right at roundabouts. Car-rental companies usually recommend that you try and avoid country roads for the first day or so until you're familiar with the car and the new driving environment.

Their advice makes lots of sense for safety's sake. When you first encounter a boreen (a narrow, rutted track with grass growing up the middle), you may well wonder how you are expected to keep to the left-hand side of the road when it's barely wide enough for one vehicle, let alone two. Panic-stricken by seeing a tractor hurtling toward them, some foreign motorists head straight for "the soft margin," better known in other countries as "the ditch." The trick to driving safely along boreens is to keep your speed down and be constantly on the watch for likely passing places such as farm gateways.

This sign indicates "Yield! Major road ahead."

Helped by grants from the European Union, Ireland has made heroic efforts to improve its road network, but there's still a long way to go. While there are short sections of motorway around Dublin, they're nothing like the freeways of North America. Unless otherwise indicated, motorway and dual carriageway speed limits are 70 miles per hour (112 km/h); direction signs are white on a blue background. Tolls are only payable at two points within the country, both are located in the Dublin area. One is on the M50 ring road between the airport and N4 interchange to the west. The other is on the R131

East Link Bridge—in both cases you'll have to pay a toll of 80p for all automobiles.

Between most towns you're likely to be driving on "N" roads: national primary routes. Here the general speed limit is 60 miles per hour (96 km/h) until entering a built-up area where it reduces to 30 miles per hour (48 km/h). Direction signs have white or yellow lettering on a green background. Unless indicated otherwise, the same speed limit applies to "R" roads: secondary routes where signs have black lettering on a white back-

You and the Irish Road

1. **What does a broken white line along the center of a road signify?**
   a) No overtaking. b) You may overtake if it's safe to do so.
   c) A dual carriageway. d) The paint ran out.

2. **What does a single continuous white line along the center of a road mean?**
   a) No overtaking. b) You may overtake if it's safe to do so.
   c) Nothing in particular.

3. **What do double yellow lines along the edge of the road mean?**
   a) No parking. b) No cycling. c) You are allowed to park if displaying a parking disk. d) Parking for tractors only.

4. **What persons have the authority to halt traffic?**
   a) The Gardaí. b) People in charge of animals.
   c) School wardens. d) Lost tourists.

5. **What is the legal minimum tread depth your tires must have?**
   a) 1.6 mm. b) 16 mm. c) 160 mm. d) There is no minimum—bald tires are OK.

6. **Approaching a crossroads with roads of equal importance, who has right of way—you or the Massey Ferguson coming down the road to your right?**
   a) You do—always. b) The Massey Ferguson. c) Whoever is quickest. d) What's a Massey Ferguson?

ground. Then there are the boreens, where direction signs of any kind at all are largely conspicuous by their absence. If you're lucky enough to find a signpost at a country crossroads, doubt it; it's not an exaggeration to suggest that the fingerpost is likely to be pointing in the wrong direction.

On newer signs, distances are given in kilometers, even though most Irish people continue to think in terms of mileage. Older signs carry distances in miles. To further confuse the visiting motorist there is also such a thing as an "Irish mile," which is slightly shorter than a conventional mile. Thankfully the

7. What is the legal alcohol/blood limit applicable to Irish drivers?
a) There isn't one. b) 800 milligrams per 100 milliliters.
c) 80 milligrams per 100 milliliters. d) You cannot drink and drive at all.

8. Who has right of way at a roundabout?
a. Traffic approaching from the right. b) You—no matter what the circumstances. c) Larger vehicles. d) Nobody— it's a free for all.

9. If you follow a sign to *An Lar,* where will it take you?
a) A hospital. b) The coast. c) A library. d) A town center.

10. What is the principal cause of tractor accidents?
a) Driving at an excessive speed. b) Driving too slowly.
c) Collisions with stray animals and rubber-necking tourists. d) Overloaded trailers.

Answers:
1-b; 2-a; 3-a; 4-a, b, and c; 5-a; 6-b; 7-c; 8-a; 9-d; 10-a.

Irish mile is a rarity nowadays and usually only spotted on centuries-old stone markers hidden in hedgerows. More confusion awaits in Gaeltacht areas where road signs are entirely in the Irish language. The most important direction sign to watch for is a red-bordered triangle carrying the words *Geill Slí.* This indicates a major road ahead and you must give way to the traffic on it.

Other rules include a minimum driving age of 17 and compulsory seat belts in both the front and rear of the car. Children under 12 aren't permitted in front seats. Documents that should be carried when driving are a valid driver's license and the vehicle log book or your rental agreement; insurance and road-tax discs also have to be displayed on the front windscreen. If you or another party is involved in an accident, then the Gardaí (police) must be informed.

Driver's Licenses

As a visitor, you're allowed to drive on your American or an international driver's license for up to 12 months. After that, well—brace yourself for some unwelcome news. Unfortunately for Americans, yours is not one of the licenses that can be exchanged for an Irish license. Residents are required to obtain a provisional license and then take the driving test. It's fairly rigorous and the pass rate remains static at around 50 percent.

In rural areas, you're likely to face a different type of traffic jam.

Issued by the motor tax offices of local authorities, a provisional license costs IR£12 and is valid for two years. Application forms need to be accompanied by a birth certificate, two passport-sized photos, and an eyesight report from your doctor or optician. If you haven't passed the driving test within the two-year time span, you can obtain another provisional license on producing a notice of failure from the driving test center.

The law requires provisional drivers to be accompanied by a qualified driver, though this rule is often blatantly ignored. Curiously enough, there are some Irish drivers who have never sat the test, yet legally hold a full license. During the late 1970s the wait for driving tests was so lengthy that the government simply gave up and issued full licenses to all and sundry on the list. It's unlikely to happen again as the wait for tests isn't long nowadays: around six to eight weeks in the provinces, a little longer in Dublin.

No matter how highly you rate your driving skills, it's advisable to take a few lessons with an instructor before taking the Irish driving test. They'll know the local test routes and what a particular examiner is likely to ask you to do. Driving lessons average around IR£15 per hour. Most people take lessons in the instructor's car, which can also be used for the test.

The driving test costs IR£30 and the ordeal lasts for 45 minutes. First the examiner tests your eyesight by asking you to read registration numbers in the car park. You'll then be asked a number of questions regarding the rules of the road and also to identify specific road signs from a chart. The actual on-the-road part of the test takes 30 minutes and you'll have to show that you can park safely as well as perform tasks such as an emergency stop and a three-point turn. Once the test is over you're told immediately whether you've passed or failed.

For more information on licenses and tests contact your local motor-tax authority or Driver Testing Section, Department of Environment, O'Connell Bridge House, Dublin 1; tel. +353 (0)1 679 3200.

Driving schools can be found through your local telephone directory's Golden Pages, but make sure they belong to an accredited body such as the DIR (Driving Instructor Register) or ACDI (Association of Certified Driving Schools).

Buying a Car

Unless you opt for a city life it will be extremely difficult to get by in Ireland without a car. Although it's possible to import your own car from abroad without having to pay duty (subject to fulfilling certain conditions such as having owned it for a year), few American newcomers would bother to do so. Due to the width of many Irish roads, driving is very difficult in the larger U.S. models (and just think of all the gas they guzzle). And where are you going to find spare parts for a Cadillac or a Chevrolet?

Furthermore, the driver's controls are on the "wrong" side, which doesn't make for safe driving. If you insist on bringing your own car, further details on the question of importing cars from abroad can be had from the Revenue Commissioners, Dublin Castle, Dublin 2; tel. +353 (0)1 679 2777.

Although new car sales are currently at an all-time high, prices are very expensive due to the tax regime. One of the smallest cars on the road, the Ford Ka, retails for around IR£8,895. Roomier midrange cars can be had for around IR£13,000: Toyota Corollas start at IR£12,750, the Mazda 626 Saloon at IR£15,600. The cheapest BMW (316I model) retails for IR£19,400.

Secondhand cars are rather more affordable. Price depends on the age and make of the car: You can spend anything from IR£700 for an 11-year-old Peugeot to IR£9,500 for a two-year-old Toyota Corolla, one of Ireland's most popular cars. Other favorites are the Ford Fiesta and Ford Escort (each priced around IR£4,500 for a five-year-old model). The vast majority of garage owners who sell secondhand cars are trustworthy—not fly-by-night characters who'll sell you a mechanically unsound heap of rust. After all, garage owners are part of the local community, too, and there's no profit in rooking the people you have to live with!

Some new residents think they're being canny by crossing the border into Northern Ireland and buying a car at British prices, which are substantially lower and can seem very tempting. Don't bother—the Revenue Commissioners will slap you with the Vehicle Registration Tax, an import tax based on the book value of each particular make of car, new or secondhand. It has been carefully crafted to wipe out any savings you make by buying outside the State. It's impossible to avoid this tax as you need to produce the car's logbook when buying a road-tax disk or renewing your insurance.

Car Tax and Insurance

All cars on the Irish road must be taxed and insured. Levied annually (or, if you wish, by the quarter), the state road tax operates on a sliding scale based on the size of a car's engine. A car with a 950cc engine such as a Ford Fiesta is taxed at IR£104 annually. A bigger car, say a Peugeot with a 1300cc engine, attracts a levy of IR£180. Road tax is paid at your local motor-tax office.

The law also compels you to have motor insurance. Get caught without it and you'll be taken to court and given a heavy fine—persistent offenders are often jailed. Cost varies enormously depending on whether you take out fully comprehensive coverage or opt for just third-party insurance. Factors such as age, driving record, type of car, and whether you hold a full or provisional license are also taken into account. For example, full insurance coverage on a new or almost new medium-range car driven by a mature driver who has never submitted a claim is likely to be in the region of IR£350 to IR£500, depending on where you live. (Dublin has a growing reputation for car thefts so premiums for city residents are higher.) If you live in a country area, third-party coverage is likely to cost around IR£200 for a mature driver with a good driving record.

A host of insurance companies operate in Ireland—Hibernian, Irish National, and Guardian PMPA, to name but a few. Instead of spending hours on the phone getting quotes, it's far simpler to call an insurance broker who'll do the job for you. You'll find brokers in every town—many are also agents for building societies and auctioneers so they're easy enough to find. Alternatively, contact the Irish Brokers Association for a list of members. They're based at 87 Merrion Square, Dublin 2; tel. +353 (0)1 661 3061.

Service and maintenance costs also need to be budgeted for. Large garages linked to specific dealerships may charge you as much as IR£200 for an annual service: new points, spark plugs, oil change, replacement filters, brake pads, etc. In contrast, a one-man-band local garage may only charge IR£80 for the exact same work. If you're happy with your local garage then use it.

Car Rental

Major international rental firms such as Hertz, Avis, and Budget are all represented in Ireland and their desks are almost the first things that greet you in the arrival hall at Dublin and Shannon Airports. You'll also find outlets in all major towns—look in the telephone golden pages under "car hire."

Weekly rental rates are punitive: around IR£250 in high season for a small car such as a Ford Fiesta; around IR£360 for a larger model like a Ford Mondeo. Out-of-season rates are around 25 percent lower. These rates include fully comprehensive insurance coverage, VAT, and unlimited mileage. The longer you hire a car, the cheaper it becomes, though it still costs around IR£800 per month for a medium-sized car like an Opel Astra.

Local rental firms often have more attractive price deals. At Dublin Airport, Access Car Rentals offer an off-season special weekly price of IR£136 for a Toyota Starlet or a Mazda 121. In county Sligo, Yeats Country Rent-A-Car quoted IR£225 for the weekly hire of a roomy Volkswagen Polo between May and September.

To hire a car, it's essential to have a valid driver's license from your country of origin and it normally must have been held for at least two years. Age requirements are generally from 23 to 70 or 75—you'll find it almost impossible to hire a car if you fall outside these limits. All major credit cards are accepted; with the international firms you should be able to rent models that have automatic rather than the normal manual transmission.

Most Irish rental firms have recovery service agreements with the AA (Automobile Association). Unlucky drivers who break down should contact the rental company as soon as possible and ring the AA's toll-free phone number: 1800 667788.

For information on renting cars in Ireland, contact the following:

Access, Suite 201, Forte Posthouse, Dublin Airport; tel. +353 (0)1 844 4848

Automobile Association (AA), 23 Rock Hill, Blackrock, Co. Dublin; tel. +353 (0)1 260 0388

Avis, 1 East Hanover St., Dublin 2; tel. +353 (0)1 605 7555

Budget, Eyre Square, Galway; tel. +353 (0)91 566376

Hertz, 149 Upper Leeson St., Dublin 2; tel. +353 (0)1 660 2255

Yeats Country Rent-a-Car, Hughes Bridge, Ballisodare, Co. Sligo; tel. +353 (0)71 67291

Taxis

In Dublin, Cork, Galway, and Limerick, taxis are metered. It's rare to come across cabs cruising for passengers: The best places to find them are at official taxi ranks and bus or rail terminals. Alternatively you can ring a particular company's central operations depot for a pick up. In Dublin, taxi charges are IR£1.90 for the first half mile and .90p per subsequent mile. Extras include .40p for each piece of luggage and extra passenger. The fare from St. Stephen's Green to Heuston Station recently cost four of us IR£5. From Connolly Station to the airport expect to pay between IR£10 and IR£12.

From Shannon Airport to either Limerick or Ennis (Clare's county town) costs IR£15 to IR£20 and you shouldn't have problems finding taxis. However, in many small provincial towns there may be only one or two firms, usually family-owned businesses where the sons and nephews do the driving. If you have a train to catch, don't leave phoning until the last minute. You may find somebody else has just booked the last available cab.

Taxis throughout provincial Ireland aren't metered so it's normal to agree to the fare beforehand. As a rule of thumb, average rates are IR£1 to IR£1.50 per mile. Like with city cabs, it's usual to tip around 10 percent. Do beware though that long-distance cab rides can be very expensive, as most drivers will calculate a price to compensate for their return trip. Quotes of IR£180 from Dublin to Cork or IR£200 from Dublin to Tralee in Kerry aren't uncommon.

10

Moving to Ireland

When moving to an English-speaking country like Ireland, it's easy to assume the words "culture shock" don't apply. OK, Irish people use a few weird words and speak with peculiar accents, but day-to-day living will be pretty much the same as back home, won't it? After all, you're simply exchanging a frenetic big-city existence for that idyllic life you've been dreaming about for years. You can picture it already—an old-fashioned farmstead on a dozen emerald acres, walking your dogs along the beach, maybe even getting a little part-time job in the local bookstore.

Hmm. Some clouds are looming over the horizon if that's your plan. Do you realize that your pets will be quarantined? Or that you cannot buy more than five acres of land without seeking special permission? And there'll be no job in the bookstore or anywhere else for that matter—not unless you buy your own business or you've got claims to Irish or any other EU citizenship.

Although the subject of employment is dealt with in Chapter 12, "Working and Investing in Ireland," it's worth pointing out right away that all non-EU nationals need work permits to take up paid employment within Ireland. This isn't something you can obtain yourself—applications must be made by *employers* before a prospective employee even arrives in Ireland. However, if you have a historic entitlement to Irish or any other EU citizenship, then the door to employment is wide open.

Residency Requirements

No visa is necessary to enter Ireland, but unless you already hold dual citizenship, you'll need to register with the authorities if planning to stay longer than three months. This rule applies to all non-EU nationals. For newcomers living in the Dublin area, registration formalities are handled by the Aliens Registration Office, Garda Síochána, Harcourt Square, Dublin 2; tel. +353 (0)1 475 5555.

Elsewhere in the country, local Gardaí (police) stations issue residency permits. Permission to stay in Ireland is renewable annually and will almost certainly be granted provided you have the means by which to support yourself. Currently there is no fee for registering. After five years you can claim permanent resident status and there's no further requirement to continue renewing your permit. You can also apply for Irish citizenship if you weren't able to claim this earlier.

Irish citizenship is a valuable thing to have as it brings with it a whole range of economic and social benefits including the right to live and work in any part of the European Union. And maybe one day your grandson may even play for the Irish soccer team—most of our heroes who currently wear the green jersey are on the team through the "Irish granny" rule. More prosaically, as an Irish citizen you'll have the right to vote (and be a candidate for elective office) in elections for both the European Parliament and at national level.

> *If either parent was born in Ireland, you're automatically deemed Irish by right of birth.*

There are a number of ways to obtain Irish nationality: in your own right; by right of a parent's or grandparent's birth in Ireland; by marriage; or by naturalization through residence. As you may already be entitled to Irish citizenship, let's look at the different ways you can stake a claim.

Citizenship by Birth
Regardless of parental nationality, anyone born in the Republic of Ireland after 1921 is considered an Irish citizen. For those born before 1921, the ruling covers the entire island of Ireland, including Northern Ireland.

Citizenship by Lineage
If either parent was born in Ireland, you're automatically deemed Irish by right of birth (the *jus sanguinis* principle). There is no need to register a claim or even to take up residency to acquire citizenship. To obtain an Irish passport, all you have to do is submit the necessary documentation to the nearest Irish embassy or consulate.

Along with passport photos, you'll be asked to produce your own birth certificate, your parents' birth certificates, and their marriage certificate. Within the United States, the current fee for processing passport applications is $77 plus $5 for postage.

Again, you don't have to be a resident in Ireland to claim citizenship through a grandparent. However, the procedure is a little different and needs to be undertaken by what is known as "foreign birth registration." Applications are processed through the local Irish embassy or consulate, or (once you are resident in Ireland) through the Department of Foreign Affairs, Consular Section, 72/76 St. Stephen's Green, Dublin 2; tel. +353 (0)1 478 0822.

A great deal of paperwork will need to be produced, both the original certificates and two copies of each document. You'll need your birth certificate, the birth certificate of the parent through whom you are claiming Irish ancestry, and that of your Irish-born grandparent.

If a birth certificate is unobtainable, a baptismal certificate may be acceptable though this is likely to slow down the process somewhat. You'll also need to produce marriage certificates for yourself (if applicable), your parents, and your grandparents. Death certificates are also required if a grandparent or the relevant parent is deceased. Costs are currently $179 for adults and $64 for those under 18.

Along with two passport-sized photos, you must also submit a photocopy of a current passport (if you have one), and photocopies of three more forms of identity such as a driver's license, social security card, pay slips, or bank statements.

You may have heard that Irish citizenship can be claimed through a great-grandparent. This was so until 1984. Unfortunately the legislation was altered and it's no longer possible for great-grandchildren to benefit from the *jus sanguinis* principle.

Citizenship through Marriage

Marriage is another route to Irish citizenship: A person married to an Irish citizen for three years or more can take up their own Irish citizenship simply by registering with an Irish embassy or consulate. If your American-born husband or wife has an Irish parent and you've been married for at least three years, you are

Your bookstore dream job requires a bit of legal effort.

immediately entitled to an Irish passport and citizenship rights. If, how-ever, your spouse's Irish ancestry is through a grandparent but he or she has yet to register a claim, you'll have to wait for a full three years after your spouse claims citizenship.

Citizenship through Naturalization

Ireland's Department of Justice handles applications for naturalization, and citizenship is granted at the minister's "absolute discretion." It's a slow process and generally takes between 18 and 24 months before any decision is reached. To be considered for Irish citizenship, the following criteria have to be satisfied:

1. The applicant is resident in the State and is 18 years of age or older.
2. During the preceding nine years, the applicant must have resided legally in the State for five of those years. The last year must have been one of continuous residence, though an absence for vacations or business pur-poses won't generally be regarded as a break in residence.
3. Applicants must satisfy the minister of their good character and also of their intention to reside in Ireland after naturalization.

The following documentation has to be submitted with an application, both the originals and a photocopy of each:

• A passport.
• Garda Síochána certificate of registration (green residency permit book).
• Birth certificate with a certified translation if not in English.
• If applicable, a marriage certificate—again with certified translation if necessary.
• Statement from the Revenue Commissioners that all due taxes have been paid. Depending on circumstances, the statement must include details of personal tax, company tax, PRSI contributions, and VAT payments.
• Documentary proofs of financial status such as bank or building-society statements.
• If applicable, pay slips or statement of earnings from an employer.

Should the minister grant your application, a fee of IR£500 becomes payable for yourself with additional fees of IR£100 each for your spouse and any children who are still minors. You'll be required to stand in open court before a District Court judge and make a declaration of fidelity to the nation and loyalty to the State.

For more information contact the Department of Justice, Immigration and Citizenship Division, 72/76 St. Stephen's Green, Dublin 2; tel. +353 (0)1 678 9711. (Calls are only accepted on weekdays between 10 a.m. and noon.)

Holding Dual Nationality

Unlike in some European countries, taking up Irish citizenship doesn't require renouncing another citizenship. Ireland's Department of Foreign Affairs has no objection to anyone holding dual citizenship, but it does advise individuals to clarify the position with home governments first.

Looking at it from the reverse angle, the U.S. government will not deem you to have committed an expatriating act simply by becoming a dual national. To lose your legal status as a U.S. national you would need to have committed treason or have formally renounced your citizenship.

You are required to use your U.S. passport when leaving or entering the United States. However, even if you decide to use your Irish passport when traveling elsewhere, you can still call on the assistance of U.S. embassies and consulates.

Another point to note is that the U.S. government still expects its overseas citizens to file tax returns, even if no tax is payable. Even so, one congressional report estimated that around 61 percent of Americans living abroad are flouting this rule. In an attempt to keep track of wayward citizens, the law requires every U.S. national applying for a passport to file an IRS information report listing foreign residences and other details that the taxman may find interesting.

Rights and Obligations

The main obligation for Irish citizens resident in the State is the requirement to undertake jury service if called upon to do so. As a citizen you'll also have full voting rights, which, for others, depends on status.

As present, only Irish citizens can vote in presidential elections or a referendum. The only resident foreigners entitled to vote in elections to the Dáil (the Irish Parliament) are UK citizens—that's because Irish citizens living in the UK also have the right to vote there. Voting in elections to the European Parliament is open to any resident holding citizenship of an EU member state.

However, you don't need to hold Irish or any other kind of EU nationality to vote in local elections—you simply need to be resident here and have your name on the electoral roll. Those who are only entitled to vote in local elections have the letter "L" after their names on the register of electors, compiled each year.

To get on the register, either contact your local council offices or fill in a form at the post office. The process of compiling the register starts in September and comes into effect the following February. To make sure you're on the electoral roll, you can check the draft register that is

Genealogy

Think back to your great-grandparents—where did they come from? Quite possibly the Emerald Isle, for it's estimated that 40 million Americans are of Irish descent. If you have Irish forebears somewhere in your background, why not take the opportunity to find out something about their lives and communities? Just imagine the thrill of glimpsing something of the world they knew—their town or village, the fields the family tilled, maybe even the local school or holy well that would have been visited on the patron saint's day.

Where do you begin? Well, you'll certainly need more information than just a family surname, so the more information you can garner about maiden names and the names of siblings, the better. There are more than 70 thousand listed townlands (parishes) throughout Ireland and it's vital to be able to pinpoint the county where your ancestor(s) was born. If you're not sure, the best place to begin your research is in the United States. The National Archives (700 Pennsylvania Ave., Washington, D.C. 20408; tel. 202/501-5400) possesses an extensive collection of immigration records and passenger lists. Another source is the Washington National Records Office (4205 Sutland Rd., Washington, D.C. 20409; tel. 301/457-7010), which holds naturalization records. These may contain the date and place of birth, occupation, and previous place of residence for each immigrant.

Armed with that sort of information, you will be able to search through Ireland's vast numbers of census returns, parish records, national school records, and many other resources, which will give clues about your other family members. Each Irish county has its own computerized genealogical database, though some are more comprehensive than others. Those interested in undertaking research work should first contact the Genealogical Office at Kildare Street, Dublin 2 (tel. +353 0-1 661 8811), which runs a general consulting service.

published on November 1. It's available for inspection in post offices, libraries, Gardaí stations, and local authority offices.

Social Welfare Perks

Depending on income, Irish citizens of retirement age (66 or over) may qualify for certain welfare benefits. As an American citizen residing in Ireland, you may also be eligible to claim them if you're receiving a Social Security pension and your weekly means is no more than IR£30 above the State's Social Welfare Pension rate. This currently stands at IR£83 for individuals and IR£135.50 for couples. Benefits include:

• Free electricity. The concession covers ESB standing charges (IR£40.50 per annum) and 1,500 units of electricity per annum, worth IR£111.45. Alternatively you could opt for an equivalent allowance for natural or bottled gas.

• If living alone, a free telephone-line rental allowance (IR£120 per annum) plus 120 free call units, currently worth IR£11.40.

• Winter fuel allowance for 26 weeks between October and May, worth IR£5 per week.

• Free TV license worth IR£70 per year.

   All these "free schemes" are administered by the Department of Social, Community, and Family Affairs, Pension Services Offices, College Road, Sligo, Co. Sligo; tel. +353 (0)71 69800.

Bringing Pets to Ireland

Sad news. You'll have to bid a tearful farewell to Rex and Tibbykins for a while. Ireland has draconian quarantine laws and all pets have to spend six months at an approved quarantine station.

   The only exceptions are racehorses (which are not considered pets) and pets entering the country from the UK. Because the UK's quarantine regulations are just as tough as Ireland's, it won't be possible for you and your pet to fly first to the UK to get around the regulations. There's no benefit in you coming to Ireland and your pet having to spend its quarantine in Britain. The reason behind the ruling is to keep both countries rabies free—the disease still surfaces in parts of continental Europe.

   Pets arriving without proper documentation will be flown straight back home at your expense—and so will you. And don't even think about trying to smuggle your pet into the country: In addition to a stiff financial penalty you'll also be risking a possible jail sentence. This book can tell you many things, but how to "live well in Dublin's Mountjoy Prison" isn't one of them!

   Quarantine fees for the six-month period are charged according to the size of the animal, but expect to pay an average of IR£1,000 for a cat and IR£1,200 for a medium-sized dog such as a spaniel. You'll also have to pay any necessary veterinary fees whilst your pet is in quarantine. As the documentation process may take as long as three months, don't delay in getting forms from either the Irish Embassy or the Department of Agriculture, Veterinary Division, Kildare Street, Dublin 2; tel. +353 (0)1 607 2862.

Customs and Excise

If you're relocating from outside the European Union, you're allowed to import, duty-free, any belongings that you have owned for at least six months. You can continue to import your personal possessions for up to one year after relocating. The only real proviso is that should you decide to sell any of your imported belongings within the first year of residence, duty becomes liable to be paid. There are some items that you'll not be allowed to import—handguns, for example.

For information on customs and excise laws, contact the Revenue Commissioners, Customs and Excise Information Office, Castle House, South Great George's St., Dublin 2; tel. +353 (0)1 679 2777.

Culture Shock

Things are not going to be the same as back at home. Take the issue of tobacco, for instance. Pubs and restaurants are *not* smoke-free zones and many Irish people (teenagers included) still puff away like the proverbial chimneys. Nobody is going to take the slightest bit of notice of your exaggerated coughing or any trenchant insistence that you have the right to breathe clean air.

Once you're inside the smoky confines of a pub, you may be surprised to find yourself sharing a table with a group of 15-year-olds. It's all quite above board—although the legal age for drinking alcohol is 18, children under the age of 15 are allowed into pubs if in the company of a parent or guardian. So long as they stick to soft drinks, those aged between 15 and 18 can spend all day and night in the pub—even if it's the roughest den in town—without any parental accompaniment whatsoever.

If you've been used to a city lifestyle, the reality of rural Ireland may provide you with rather more than you bargained for. The countryside isn't a picture book; it's a working environment. Cows smell, pigs smell, and you'll undoubtedly smell a bit too if your next-door neighbor is a farmer who regularly sprays slurry (a fertile mix of animal dung and urine) on his fields. The joys of rural life don't only include cockerels crowing away at the unearthly hour of five in the morning, but the summertime sounds of agricultural machinery grinding away at two, three, and four in the morning, too. Due to the fickle weather, farmers often work through the entire night to get the hay in. You'll just have to put up with a few nights of disturbed sleep.

Countryside properties don't come with quite the same services as in towns or cities. Unless you buy a village house, it's unlikely that there will be any streetlights on the roads, and everywhere may seem rather spooky on moonless nights. Of course, the great benefit of living in a place with no light pollution means you'll be able to step outside and look at the stars—when was the last time you did that? Another surprise to city dwellers is the complete absence of sidewalks: A country stroll usually entails leaping into the hedgerow every time a car whizzes past.

No streetlights, no sidewalks, and no sewage-treatment plants either. Rural Ireland hasn't got a proper sewage system. Even if you've bought a trophy property costing IR£1 million, you'll still be in the same position as a buyer with a IR£20,000 cottage—you'll need a septic tank in which to store all that stuff most people don't talk about in polite society. Connected to the house by a waste pipe, septic tanks are buried in the ground: You'll know if yours needs emptying when the contents start to seep into the garden or back along the outflow pipe. Though it sounds a bit of a nightmare, it isn't something to constantly fret over. In general, a septic tank only needs emptying once every 10 years and it isn't something you'll have to do yourself. Neighbors will give you a local contact name—expect to pay in the region of IR£50 to IR£60.

Free-ranging cattle (that just might range into your yard!) are part of the charm of country living.

Thought chimney sweeps only belonged in the pages of Dickens? Think again. If you have open fires, chimneys need to be swept free of soot twice a year. For around IR£30 you can buy rods and brushes and do the task yourself. Or you can contact a chimney-cleaning service or an old-fashioned local sweep who will charge around IR£35 to IR£50 for the average-sized cottage or bungalow.

Dressing for the Occasion

Ireland is a jeans-and-sweater type of country: Casual gear does for

Weird Words

No parking lots for drivers, no sidewalks for pedestrians. Restrooms? Forget it. Nor are we familiar with gas stations, drugstores, or diapers. As a **blow-in** (foreigner), you'll need to get used to some strange new terminology.

Want to fill your car with gas? No, no, no. You want **petrol** or **diesel**. And you put your **messages** (groceries) in the car **boot**, not the trunk. The fender is the **bumper** and the hood is the **bonnet**.

You buy medicine at the **chemist** and stores are always called **shops**. **Minerals** are soft drinks such as cola and lemonade, **rashers** are bacon, and **courgettes** are what you call zucchini. Babies will need to get used to wearing **nappies**, not diapers. A new pair of pants? If you mean **trousers** or **slacks** say so. **Pants** are something you'll find in the men's underwear department.

Why do you want to go to the bathroom if you don't intend having a bath? The door marked **W.C.** (water closet) is a **toilet, lavatory, loo**, or, if you've fallen into rough company, the **jacks**. It is not, repeat *not*, a restroom.

Any tool that us **culchies** (country bumpkins) forget the name of is a **yoke**, as in "Pass me that yoke." Any person whose name you can't remember is **yer man** or **yer woman**. Naughty kids are **bold** and anybody who seems unwell probably looks **well shook**. If you're tired, you're **banjaxed**. However, if your radio or TV is **banjaxed**, it's broken or damaged. (Though cruder people will tell you it's **bollixed**.) And if somebody asks if you're enjoying the **crack** (*craic*), don't be alarmed. It's not a reference to illegal substance abuse, but a harmless word for sharing a joke or having a fun time.

Scheme is another word that sends American eyebrows into orbit. In Ireland you'll see it everywhere: health-insurance schemes, drug-subsidization schemes, community-employment schemes, seaside-resort schemes. Scheme never signifies anything dubious; it's simply an alternative word for a plan or project.

almost all occasions. Even in cities such as Dublin and Cork, there are few fashion victims and most people dress very informally. Of course, different standards apply to management and professional people so you should certainly wear something a bit more formal if you intend conducting any business here. People also generally make an effort to dress up at weddings, special social functions, theater trips, and for dinner at a classy restaurant. Otherwise the rule is "come as you are."

Leaving aside Dublin's chattering classes, Ireland doesn't really have a dinner-party culture (in rural areas dinner is the meal you eat at midday) and most social contact with neighbors is down at the pub. Village pubs operate as community centers and you'll often find they're the venue for quiz nights, charades, and card games, as well as live music. You don't have to drink alcohol if you don't want to—it's quite common to see people drinking soft drinks, tea, or coffee. In West Ireland especially, many pubgoers give up alcohol completely for the 40 days of Lent. Well, almost completely—the Church allows a special dispensation to break the Lenten fast on March 17, St. Patrick's Day.

Support Groups

You are not alone. U.S. expatriates and retirees can touch home base through the Irish-American Society, a support group offering advice, get-togethers, business contacts, etc. The group sponsors Thanksgiving with a dinner hosted by the U.S. ambassador to Ireland. The society holds an Independence Day barbecue, barn dance, and fireworks display at Dun Laoghaire, county Dublin. For more information contact Joan Hanley, 16 Dargle Wood, Templeogue, Dublin 16; tel. +353 (0)1 494 4091.

Ex-servicemen and women can join the American Legion, which has branches in Dublin, Claremorris in county Mayo, and Killarney in county Kerry. They'll keep you informed on U.S government policy toward veterans and pension entitlements and also about various Legion get-togethers. Contact John N. Power, Adjutant, 11 Skiddy's Homes, Pouladuff Road, Cork; tel. +353 (0)21 314188.

The American Women's Club of Dublin produces a monthly newsletter for members and organizes lectures, tours, and courses on different aspects of Irish culture. Contact them at 40b Dartmouth Square, Dublin 6; tel. +353 (0)1 676 6263.

Depending on your business interests, you may want to contact The American Chamber of Commerce Ireland, which promotes cultural and commercial exchange between the two countries. Reach them at Heritage House, 23 St. Stephen's Green, Dublin 2; tel. +353 (0)1 661 6201.

A list of clubs and societies with U.S. links can be had from the American Embassy at 42 Elgin Road, Dublin 4; tel. +353 (0)1 668 8777.

Housing Considerations

To rent or to buy? If Ireland is new to you, it makes sense to rent a property for an initial six- or twelve-month period so you can get to know the country and its people. Even if you eventually intend buying or building a home, renting allows ample time to visit different counties and find the right property at the right price. You don't want to be rushed into a hasty decision you might later regret—it's all too easy to do if you're here on a two-week summer-vacation trip when skies are that special shade of duck-egg blue, roses are in full bloom, and everywhere looks its idyllic best.

Bear in mind that the country's slow pace of life won't suit everybody. Nor will the climate: The winter skies of northern Europe can often be gray and dreary. Buying a house isn't like buying a new pair of drapes: It's a major financial commitment. Do ensure the Emerald Isle is the ideal home for you in January as well as in flaming June.

Also bear in mind that certain parts of the country are much less accessible price-wise than others. Dublin and its satellite counties of Meath, Kildare, and Wicklow are very much overpriced (consequently, I don't discuss them in Chapters 13 through 16, "Prime Living Locations"). But affordable cottages in lovely rural locations can still be found in most other parts of Ireland—if you know where to look.

The Rental Market

Renting isn't complicated, but over the long term it can be expensive. Ireland's rate of home ownership is put at 83 percent—one of the world's highest—so there's never a huge glut of rental property available. Unlike in Germany, where only around 40 percent of families own homes, few Irish people rent for life.

In some areas, rents have almost doubled over the last three years. The booming housing market has led to an increased clamor for affordable rental accommodation, particularly from young Dubliners on modest incomes. Depending on size, quality, and distance from the city center, most houses in the Dublin catchment area fetch between IR£550 and IR£1,200 per month. Apartments start at around IR£450 per month, but you can expect to pay closer to IR£600 per month along the quays or in the fashionable Temple Bar quarter.

A Dublin rental property provides an excellent base for house-hunting forays along the east coast and into rural counties such as Kilkenny. To cite a few examples of costs, a two-bedroom furnished apartment in the capital's seaside suburb of Bray was recently advertised for IR£550 per month. In the heart of the city center, another two-bedroom furnished apartment with views of Dublin Castle and Dame Street was available for IR£750 per month. IR£600 is the monthly rent of a three-bedroom furnished house in outlying Blanchardstown. Or, for a country home within easy striking distance of Dublin, you could rent a charming three-bedroom gate lodge in county Kildare for IR£550 per month.

Your tastes might lead you to a thatched cottage in Spiddal, county Galway.

Within Dublin, both private landlords and realtors advertise in the classified sections of newspapers like the *Irish Independent*, *Irish Times*, and *Evening Herald*. Although they mostly handle property sales, some realtors have their own rental departments.

The following Realtors can provide you with current rental information:

Christies Property Services (rentals), 97a Morehampton Rd., Donnybrook, Dublin 4; tel. +353 (0)1 667 0099

Daphne L. Kaye & Associates (rentals), 1 Brighton Rd., Foxrock, Dublin 18; tel. +353 (0)1 289 4386

Hooke & Macdonald, 52 Merrion Square, Dublin 2; tel. +353 (0)1 661 0100

Lisneys, 24 St. Stephen's Green, Dublin 2; tel. +353 (0)1 668 2111

In provincial towns and cities, the costs of monthly rental can be anywhere between IR£250 and IR£800. As in Dublin, much depends on the size of the property, whether it's furnished, and where it's located. Galway townhouses and apartments typically fetch between IR£450 and IR£650. Prices here are at the higher end of the provincial lettings market because of various factors such as demographic growth rates, good employment prospects, and Galway's status as a university town.

Around smaller towns such as Sligo, Clonmel, and Tralee you can find nice townhouses and country bungalows for between IR£280 and IR£400 per month. Remote rural cottages sometimes surface for as little as IR£100 per month, though these will undoubtedly require a bit more work in tracking down. Again, the best way to find rental properties is by scanning the classified sections of local newspapers or by contacting agents in an area that appeals to you. Although provincial realtors don't have specific letting departments, most generally have a handful of rental properties on their books.

If your heart is set on Kerry, try James North (33 Denny Street, Tralee, Kerry; tel. +353 0-66 22699). At the time of writing the agency's portfolio included a furnished one-bedroom bungalow near Tralee town for IR£290 per month. Or consider Kinsale, the star turn of county Cork's historic harbor towns. For an evocative address, how can you beat Lobster Cottage, World's End, Kinsale? A three-bedroom cottage, it rents for IR£600 per month. For IR£400 per month you could settle into a one-bedroom apartment on Market Quay, in the center of Kinsale town. Both these and other Kinsale properties are available through Sheehy Bros., 10 Short Quay, Kinsale, Co. Cork; tel. +353 (0)21 772338.

Going by my own experience, it shouldn't be difficult to get settled in fairly quickly. Before buying our own cottage near Lough Key in county Roscommon, we rented a house in Sligo for six months, a place we knew well from previous holidays. On day one, over on a house-finding trip from England, I walked into an estate agent's office in Sligo town. That same January afternoon he drove me out to see a property, a furnished country house four miles from the town center. I was introduced to the house's owner who spent most of her time in Boston.

On day two I accompanied my prospective landlady to her solicitor's office where we signed a lease. I handed over two months' rent, half of which took the form of a deposit—returnable providing we didn't damage the house or its contents. The following week we were here in Ireland, living the country life, and our daughter was discovering the weird new world of an Irish convent school!

Providing the rent is paid, tenants are well-protected under Irish law. The landlord is obliged to provide a rent-book or written lease that includes the duration of the tenancy, the amount of rent, and when payment is to be made and by what means—cash, direct deposit, check, etc. The terms of the lease should also include arrangements regarding utility bills, the amount and purpose of the deposit, and whether pets are allowed.

Signing a lease legally obligates you to pay the rent for any agreed period, regardless of whether you move on within the next few weeks. An aggrieved landlord is within his rights to track you down and demand any missing payments if you decide to leave early. Of course, it's quite likely that you'll be able to come to an amicable arrangement should you find a suitable property to buy before the rental lease expires.

Short-term Rentals

For short-term rentals, why not consider a holiday let? Although many properties listed in tourist brochures may seem pricey, rates fall dramatically during the low season. It may even be possible to negotiate an advantageous two- or three-month rental deal with the property's owner—you'll never know until you ask.

A good place to start is with the tourist board's self-catering accommodation guide, priced at IR£4 and available at all Bord Fáilte offices. This weighty tome lists hundreds of holiday rental properties and includes owners' contact numbers. As all properties marketed through Bord Fáilte must meet certain standards, you can be sure that these homes will be warm and well-decorated with all the necessary conveniences.

Taken on brochure price, garden apartments at Courtmacsherry village in county Cork cost IR£90 per week throughout February and March. The apartments sleep between two and six people and are fully equipped, but note the price jumps to IR£350 per week during July and August. Contact Brookhill House, Courtmacsherry, West Cork; tel. +353 (0)23 46177.

In county Clare, Ballyvaughan is an attractive fishing village on the edge of the Burren where rare wildflowers bloom among the rocks. Here cottages sleeping two rent for IR£110 per week during February. For these and more holiday properties in the Midwest contact Holiday Villages Ireland, Caher Road, Mungret, Co. Limerick; tel. +353 (0)61 302711.

In the heart of Connemara's Gaeltacht, Hotel Carraroe has a small holiday cottage development with prices at IR£100 per week during February and March (IR£395 per week July and August). I stayed here one Easter myself—don't miss the exhilarating walks along the coral strand and the traditional music in the village pub, An Cistin (The Kitchen). Contact Hotel Carraroe, Carraroe, Connemara, Co. Galway; tel. +353 (0)91 595116.

Buying Property: Choices and Costs

Irish property comes in myriad enticing guises, from traditional farm-houses to cozy modern bungalows and rambling Georgian mansions clad in skeins of ivy. It's even feasible to buy a plot of land in a glorious location and build that dream home you've always had in mind. The Republic's 26 counties are a treasure chest of beguiling buys, though some areas are a lot more affordable than others. Like everywhere else, Ireland has its million-aire homes and property hotspots. The east coast in particular has seen a phenomenal rise in house values over the past three years, by as much as 60 percent in some localities.

Turf smoke curling above a roof of golden thatch? For many overseas buyers the ideal Irish home is a simple whitewashed cottage standing on its own emerald-green acre. Really old-fashioned cottages have what's known as a half-door—the top half can be opened to let in the light and sunshine while the bottom part keeps out the geese and chickens clucking in the yard. Of course, another requirement is a spectacular lookout: a rugged landscape of shimmering ocean and brooding mountains. . . .

If you can handle the trauma, buy a property needing plenty of work—you'll almost certainly see an imme-diate profit if you restore a place and then resell.

Be warned. Thatched cottages in the fairylands of Connemara now sell for telephone-number–length price tags; it seems ironic that these traditional dwellings were once the exclusive preserve of the poor. Every romantically inclined foreigner is chasing the same dream and any cottage coming onto the market is soon snapped up. In the Galway region, the cheapest thatched

The DOs and DON'Ts of Property Buying

- DO thoroughly investigate an area where you intend to buy, and visit it at different times of the year.
- DO talk to locals—they'll know what similar houses in the locality are selling for.
- DO visit a number of estate agents to compare properties and prices.
- DO use professionals and have legal title to a property approved by a solicitor.
- DO remember you haven't legally secured a property until both buyer and seller have signed formal contract documents. Oral agreements count for nothing.
- DO arrange insurance coverage. Ideally it should be in place on the day you visit the solicitor's office to sign the final contract.
- DO ensure money is transferred through correct banking channels with a proper record of the transaction.
- DO make sure sufficient funds are available if buying at auction—successful bidders have to pay 10 percent of the purchase price on the day of sale.
- DON'T buy sight (or site) unseen.
- DON'T buy when on holiday—arrange a proper house-hunting trip. An even better idea is to rent a house before you buy.
- DON'T write to estate agents asking for details of "quaint little cottages in western Ireland." They'll require you to be far more specific regarding locality and price range.
- DON'T be unrealistic. You won't find a chocolate-box thatched farmstead for IR£25,000.
- DON'T shave on costs—get that surveyor's report.
- DON'T forget to allow for additional fees and charges.
- DON'T go building your dream home without first obtaining planning permission.
- DON'T even think about attending an auction if you're one of life's impulsive characters.

cottage I've seen recently (IR£72,000) was at Headford in the mountainless eastern part of the county. For a cottage in picture-perfect condition in popular Connemara villages such as Clifden or Oughterard, the currency of nostalgia won't get you very far. Buyers are willing to pay as much as IR£170,000.

If your heart is set on this type of home but funds are tight, the best county in which to search is Donegal. Thatched cottages in so-so condition still surface for as little as IR£35,000 but, as in Connemara, you must be prepared to move fast. However, do note that the typical Irish cottage is not a magic home whose living space will somehow miraculously expand the moment you've bought it! Rooms are often poky and there won't be much storage space.

Other properties that attract foreign attention are the houses of the Anglo-Irish Ascendancy. Many well-heeled buyers cherish the dream of stepping over the threshold of history into a handsome Georgian rectory buried deep in hunting country—the kind of house where you receive your guests in an elegant high-ceilinged drawing room, play croquet on the lawn, and keep horses in a lush green paddock. What will such a property cost? Well, an eighteenth-century rectory in the Donegal highlands on two and a half acres bordered by a river choked with salmon is priced at IR£250,000. Period properties don't come cheap and affluent buyers are prepared to spend even more to be within easy reach of Dublin. A restored 1830s country rectory in county Offaly (40 miles from the capital) recently sold for IR£325,000.

If you're interested in period country houses (and have at least IR£100,000 to spend), a number of agents specialize in these types of properties. All the following produce glossy brochures covering properties countrywide:

Ganly Walters, 37 Baggot St. Lower, Dublin 2; tel. +353 (0)1 662 3255

Hamilton Osborne King, 32 Molesworth St., Dublin 2; tel. +353 (0)1 676 0251

Jackson Stops, 51 Dawson St., Dublin 2; tel. +353 (0)1 677 1177

More cost-conscious buyers may prefer to breathe in the ozone of West Cork where sheltered coves string the coastline and village houses are gaily washed in rainbow shades of teal blue, salmon pink, and buttery yellow.

If you can handle the trauma, buy a property needing plenty of work—you'll almost certainly see an immediate profit if you restore a place and then resell. Admittedly you may need vision to see the true potential of many rundown properties, but part the cobwebs and you can still find farmhouses needing modernization in this wonderfully scenic area for between IR£25,000 and IR£40,000.

As most buyers want a home that's ready to move into, you can make substantial gains by buying a house in sad repair and then fixing it up. Ireland's restoration projects are literally endless—maybe your idea of bliss is to renovate a quaint old farmhouse down in the strawberry fields of county Wexford or an old schoolhouse in lakeland Leitrim. And, for the really adventurous, there's even the opportunity to capture a tumbledown castle and bring it back to its former glory days.

Many foreigners who settle here are individualistic types with a taste for rugged simplicity rather than a hunger for bright lights and the high life. There are no real purpose-built communities where little knots of Americans, Germans, or Brits have created a home-from-home expatriate lifestyle such as you find in places like Mexico's Lake Chapala, Portugal's Algarve, and the Costa del Sol in Spain. Buy a house in Ireland and you really are buying into the local community.

A downside to the country's economic success is the fact that buyers need to search harder to find good-condition property bargains in Ireland's best-known counties. Wealthy Irish city-dwellers are now in the market for second homes in scenic areas and fierce competition is driving prices skyward, especially for refurbished homes around the most sought-after villages. Ten years ago you were spoiled for choice if you wanted to buy a sound little cottage on an acre of land for under IR£20,000. Unfortunately those days have long since passed into the history books.

The property wave shows no signs of ebbing and residential values in most counties are still on the upward trend. The latest statistics translate the cost of buying a new home nationally at IR£81,276. Average prices from selected cities are the following: Dublin, IR£95,998; Cork, IR£74,613; Galway, IR£88,555; Limerick, IR£73,338; and Waterford, IR£74,537. The average for other areas is IR£76,221.

For secondhand homes the national average is IR£80,774. Broken down on the same basis, the average price for Dublin comes in at IR£104,196; for Cork, IR£70,739; for Galway, IR£83,569; for Limerick, IR£57,807; for Waterford, IR£57,048; and for other parts of the country, IR£67,755.

Although statistics provide a useful yardstick, they don't give the full picture. While you can easily pay IR£120,000 for a small, mint-condition bungalow in the commuterland counties of Meath and Kildare, look elsewhere and almost identical properties can still be had for IR£40,000. Exceptional value-for-money continues to exist in counties Roscommon and Leitrim where rural depopulation has left the price of many old-fashioned properties in the doldrums. Root about here and you'll still find country cottages carrying IR£20,000 price tags.

Another good hunting ground is the border county of Cavan. And put South Sligo and the eastern halves of counties Donegal, Mayo, and Clare on your list, too. Any location within these counties is within easy reach of the dramatic western seaboard, though you'll pay more for properties with an ocean view.

Basically it all comes down to location, location, and location. A village property will always be more expensive than a remote cottage embedded in the middle of nowhere. Plots of land beside the Atlantic and backdropped by mountains are likely to cost at least three times as much as sites of similar size deep in the landlocked midlands. And although Dublin is undoubtedly driving the country's property engine, many provincial towns are experiencing what our realtors describe as "buoyancy." The Killarney Lakes in Kerry, the Galway coastline, the harbor towns of county Cork, and the wild green glens of Wicklow are all localities where vendors can and do demand a high premium for properties.

Further information about property prices can be found in the "Prime Living Locations" chapters, but here are a few examples of what your money would have bought recently:

Under IR£25,000

IR£8,000: Former schoolhouse near Dromahair in county Leitrim.
   Somewhat dilapidated but with great potential for development into a crafts studio, arts center, or even a house. Electricity is already on-site.

Buy or rent a home like these in ancient Kinsale, county Cork.

IR£11,500: Unrestored cottage in south county Sligo.

IR£12,000: Stone-built country cottage between Kiltimagh village and Knock shrine in county Mayo.

IR£17,500: Stone-built cottage for renovation, six miles from Ennis in county Clare.

IR£22,000: Two-bedroom semidetached property in Buncrana, a seaside town on Donegal's Inishowen peninsula.

IR£25,000–50,000

IR£30,000: Old-style cottage in good repair at Georgetown Kill, three miles from county Waterford's coast.

IR£35,000: Two-bedroom cottage in a quiet rural location near Listowel, county Kerry.

IR£39,000: Three-bedroom townhouse in Bantry, county Cork.

IR£45,000: Beachside bungalow in the scenic Killala Bay area of north Mayo.

IR£45,000: Renovated cottage in Courtnacuddy village, county Wexford.

IR£50,000–75,000

IR£55,000: Renovated cottage near Pontoon Bridge and the shores of Lough Conn in county Mayo.

IR£60,000: Four-bedroom bungalow overlooking Mulroy Bay, county Donegal.

IR£62,000: Four-bedroom cottage at Doolin in county Clare, a village famed for its "singing" pubs and terrific views of the Aran Islands off the coast.

IR£65,000: Modern five-bedroom home in picturesque Ardara, a village at the center of Donegal tweed-making.

IR£65,000: Renovated three-bedroom house plus stable on one and a half acres near Ballinasloe on the Galway/Roscommon border.

IR£75,000–100,000

IR£72,000: Thatched cottage at Headford, county Galway.

IR£80,000: Two-bedroom thatched cottage near Oranmore, county Galway.

IR£90,000: Luxury bungalow in county Sligo with magnificent views of the ocean and Benbulben Mountain.

IR£95,000: Two-bedroom bungalow with views of the Wicklow coast in the garden village of Kilpedder.

IR£98,000: 200-year-old Rosebank Cottage, a refurbished two-bedroom dwelling with a thatched roof near Athy, county Kildare.

IR£100,000-plus

IR£120,000: Georgian house in need of internal renovation on a one-acre
  site near the pretty Kilkenny village of Inistioge and the river Nore.

IR£139,000: The Old Forge at Ratharney, county Longford. A fully
  restored cut-stone cottage, this former blacksmith's house dates from
  1637.

IR£149,000: 1820s thatched house in Balrothes, north county Dublin, 30
  minutes from the city.

IR£180,000: Eighteenth-century farmhouse and nine acres of grazing land
  in county Wexford. The house has uninterrupted sea views as well as
  direct access to a private beach.

IR£185,000: Three-bedroom home close to the south strand in Skerries, a
  county Dublin fishing village. Sea views stretch north to the Mourne
  Mountains and out to Lambay Island.

Buying a Site

If you've found the perfect location but no properties on the market suit
your requirements, you may want to purchase a plot of land and have a
house built to your own specifications. An important point to note is that
all buyers, whatever their nationality, must obtain planning permission
from the local authority before starting building work. Once you start
scouring the listings of sites for sale, you'll notice that the more expensive
sites are in highly desirable scenic areas and carry the magic words "with
Full Planning Permission approved."

Just because a site is for sale doesn't necessarily mean you'll be given
the green light to build upon it. Ireland now has rigorous planning laws
and flouting of the regulations can lead to heavy fines. Lax standards in the
past resulted in some charmless areas of "ribbon development" whereby a
number of coastal areas got brutalized by a seemingly endless string of
houses of very dubious architectural merit. Traveling the coast-road
approaches to Galway City can be a shock to those who remember the
days when local people lived in simple cottages instead of huge Spanish-
style haciendas complete with incongruous Georgian porticos.

Although it's possible to submit a planning application yourself, the
devil is always in the details and a fair amount of specialized knowledge is
required. Most people leave it in the hands of an architect or builder—your
estate agent will introduce you to firms they have dealt with before. One of
the first things they'll do is check that building proposals don't conflict
with the local authority's Development Plan that lays down guidelines per-
taining to the area. After submitting plans, they can then seek Outline
Planning Permission (OPP), which essentially establishes approval as to

the general nature of the project (OPP for a three-bedroom residence, for example). Or they can go ahead and apply for the most common type of permission—Full Planning Permission, which entitles the applicant to start building their new home. They (or you) will also need to have a notice of the proposals published in the local newspaper as well as on a board beside the site. This is to give any interested parties advance warning of your plans and to allow them the chance to object.

Once Full Planning Permission has been obtained, it generally applies for a term of five years. If the house hasn't been completed within this time span, it's necessary to make a renewed application for planning permission.

How much it will cost to have a house built obviously depends on the type of residence you have in mind—a two-bedroom bungalow-style home averages around IR£40,000. The cost of the land that you aim to build on is another matter entirely. Land zoned for development carries a far higher price than farmland, mainly because buyers aren't usually given permission to build brand-new housing upon agricultural land. Cow byres, yes. Cottages, no. Just because you read an article in the *Farmer's Journal* saying that county Wexford farmland is fetching IR£3,500 an acre doesn't mean that *all* land in Wexford averages that amount. When it comes to land zoned for development, the reality hereabouts is around IR£17,500 for a half-acre plot with sea views.

Looking elsewhere, three-quarter-acre sites where Full Planning Permission has already been obtained can be had for IR£10,000 to IR£12,000 in rural county Mayo. However, you'll pay at least double that amount for a prime site of similar size overlooking island-studded Lough Corrib in county Galway or county Clare's Lough Derg.

If you want Atlantic views, half-acre sites near Kinsale in county Cork are currently selling for IR£33,000. Around Dublin and the east coast, vendors can practically name their price for sites in the right location. A 20-acre site at Greystones, county Wicklow, recently sold for IR£1.2 million.

It's also necessary to obtain planning permission if you intend to do major work on an existing building—for example, adding an extension or converting old stables into a residence. Once alterations are complete, you must make sure your builder gives you a Certificate of Compliance to show that Planning Permission had been granted and work was carried out according to any specific regulations laid down. Keep this certificate with the property deeds because it's an important document that needs to be produced should you eventually wish to resell.

Planning application fees are currently IR£42 for new houses and IR£21 for domestic extensions. Plenty of information can be obtained from local authority offices or from the Department of the Environment, Custom House, Dublin 1; tel. +353 (0)1 679 3377. Helpful booklets are "A Guide to

Planning Permission (PL1)"; "Making A Planning Application (PL2)"; "Building A House: The Planning Issues (PL4)"; "Doing Work Around The House: The Planning Issues (PL5)"; and "A Guide To Building Regulations (PL11)."

If you want to discuss ideas with an architect, lists of accredited members for a particular locality can be had from the Royal Institute of Architects of Ireland, 8 Merrion Square, Dublin 2; tel. +353 (0)1 676 1703.

Nonnationals Buying Property

As an American, there's nothing to stop you from buying a house or site in Ireland providing that the amount of land amounts to less than two hectares (five acres). If, however, the property comprises more than five acres and is outside the boundaries of a town or city, you'll need to seek the consent of the Land Commission. This is a government body, part of the Department of Agriculture and Food.

These regulations apply to all non-EU nationals. Although each situation is considered on its merits, note that permission is not always forthcoming, particularly if it concerns the sale of a large tract of quality farmland. On the other hand, if a property includes a substantial amount of "wilderness" land, you shouldn't encounter any problems. Basically it comes down to what the land was previously used for and what you, the prospective new owner, intend to do with it.

Those who hold dual Irish nationality or can claim citizenship in any other EU country may purchase as much land as they wish in any area whatsoever without seeking government permission. Once you have been resident in Ireland for seven years, you are also exempt from these special regulations. Another point to note is that the proviso doesn't apply to any house with a large acreage that falls within a town's boundaries.

For further information contact the Land Commission, Department of Agriculture and Food, Government Buildings, Farnham Street, Cavan, Co. Cavan; tel. +353 (0)49 61022.

Legal Title of Property

Most residential properties in Ireland are registered as freehold. This means that title to the property can be held forever and is entirely free of rent. Whether you eventually sell on a property or bequeath it to your heirs, its legal title always remains as freehold.

You're more likely to come across leasehold titles in relation to city-center houses or commercial properties. A leasehold title can be set at anything from 250 years to 999 years and usually comes with an annual

Truth in Advertising

Some Irish realtors have a passion for purple prose. Others—well, let's just say a few have been known to be somewhat economical with the truth. So beware of what all those enticing descriptions may really mean.

"Uninterrupted views" *(Of the gasworks/abattoir/ lunatic asylum)*

"Garden requires a little attention" *(Welcome to Ireland's version of the Amazon rain forest)*

"Oozing with old-fashioned charm" *(Plumbing dates from the 1740s)*

"Perfect for a handyman" *(Completely derelict)*

"Must be seen to be believed" *(I can't believe that this dump costs IR£100,000 either)*

"Wonderfully compact" *(Would only suit a midget)*

"Very secluded location" *(25 miles from anywhere)*

"Renowned wildlife habitat" *(House infested with mice, cockroaches, and death-watch beetles)*

"Ready to walk into" *(No front door, no back door, cows using the kitchen as a byre)*

"Fishing on the doorstep" *(Area prone to flooding)*

"Awaits a discerning buyer" *(Nobody else has been fool enough to make an offer)*

"Clifftop cottage—attractively priced for quick sale" *(Due to expected fall into the ocean within the next two years)*

"Totally unvamped" *(Woodwormy floorboards, dry rot behind the plasterwork)*

"Tastefully decorated" *(If your tastes run to shocking-pink decor and mirrors on every ceiling)*

"With some unusual features" *(Such as the gaping holes in the roof)* ground rent that is payable to the titleholder. The years that are left to run on any lease invariably affects the price of a property, but it's occasionally possible to buy out the lease and obtain freehold title. As leasehold titles can be complicated, do seek legal advice before signing any contracts.

How to Buy Property

Irish properties are mostly sold through estate agents (realtors), also called auctioneers. Unfortunately, there is no real multiple-listings system like in the States and most agents have their own particular little cache of properties. This means buyers have to do a lot of legwork getting around the various offices. Most agents belong to professional bodies such as the IAVI (Irish Auctioneers and Valuers Institute) or IPAV (Institute of Professional Auctioneers and Valuers). Members must adhere to certain standards of practice and are bonded by deposit-protection funds. As a buyer, you won't be liable for the estate agent's fee for selling a property. This is met by the vendor and generally amounts to between 2.5 percent and 3.5 percent of sale price.

The main method of sale for residential properties is through "private treaty," whereby a suggested price level is placed on the property. This is only a guideline price and a property may eventually change hands for more or less than the price you'll see advertised in an estate agent's window or newspaper. It's quite acceptable to make an offer, particularly if a house has been on the market for some time; the owners may be prepared to accept a lower sum than the guideline price.

A guideline price isn't binding on the vendor so ensure any agreement is put in writing. Oral deals are not legally enforceable. Have you heard the term "gazumping"? What it means is the acceptance of a higher offer by the seller, despite having verbally agreed to sell their property to someone else. Gazumping does happen, particularly in today's market where house values are continually rising.

Secondhand properties are sold according to the principle of *caveat emptor*—buyer beware. So, do make sure that any contractual agreement you sign is "subject to surveyor's report." Whether you're interested in an IR£30,000 cottage or an IR£300,000 mansion, it would be senseless to go ahead and buy without first engaging a surveyor or architect to check for structural defects. A surveyor's report may save you a lot of money as well as a lot of heartache in the long run.

Do *you* know if a house's foundations are crumbling away? The vendors (and their estate agent) are under no legal obligation to tell you if it is. Should a surveyor actually uncover a horror story, you're entitled to withdraw your offer and get your deposit back—that is if you've insisted that the contract covers this eventuality, of course. Surveyors' fees average IR£150; a list of members can be obtained from the Society of Chartered Surveyors, 5 Wilton Place, Dublin 2; tel. +353 (0)1 676 5500.

Before agreeing to buy any property and hand over the usual 10-percent deposit, it's wise to consult an Irish solicitor (lawyer) of your own to ensure your interests are properly protected. Although it's not essential, most buyers use a solicitor to handle the actual conveyancing of a property—i.e., drawing up a formal contract and getting the deeds transferred into their name.

As well as helping with negotiations on the purchase price, the deposit, the date you can take possession, and any special contract conditions, your solicitor will check to ensure the title of the property is free and clear. If necessary, he or she can also obtain permission for the sale from the Land Commission.

The entire process normally takes between six and eight weeks. The balance of the purchase price is only paid to the seller when your solicitor is satisfied that you are acquiring good and marketable title to the property.

Your estate agent should be able to point you in the direction of a local solicitor. Alternatively get a list of members from the Law Society of Ireland, Blackhall Place, Dublin 7; tel. +353 (0)1 671 0711. The standard fee charged by solicitors is IR£100 plus 1 percent of the purchase price, plus the 21-percent Value Added Tax (VAT), which has to be added to all professional charges. It all sounds horribly baffling and expensive but on an IR£30,000 property, fees would amount to only IR£400 and VAT of IR£84. That's IR£484 in total.

Auction Sales

Around 6 percent of Irish properties are sold at auction and it's these sales that tend to hog the headlines. In general, the type of properties that come under the hammer include a varied selection of Dublin houses, large country mansions and estates, farms with substantial grazing land, and business concerns such as busy town-center pubs or hotels in well-known tourist locations.

Auction properties are advertised four to six weeks in advance of the sale date, which gives time for potential buyers to evaluate a property and get a surveyor's report. In the past, some vendors sold at auction because their house had languished on the market for years and any sale price was better than no price at all. Nowadays things are different. In an ever-soaring market it can be difficult to put a value on certain types of property and auctioneers are achieving fantastic results for clients who choose to sell by this method, often 20 percent and more above guideline prices. Astute vendors are also aware that people tend to get carried away at auctions, often bidding more than what a property is really worth.

The "reserve" placed on a property is the minimum price a seller will accept. Reserve prices can differ from advertised guideline prices, as the seller isn't obliged to decide what the reserve price is until the actual day of the auction. An IAVI directive states that the guideline figure should be within 10 percent of what the auctioneer reckons the reserve price will be. As this doesn't always happen, some would-be buyers suffer immense disappointment when the prize property sells for far more than they anticipated. To rub salt in the wounds, nobody is going to refund their out-of-pocket expenses for valuation and surveyor's reports.

Consider these examples of how guideline prices can differ from the actual auction prices achieved on the day of sale:
• A Victorian townhouse in Dublin 6, guideline price IR£360,000. Sold at auction for IR£461,000.
• A four-bedroom modern residence in Dublin 18, guided at IR£330,000. Under the hammer for IR£420,000.
• Monkstown farm, county Dublin, guided at IR£500,000. Auctioned for IR£740,000.

Should you decide to buy at auction and your bid proves to be the

Buy a bit of land and build your dream home.

highest acceptable offer, the purchase contract has to be signed then and there. You must also pay a 10-percent deposit immediately. The balance becomes due when all the legalities have been completed, usually six to eight weeks down the road.

Unlike with private treaty sales, you cannot contract to buy subject to a surveyor's report being satisfactory. This should have been done before the sale date, allowing you to bid unconditionally. If you cannot complete the sale, you can wave farewell to your 10-percent deposit.

Other Charges

Along with solicitors' and surveyors' fees, a number of other outlays are involved. Registration fees can be of two types and your solicitor will advise you which one is appropriate. Land Registry attracts a levy of IR£250 and includes registration of any mortgage. The cheaper option, Registry of Deeds, costs IR£26 if the purchase is outright, IR£52 if a mortgage is involved.

Stamp Duty

This is essentially a government purchase tax and is payable as follows:
• Purchase price up to IR£60,000: 0 percent
• Purchase price IR£60,001 to IR£100,000: 3 percent
• Purchase price IR£100,001 to IR£170,000: 4 percent
• Purchase price IR£170,001 to IR£250,000: 5 percent
• Purchase price IR£250,001 to IR£500,000: 7 percent
• Purchase price over IR£500,000: 9 percent

Although Stamp Duty isn't levied on the actual construction of new homes, it does apply to the purchase price of sites. However, only very substantial or expensive plots of land attract Stamp Duty. Relief from Stamp Duty is also available to first-time buyers of any new home if the floor area is less than 125 square meters. If the floor area is greater than this, the duty becomes payable on 25 percent of the house price or the site value—whichever is greater.

The above fees, payable through your solicitor, are made on the day when final contracts are exchanged.

Application Fee

This will only concern you if you've arranged finance or a mortgage to buy a property. Charged by banks and building societies, it's sometimes levied as a percentage of the loan (typically .5 percent) or a flat fee of IR£100 to IR£150.

Valuation Fee

Again, this only applies if you're arranging finance. All lenders require prospective mortgagees to pay for a valuation report on how much any property they seek a loan against is worth. Fees are typically IR£100 plus a VAT of 21 percent.

Mortgage Stamp Duty

Borrowers pay an additional government levy of .1 percent (up to a maximum of IR£500) on all mortgages over IR£20,000.

House Insurance

For peace of mind, get your house insured. You should arrange coverage from the moment you sign the final contract. In general, premiums are lower in rural areas where rebuilding costs are cheaper and the risk factor of burglaries is slight.

In Dublin, to insure a house for IR£100,000 (structure IR£80,000, contents IR£20,000) costs between IR£175 and IR£275 per annum. In country areas, coverage of IR£80,000 (structure IR£60,000, contents IR£20,000) costs between IR£105 and IR£180 per annum.

Many insurance companies compete for business and it's possible to get some good discounts. AMEV, for example, allow a 21-percent discount for clients who are over 45 years of age and own a burglar alarm. Guardian PMPA offers a 20-percent discount to customers who have already taken out car insurance with the company. As offers differ from year to year, shop around to get quotes—the best way is by using the Golden Pages of the local phone directory. As with car insurance, the umbrella organization for brokerage firms is the Irish Brokers Association. For a list of members, contact them at 87 Merrion Square, Dublin 2; tel. +353 (0)1 661 3061.

Property Taxes

Even if you own a million-dollar mansion, property taxes aren't something you need to worry about. Although high-value properties did once attract an annual levy, all property taxes have since been abolished. Rates (local authority charges) only apply to commercial property, not the residential sector. They vary from county to county; for a small business such as a pub, expect to pay annual rates somewhere in the region of IR£250 to IR£500.

Water is there for the taking, unless you belong to one of the country's small number of private water schemes. Charges average IR£100 per year, but even these schemes are expected to become free of charge shortly.

Unless you fancy the idea of buying a trailer and hauling all your household rubbish along to the local tip (dump), you'll have to pay for refuse collection. Charges are set by local authorities and private contractors and are levied at an annual rate of between IR£70 and IR£150.

Working and Investing
in Ireland

None of us can live on fresh air alone. If you're reluctant to bid farewell to the nine-to-five grind, maybe now is the time to think about becoming your own boss. And if you enjoy playing the stock market, don't ignore the roar of the Celtic Tiger. A portfolio spiced with some well-chosen Irish investments could prove to be the pot of gold at the end of the rainbow.

Work Permits

Unless you can claim Irish or other EU citizenship, you'll need a work permit to obtain paid employment in Ireland. You can't apply for one yourself—work permits are only issued to employers, not employees.

Employers have to contact the Minister for Enterprise, Trade, and Employment before any prospective employee arrives in the country. A work permit only gets issued if the ministry is satisfied that an employer has taken all reasonable steps to recruit a suitably qualified person from Ireland or the European Union.

Yes, Americans do work here, but most are employed by large U.S multinationals in positions requiring high levels of know-how. If you're a computer whiz kid, involved in scientific research, or a manager who has already climbed a good way up the corporate ladder, you're undoubtedly a highly valued member of the workforce. No doubt your skills will be needed for the success of your company's Irish operations and your employer shouldn't encounter any difficulties in obtaining a work permit for you. However, even if you already work for a U.S. multinational with an Irish outlet, work permits are not issued for more run-of-the-mill jobs. Numerous overseas companies set up in Ireland to avail of generous grants, incentives, and tax breaks. What Ireland gets from the deal is new jobs for the local workforce. If an employer requires manual, clerical, secretarial, and other staff, the company must make these positions available to Irish or other EU nationals.

For more information contact Work Permits Section, Department of Enterprise, Trade, and Employment, Room 105, Davitt House, Adelaide Road, Dublin 2; tel. +353 (0)1 661 4444.

Self-Employment

Self-employment is a different kettle of fish entirely. New country, new career? If you have an entrepreneurial flair and like the idea of working for yourself, you can do so. Maybe you've been toying with the notion of going into the antiques trade, starting a boatbuilding business, or owning a restaurant, coffee shop, or pottery studio. Or maybe you're the crafty type who could design greetings cards decorated with pressed wildflowers or carve mythical figurines from pieces of bog oak. And here's an idea—how about providing a relocation service for other Americans wanting to move to Ireland?

Anybody out there with a "green thumb"? Well, please come and open a good plant and tree nursery in my locality. Get that permission from the

---

New country, new career? If you have an entrepreneurial flair and like the idea of working for yourself, you can do so.

Land Commission to buy a large plot of the Irish countryside and you may even want to consider growing mushrooms on a commercial scale—a Jordanian immigrant in my own area is doing just that. Making a living from the land doesn't have to mean crops and cattle. Agribusiness ventures take in everything from quail-egg production to making goat cheese to running boarding kennels for pets. I know an English couple in Leitrim who make a living from growing herbs, and one Swiss lady in Roscommon has set herself up as a traditional harness- and saddle-maker.

Pubs and guesthouses are homes with an obvious in-built business potential. If a home with an income sounds like your type of thing, why not

Creative thought could bring you your ideal job.

consider a small shop? Many retail outlets have owner-accommodations above the actual business premises. You'll be amazed at how many Irish towns are crying out for a health-food store, for instance. At present, we shoppers in Boyle and Carrick-on-Shannon have to make a 40-mile round trip to Sligo for our lentils and goat-milk yogurt.

Leaving aside the question of whether to buy an existing business or start an entirely new venture, as an American citizen you're first going to have to jump through the bureaucratic hoops. For EU citizens there are no restrictions: Any Dutch, German, or British national can start enterprises without having to seek what's known as "Business Permission." So, if you can claim Irish or other EU citizenship, do so—this slashes through all the red tape at a stroke.

Obtaining Business Permission

In the tortuous prose of governmental directives, Business Permission is "the permission of the Minister of Justice, expressed in writing, to allow a particular person or group of persons to engage and become established in business in the State for a particular period of time." All non-EU citizens need to obtain such permission.

Business Permission isn't granted automatically and a lot will depend

on the nature of any proposed venture. In general, you must satisfy the Ministry of Justice that the granting of approval would:
• Result in the transfer to the State of capital in the minimum sum of IR£300,000. This minimum investment can be waived if (a) the minister is satisfied the application is justified for the purpose of pursuing activities as self-employed persons, or (b) that you are the spouse or a dependent of an Irish or EU national.
• At the very least, maintain existing employment within an existing business.
• Add to the commercial activity of the State.
• Allow the business to substitute Irish goods for goods that would otherwise be imported.
• Be a viable trading concern and provide the applicant with sufficient income to provide for him/herself without resorting to noncontributory social welfare, or paid employment for which a work permit is required.

All applications for Business Permission must have the following documentation:
• A passport or national identity papers.
• A registration certificate if you are already living in the State.
• A statement of character from the police authorities of each country in which you have resided for more than six months during the 10 years preceding an application.
• A business plan, preferably endorsed by a firm of accountants.

Applicants normally receive the minister's decision within one month. On receiving approval, you're allowed to start your business or commence trading immediately, but will need to register (or renew an existing registration) with the Gardaí in the area in which you intend to live and work.

Permission to reside in the State is given in conjunction with the validity of Business Permission, initially a period of one year. One month before Permission expires, you'll need to reapply to the Justice Ministry to renew your permit and also to submit audited accounts and evidence of compliance with tax laws. If everything is in order, Business Permission will be renewed for five more years.

You can obtain detailed information about Business Permission from the Immigration Division, Department of Justice, 72 St. Stephen's Green, Dublin 2; tel. +353 (0)1 678 9711.

More Red Tape

How much time you'll need to spend on paperwork will depend on the type of business. You'll certainly have to keep accounts and comply with

Starting your own niche business with local employees requires being up on Irish employment legislation.

applicable legislation. Regardless of your citizenship status, it's vital to ensure that any requisite planning permissions have been obtained, all safety requirements have been met, and tax certificates are in order.

The size of any business will dictate whether you need to employ staff. For instance, that tree nursery somebody is going to come and thrill me with would probably be fine for a couple to handle on their own. But what about a busy guesthouse? You may wish to bring in an extra pair of hands to help serve breakfasts and clean the rooms. When it comes to employing help, Ireland is no different than most other countries in that an underground economy does exist. Needless to say, wages are often paid without tax deductions but *this is illegal* and you'll be putting your Business Permission at great risk.

Although there's no national minimum wage, there are certain sections of the economy where statutory minimum rates *do* apply. The largest is the agriculture sector—should you decide to go ahead with those mushroom tunnels and employ people to pick them, you'll need to pay your workers a minimum of IR£3.91 an hour to do so. The whole arena of employment legislation is complex but you must certainly know your employee's rights regarding hours worked, holiday entitlements, and dismissal procedures. Get it wrong and you could be paying out staggering sums of compensation.

If you do employ people, you'll not only need to take care of your own income tax, you'll need to ensure the correct amount of tax is deducted from your employees' wages too. It's your responsibility to pay it to the taxman so get acquainted with the 60-page "Employer's Guide to PAYE," obtainable from the Revenue Commissioners.

Enter the VAT Man

Any business with an annual turnover of more than IR£20,000 for goods or IR£40,000 for services needs to register for Value Added Tax (VAT).

How Much Does It Cost to Buy a Business?

- Retail premises in **Mohill, county Leitrim**. The store has extra income potential from first-floor letting accommodation. Price: IR£80,000.
- Sports shop in **Banagher, county Offaly**, with three-bedroom flat above. Price: IR£120,000.
- Rural grocery and newsagent with residential accommodation at **Geevagh Cross, county Sligo**. Price: IR£80,000.
- Town-center pub in **Boyle, county Roscommon**, with owner accommodation. Price: IR£175,000.
- Café and delicatessen in **Ennis, county Clare**. Price: IR£160,000.
- Small rural pub and grocery business with family residence in **Templemore, county Tipperary**. Price: IR£115,000.
- Town-center pub with two-bedroom owner's apartment in **Ferns, county Wexford**. Price: IR£180,000.
- Rural pub in **Fiddown, county Kilkenny**, on the main Limerick road. Price: IR£220,000.
- Truffles, a bistro-style restaurant in **Sligo town**. Price: IR£170,000.
- Five-bedroom B&B property with separate apartment at **Ardeanig, county Kerry**. Price: IR£150,000.
- The Crooked Billet, four-bedroom guesthouse in **Kinsale, county Cork**. Price: IR£165,000.
- Five-bedroom guesthouse in **Cong, county Mayo**. Price: IR£120,000.
- Six-bedroom guesthouse at **Macroom, county Cork**. Price: IR£145,000.
- Lighthouse View, small B&B residence near **Clifden, county Galway**. Price: IR£135,000.
- Rural pub and grocery business with owner accommodation near **Roscrea, county Tipperary**. Price: IR£140,000.

Essentially this is a hidden sales tax collected by suppliers of goods and services on behalf of the Revenue Commissioners.

VAT is undoubtedly the self-employed person's biggest headache. For example, running a pub or a restaurant entails a lot more than simply dispensing hospitality—like it or not, part of the job involves becoming an unpaid tax collector. Valuable time needs to be spent updating records in readiness for the VAT officer's regular inspections. It's not an easy task when there are five general rates of VAT in operation.

Although you will eventually be passing this tax on to customers, wholesalers and distributors also charge *you* VAT on stocks supplied. When calculating the amount of VAT to be levied, you deduct the amount you have been charged from the amount payable. Should you mistakenly pay out more in VAT than necessary, the good news is that you can claim refunds.

Plenty of advice is available at local VAT offices. Addresses are given in the 68-page "Guide to VAT" available from the Revenue Commissioners (Indirect Taxes), Stamping Building, Dublin Castle, Dublin 2; tel. +353 (0)1 6792777.

The Bed-and-Breakfast Business

Along with local holidaymakers, Ireland receives more than 4 million foreign visitors each year—and they're all looking to sleep somewhere. As many vacationers opt to stay in private family homes rather than hotels, if you can keep house and cook a hearty breakfast this may be the perfect little business venture for you. The potential for making money certainly exists. Especially during high summer, demand for lodgings often exceeds supply and it can be extremely difficult to find a B&B with vacancies in the popular coastal towns and villages of Galway, Kerry, and West Cork. On my last trip to county Cork in August, I found every B&B in the harbor villages of Schull and Baltimore completely booked out.

A home that pays for itself is a beguiling prospect—owning a B&B can supplement a pension income and may even help to fund the purchase of a house. However, the key to financial success is choosing the right location—most holidaymakers look for lodgings within easy walking distance of towns with plenty of restaurants and music pubs. A house that's eight miles down a country road is only likely to get paying guests when the choicer locations nearer town have been taken.

Dublin aside, Ireland's west and southwest regions have the greatest appeal; areas such as the border counties and midlands don't register as high in the public imagination. Remember the vast majority of non-Irish visitors never venture into unfashionable counties such as Roscommon and

Cavan. Suitable properties will be less expensive in these counties, but you won't find many bed-and-breakfasters ringing the doorbell. And note that trade is seasonal: Statistics indicate that even B&Bs in prime touring locations only achieve full occupancy 180 days of the year.

Depending on facilities available, most B&Bs charge between IR£17 and IR£20 per person, per night. Those providing evening meals charge an additional amount—usually between IR£7 and IR£12. Homes don't have to conform to any particular architectural style: They range from townhouses to farmsteads and modern bungalows. If the idea of running a B&B business captures your imagination, avoid hotels and stay in a few private homes yourself. It will give you the best idea as to the standard of accommodation and service you'll need to provide.

Although not all B&Bs are registered with Bord Fáilte (the Irish tourist board), getting your name on their accommodations lists will almost certainly deliver more guests. To be on the register, homes must meet certain minimum standards and for starters need at least three guest bedrooms. For exact requirements regarding room size, facilities, etc., contact Bord Fáilte, Baggot Street Bridge, Dublin 2; tel. +353 (0)1 602 4000. Advisory visits to prospective guesthouse owners currently cost IR£50, and a further IR£50 is levied when a home becomes eligible for listing. This fee is payable annually.

You could buy a B&B that already has an established trade or purchase an ordinary residential home and then refurbish it to tourist-board standards. In both cases, the cost of any property will depend on house size, existing facilities, state of repair, and, most important of all, location.

The Labor Force

Although on a downward trend, unemployment still blemishes the economy. More than 10 percent of the available labor force is currently jobless: 171,600 people in total. The percentage figure is often extremely high in rural counties and the inner city. To alleviate the problem, the government has set up a large number of "Social Employment Schemes" that are partly funded by the European Union. Schemes range from wall-building to helping out in senior citizens' day centers to collecting genealogical data. Workers generally work one week in two but are paid the same amount on nonworking weeks. Rates are slightly higher than unemployment benefits: A married man receives IR£129.50 weekly with additional supplements depending on the number of children in the family.

Much of Ireland's labor force is unionized and very happy to be so. Any liberal leanings you may have will be tested when you find yourself stuck at the airport, unable to leave the country because aircraft maintenance crews have downed tools. And you're unlikely to be humming *The Red Flag* if your mail has been gathering dust in a sorting office for three weeks and more. These things can and do happen. Although not up to the same level of bloody-mindedness as their French comrades, Irish unions can be fairly bolshie.

Despite all the shouting about the Celtic Tiger, there has been growing unrest among an aggrieved public-sector workforce, many of whom feel they aren't getting a fair share of the economic cake. Pay disputes have led to strikes and threatened strikes amongst the ambulance service, sewage and water workers, train drivers, airport baggage handlers, and refuse collectors. The Gardaí (police) also joined in the act. Legislation prevents them from taking strike action, so, to make their point, thousands phoned in sick on two occasions. With senior officers left holding the fort, most places had no police on the streets whatsoever. People found this an alarming state of affairs and were thankful the country has a relatively low crime rate. Should you hear the term "blue flu," it doesn't refer to some strange disease but to police officers feigning illness.

Economy

Many foreign investors still think Ireland's economy is solely agricultural—a place whose only exports are pigs, butter, and potatoes. While it's true that the country is nowhere near as industrialized as the rest of Europe, immense changes have occurred in recent years. Agriculture is no longer the mainstay of the economy, though it does, of course, remain a key contributor. Within this sector, the emphasis isn't just on livestock farming but also on large-scale production of wheat and barley. The food processing industry is equally important and big companies like Kerry Group and Avonmore Waterford have stock-market quotes.

Did you know that Ireland is the world's second-largest exporter of computer software after the United States? The information-technology business is going gangbusters and benefiting both indigenous companies and big multinationals. Employing around 19,000 people, the software export sector garners an estimated IR£4.4 billion worth of annual business. The boom has come about mainly through offering attractive tax-advantageous packages for foreign companies to relocate to Ireland, but successive governments have also operated a tireless policy of promoting the country's advanced technology services. The Industrial Development Agency (IDA) and Enterprise Ireland do much sterling work behind the scenes.

The Republic's big advantage in attracting inward investment is through charging multinationals a very low level of Corporation Tax. Although this is set to rise from 10 percent to 12.5 percent, it's still an

So You Want to Buy a Pub?

Pubs have become amazingly expensive and few sell for less than IR£100,000 nowadays. Anything below that price undoubtedly has very few customers and so turnover will be extremely modest. And while a quiet pub may suit a first-time buyer, it's unlikely to prove to be a little gold mine. With many Dublin pubs achieving a price of IR£1 million and more, buyers have been looking to the provinces. Consequently prices have rocketed there, too. The selling price depends on various factors: turnover, quality of the premises and owner accommodation, location, and potential for increasing profits such as through food sales or functions. One of the largest agents handling the sale of pubs countrywide is **Gunnes** (Licensed Division), 18-22 Pembroke Rd., Ballsbridge, Dublin 4; tel. +353 (0)1 668 2588.

Other names in the pub property market include **Irish Pub Sales** (Church St., Athlone, Co. Westmeath; tel. +353 0-902 73838), an umbrella organization for pub realtors throughout the country. They'll let you know which of their members serves a given area. The Carlow branch always seems to have some nice propositions for first-time buyers in the southeast corner of the country: For a pub there contact **George Sothern**, Irish Pub Sales, 37 Dublin St., Carlow Town, Co. Carlow; tel. +353 (0)503 31218. **Rooneys**, 99 O'Connell St., Limerick; tel. +353 (0)61 413511, has a good selection in counties Limerick, Tipperary, and Clare. In the midlands try **John Earley**, Goff St., Roscommon Town, Co. Roscommon; tel. +353 (0)903 26579.

enticing deal for companies looking for a gateway into the wider European marketplace.

Continuing growth doesn't just depend on the IT sector. Ireland is also a base for many foreign companies involved in telecoms, chemicals, pharmaceuticals, and textiles. Exploration companies have found a number of oil and gas deposits off the southern coastline. In the service sector, banking and insurance companies keep churning out huge profits and Dublin itself is the home of an International Financial Services Center, the IFSC. International banking companies in the IFSC operate there on an offshore basis, which means foreign investors can roll up profits tax-free. However, Irish people cannot take advantage of offshore accounts in their own country. Residents wanting to hold offshore investments have to look to places like the Channel Islands or Isle of Man.

Although the economy has turned in a stellar performance in recent years, few outsiders ever associate the Emerald Isle with major profits and prosperity. Yet this is the fastest growing economy in Europe and last year gross domestic product rose by 10 percent, three times the European average. Consensus for GDP growth in 1998 is put at 12.5 percent with most financial commentators expecting that Irish participation in EMU and the single currency will bring about lower interest rates, thus giving another shot in the arm to the economy.

A thriving economy goes hand in hand with rising house values and the Dublin market has delivered huge windfalls for property investors who got in on its recent soaring act. Over the 30 months from January 1996 to July 1998, the average gain has been 66.7 percent. Some investors have done even better with trophy houses in prime locations doubling and even trebling in value. Can these massive rises continue? Isn't the bubble going to burst? Well, the pundits were asking those questions last year and the year before that, too.

There's no sign of any slowdown yet. One buyer parted with IR£5.9 million for a house in Sorrento Terrace, a fashionable parade in the capital's seaside suburb of Dalkey. In the Dublin 15 district, a very ordinary three-bedroom bungalow on half an acre changed hands for IR£770,000. It's an unimaginable sum for those of us who live west of the river Shannon, but in the Dublin marketplace a house has to be well in excess of IR£1 million to make headlines.

The Stock Market

It's the same story with equities—the only way to describe the figures for stock market growth is spectacular. At the end of 1995, Dublin's ISEQ Index closed at 2,216. In January 1997 it stood at 2,860, an increase of almost 29 percent in 12 months. In April 1998 it touched 5,461, and though the Index has since experienced a "correction," the economy continues to surge ahead. With the advent of the European single currency, Irish exporters will find it easier to sell products to other EU countries, perhaps even at the expense of British competitors who aren't part of the single currency club. At the moment, Ireland's main trading links are with the UK, which buys around 35 percent of exports, followed by Germany and the United States.

Shares in most Irish companies have already come up trumps for both short-term speculators and those who are in for the long haul. For instance, if you had bought IR£1,000 worth of stock in the insurance company Irish Life at the beginning of January 1997, you could have sold in April 1998 for IR£2,616. Taken over a 10-year period, an IR£1,000 stake in Allied Irish Banks would have grown to IR£6,482 and yielded almost IR£900 in dividends. Results have been the same with most quoted stocks, not just those in the financial sector. IR£1,000 worth of stock in Jury's hotel chain grew to IR£5,781 in the last decade.

Over the long term, equities have outperformed other types of investments such as property, bonds, and savings accounts. However, nothing can ever be taken for granted and shares can go down as well as up. At the

Acquiring an established pub requires less initial effort, but costs commensurably more.

time of writing, world stock markets (Ireland's included) were reflecting the uneasy political situation in Russia.

Buying Irish Shares

There are many ways to purchase Irish equities. The first, direct investment in a company, is when a stockbroker buys a designated amount of shares on your behalf. As most Irish stockbrokers also deal on the London market, you're not necessarily limited to the small number of stocks that make up Dublin's ISEQ Index. Some homegrown companies have bypassed the Irish marketplace completely and gone instead for a sole London listing.

Dealing costs vary widely. Any transaction, no matter how small, costs a minimum of IR£60 in commission fees if done through the Bank of Ireland, which has its own stockbroking arm. On the other hand, if you choose an execution-only broker, dealing costs will usually be much less expensive. The brokerage company I use is Fexco, which currently charges commission fees of IR£12.50 on deals of IR£1,000 or less. Contact them at Fexco House, Ely Place, Dublin 2; tel. +353 (0)1 661 1800.

Other stockbrokers who welcome small investors include:
- **BCP Stockbrokers**, 72 Upper Leeson St., Dublin 4; tel. +353 (0)1 667 1500
- **Bloxham Stockbrokers**, 2/3 Exchange Pl., Dublin 1; tel. +353 (0)1 829 1888
- **Butler & Briscoe**, 3 College Green, Dublin 2; tel. +353 (0)1 677 7348
- **Goodbody Stockbrokers**, 122 Pembroke Rd., Dublin 4; tel. +353 (0)1 667 0400

Despite the risk factor of equities, the government also takes a bite out of your investment. Stamp duty is 1 percent: on a IR£700 deal you pay tax of IR£7. When selling shares, you'll be subject to Capital Gains Tax (CGT) on any profits made. The current rate of personal CGT is 20 percent, but you're allowed an annual allowance of IR£1000 before paying tax. If you've made losses on other shareholdings during the tax year, these can be offset against a CGT bill. (Ireland's CGT allowance is hardly generous—even under a Labour government, investors across the water in Britain are allowed to make profits of IR£6,800 before paying CGT.) More tax is due if a company pays shareholders dividends—either 24 percent or 48 percent, depending on your income tax bracket.

Spreading the Risk

An alternative to direct equity investment is pooled investments. You may already be familiar with these if you hold U.S. mutual funds. In Ireland, mutual funds are called unit trusts and unit-linked funds. The money paid by investors is pooled together in units in the investment company's assets which can include property, equities, and government gilts from both Ireland and overseas. With these types of investments, the tax liability (24 percent) on profits is paid by the investment fund and you won't have to meet a personal CGT bill. In general, banks, building societies, and life-insurance companies sell pooled investments. Some funds concentrate solely on holding Irish assets while others hold baskets of British, Continental European, or worldwide stocks.

Although most life-insurance companies require a minimum of IR£2,000 to IR£5,000 from investors looking to stash away a lump sum in unit-linked funds, Bank of Ireland and Allied Irish Bank also have plans whereby you can make monthly investments (IR£50-per-month minimum). This is a good way to invest for the long term because if the stock market heads south, your monthly investment buys more units. The recommended holding term is five years at least, but there's nothing to stop you from cashing in units earlier.

Seeking the right product in what can seem a bewildering financial maze does take time. One of the most tax-efficient packages available is a PEP, a Personal Equity Plan. Similar to a unit trust in that it holds a broad mix of stocks, you can realize greater profits with a PEP because the fund pays a lower 10-percent rate of tax on profits instead of the normal 24 percent. To qualify for this special tax rate, at least 55 percent of the fund has to be invested in Irish equities, 10 percent of which must be in stock of developing companies. Again, you can alleviate the horror of finding you've put a lump sum into a plunging stock market by making monthly investments: IR£100-per-month minimum with Bank of Ireland and Allied Irish Banks, IR£50-per-month minimum with the Educational Building Society (EBS). A PEP with the EBS has the added attraction of a 3-percent bonus if held for 10 years.

Another type of stock market–related investment is a tracker bond. Most trackers carry a two-pronged guarantee, the most important being that your original capital is returned after the set term of the investment. Any guarantee on profits depends on the index (or indices) the bond is "tracking" rising—should the chosen stock market commit suicide, at least you get your money back. The term of a bond can be from three to five and a half years and will be linked to the performance of one or more of the world's bourses such as the DAX Index in Frankfurt or the FTSE 100 in London. Again, all major banks and insurance companies market tracker bonds.

Prime Living Locations

Although this section doesn't detail all of the Republic's 26 counties, it will give you a good indication of price levels in the places that most foreign buyers are drawn to. Of the unmentioned counties, some are downright unaffordable. Others don't offer a great deal in the way of scenic splendor—unless you have a peculiar yearning for endless vistas of sugar beet fields or flat brown boglands being plowed up by industrial machines. That's not to say you won't find attractive homes in the unmentioned counties. Ardagh in county Longford, for example, really is as pretty as a picture and it deserved to scoop the title of Ireland's tidiest village in 1998.

Dublin and its satellite counties (Meath, Kildare, and Wicklow) are very much over-priced. House values in the east of Ireland have absolutely rocketed over the last two years and most young Irish buyers are saddling themselves with huge mortgages simply to get on the first rung of the housing ladder. Leaf through the property sections in the *Irish Times* and *Irish Independent* and you would think that the streets of the capital must be paved with emeralds. Poky row houses, originally built for artisans, fetch IR£100,000 and more. A three-bedroom family residence in a suburban residential area easily achieves IR£170,000. In the most sought-after Dublin neighborhoods you can expect to pay around IR£250,000 for a four-bedroom detached residence on the city's northside and IR£400,000 for a similar property on the more fashionable southside. One buyer recently parted with more than IR£5 million for a house in the seaside suburb of Dalkey. Want to buy a Dublin guesthouse? Be warned that they sell for scary sums and one in the Clontarf area of north Dublin made IR£850,000 at auction. Most pubs sell in excess of IR£1 million.

I've seen "retirement location" pages on the Internet indicating pretty stone cottages in Dublin's surrounding countryside sell for between $10,000 and $20,000 (IR£14,000 to IR£28,000). The authors neglect to say where exactly these cottages are located and which agents are selling them. It's not surprising—the $20,000 east coast cottage is nothing but a figment of the imagination. Please don't come to Ireland expecting to find such bargains because you'll be doomed to disappointment. Anything remotely habitable in the Meath, Kildare, and Wicklow countryside fetches at least $120,000. All these counties are within easy commuting distance of the capital and buyers are paying premium prices.

My advice is to head away from the capital and its commuter belt. Even high-profile counties such as Kerry and Cork aren't necessarily beyond most people's pocketbooks if you look to places like Listowel and Bantry instead of the guidebook localities. Be adventurous! Take a foray up to Ballina and the unsung shores of north Mayo where cozy bungalows with Atlantic views sell for really enticing prices. Prefer an Ireland scattered with low hills and little loughs? Try Cavan, undoubtedly the most undiscovered county of all. Affordable cottages in lovely rural locations can still be found in most parts of Ireland—if you know where to look.

The Western Seaboard

O nce visited, never forgotten! A land of stone-walled fields and
melancholy mountains, Ireland's wild West offers up all the wilderness you could ever wish for. If you're nostalgic for the traditional Ireland
of ancient ways and curious festivals, this beautiful region will almost
certainly fit the bill.

County Galway

Few counties can rival Galway for scenic splendor, particularly on cloudless
days when the mirror-clear light lends everywhere the qualities of feyness
and illusion. Forty shades of green? Galway's canvas is painted in a myriad
changing hues: the mountains of the Twelve Bens etched in delicate blues
and violets, the uplands a bronzed carpet splashed with golden gorse and
the white flecks of sheep. As spring turns to summer, pale water lilies bro-
cade the loughs, and the countryside around Kylemore Abbey explodes in
a pink bonfire blaze of wild rhododendrons. Follow the whiff of ozone
westward and the colorfest is completed by white coral strands and shadowy humped islands that drift like whales in the blue-green swell of the
Atlantic.

For many people, the very essence of Irishness seems rooted in this
western county and it's a popular location for both foreign buyers and
wealthy Dubliners seeking holiday homes. Both sets of buyers tend to
yearn for old-fashioned cottages and farmsteads in the legendary lands of
Connemara, the name given to the scenic northern region of the county.
For local buyers, proximity to Galway City is a top priority and most prefer

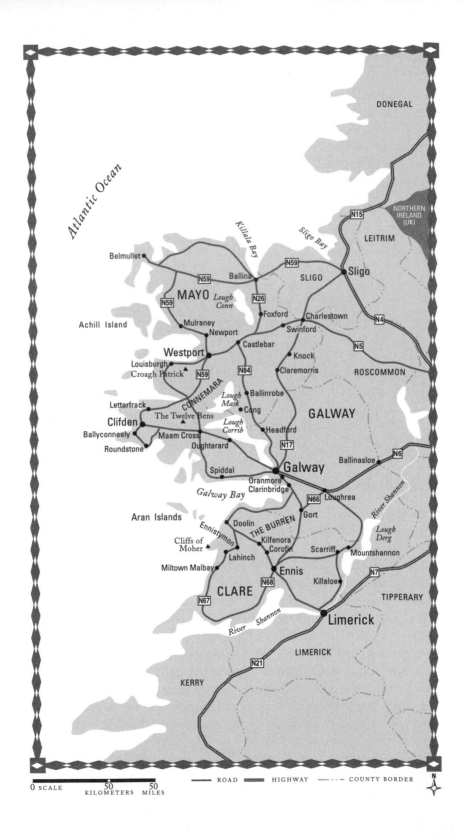

modern homes, usually a newly minted bungalow. While it's true that these types of residences hold little appeal for traditionalists, there's no denying that they're far warmer and cozier than the vernacular thatched dwellings of times past.

Although house values within the county are considered expensive, there *is* a two-tier market. An hour's drive from the coastline, the small sleepy towns of agricultural eastern Galway aren't on the tourist trail and houses are thus a lot more affordable. Even if Connemara is beyond your price range, you can still have a piece of Galway at prices that won't break the bank. Look to the "Fields of Athenry" (yes, Athenry exists) and countryside areas around towns such as Ballinasloe, Headford, and Loughrea.

Galway City

The West's self-styled cultural capital is a medieval seaport city of twisty, atmospheric laneways and scores of traditional-music pubs. Galway's origins date back to the thirteenth century when a settlement grew up around a castle built by Richard de Burgo. As a trading port, the city developed strong links with other European maritime cities, and it's widely believed that Columbus came here before his epic voyage to the Americas.

A stone's throw from the bus and railway stations, the hub of today's city is Eyre Square. Here you'll find all of the big banks and building societies, the grand old edifice of the Great Southern Hotel, and also a monument to the *Galway Hooker*—not an infamous lady of the night, but one of the local sailing boats! Interesting pubs and little specialty shops are found on the prosaically named Shop Street, which links Eyre Square to Spanish Arch and the Corrib River, where old wharfside warehouses have been transformed into attractive apartments. Delve into the adjoining laneways and you'll come across tempting little courtyard restaurants and bistros, many of which specialize in seafood.

University students add year-round vibrancy to the place, but it's in summer that things get really hectic. Galway's arts, music, and theater scene has gained legendary status, and legions of tourists from all over the globe arrive to experience festival fever—everything from horseracing to oyster extravaganzas. The 12-day arts festival in July is always tremendous fun so don't miss it. Its highlight is a colorful street pageant, and previous themes have centered on Noah's ark and the Fairy Horde.

House prices in Galway City and its suburbs reflect the fact that there has been a population explosion: up from 25 thousand inhabitants in the 1960s to around 60 thousand today. Over the past 10 years, Galway has held the title of Ireland's fastest growing city, largely due to an influx of jobs in both tourism and information technology. Major U.S. companies such as Intel, Compaq, and Boston Scientific all have bases here. General engineering (26 percent), information technology (25 percent), and health-care products (17 percent) are the dominant sectors. With growth expected to increase further, the city is constantly drawing people into its employment orbit and once sleepy communities like Oranmore, Spiddal, and the oyster village of Clarinbridge have become an inextricable part of the western commuter belt.

Official statistics put the average price of the new homes in the Galway region at IR£88,555; secondhand homes at IR£83,569. However, that's the average for the whole county. Estate agents' guideline prices for solid family homes near the Galway city center are more likely to be pitched somewhere between IR£80,000 and IR£150,000. In the city's sought-after residential neighborhoods such as Taylor's Hill, Kingston Road, and Threadneedle, the price of Victorian and Edwardian townhouses can easily soar above the IR£300,000 mark.

Due to the high cost of development land around the city (between IR£100,000 and IR£120,000 per acre), the majority of new developments are apartments. Again, prices aren't cheap with one-bedroom townhouse apartments in the Quays area starting at IR£75,000 and two-bedroom apartments fetching IR£120,000-plus. Monthly rents for most properties are in the IR£400 to IR£600 category.

Move away from the city environs and prices vary from IR£25,000 for an isolated cottage in *extremely* sad repair to IR£500,000 or more for a lovingly restored Georgian mansion in a desirable setting. If you fancy building a dream home here, the average price of a half-acre site with a sea view is IR£30,000, but it can be a lot more. Depending on size and location, refurbished cottages and houses mostly fall into the IR£50,000 to IR£150,000 bracket. The typical two- or three-bedroom bungalow fetches IR£60,000 minimum and invariably carries a substantial premium if in a prime scenic area. To cite a typical example, a three-bedroom country bungalow on an elevated site of slightly more than half an acre is priced at IR£120,000. More than anything else, what buyers pay for is location: With views of mountains and ocean, the bungalow is two miles from Clifden, the main tourist center of Connemara. This area is renowned for its beautiful beaches, and a further attraction is the nearby championship golf course at Ballyconneely.

County Galway's mountainous fringe, Connemara, lies west of Lough Corrib and has long been a popular location with foreign buyers. More a state of mind than a map reference, its haunting beauty inspires both joy and melancholy as well as the urge to grab a paintbrush. Many first-time visitors are surprised that Connemara isn't a county in its own right, for this seems to be the Ireland of donkeys, turf stacks, and little whitewashed cottages that imagination promised.

The well-trampled routes are in north Connemara, mostly around Clifden and the villages of Roundstone, Ballyconneely, and Letterfrack. Clifden, home of the Connemara Pony Show, is an exceptionally pretty community where houses are washed in an artist's palette of forget-me-not blue, salmon pink, and pale primrose yellow. The town's plethora of craft shops, sweater outlets, pubs, and restaurants suggests that North Connemara isn't exactly virgin territory, and estate agents' listings soon confirm that there's no such thing as bargain properties hereabouts. West of Clifden, a two-story farmhouse in need of repair is priced at IR£150,000, and a modest little two-bedroom cottage near Ballyconneely at IR£90,000. And although no planning permission for any new residence had yet been given, a one-acre site containing the ruins of an old cottage near Roundstone recently sold for IR£120,000. Roundstone is particularly easy to fall in love with—it's a quaint fishing village with a toy-town harbor where you can watch nets and lobster pots being repaired.

Another Connemara village that demands buyers to have fairly deep pockets is Oughterard. Its location is magical—on the western shore of Lough Corrib, which is peppered with uninhabited wooded islets and home to flocks of wild swans. This is the heart of thatched cottage country, but unfortunately these storybook dwellings command prices of IR£100,000-plus and tend to get snapped up like hotcakes. In good condition, a three-bedroom thatched cottage near Oughterard carries a guideline price of IR£165,000.

The countryside south of Maam Cross remains more of an uncharted wilderness. Here Connemara's coastline breaks up into a filigree fretwork of peninsulas with islands chained fast to the mainland by stone causeways. This is Iar Connacht—wild, isolated, and veined with some of the most penitential roads in Ireland. It's a buyer's best bet for obtaining an affordable slice of Connemara with "renovation project" cottages occasionally surfacing for IR£30,000. The cozier comforts of a modern bungalow cost around IR£65,000 to IR£75,000 in these parts: not too high a price considering that most houses in this mazy land of waterscapes have at least one view of the sea.

The Irish word for "west," *Iar* also means "the end," a place where everything runs out. A Gaeltacht enclave where most inhabitants speak Irish as their first language, Iar Connacht can evoke fear and dread in urban teenagers. During the summer holidays, scores of city schoolchildren are packed off here to improve their language skills. Boarding with local families, both eager and reluctant students are thoroughly immersed in their native tongue.

Not every youngster appreciates the south Connemara experience. No cable TV or discos, just Gaelic games, *ceilidh* nights, and the jabber of Radio na Gaeltachta. Irish summer schools bar English-speaking for the duration and also frown on what is quaintly termed "keeping company" with the opposite sex. Rebellious offenders are sent home and, as fees are nonrefundable, parental reaction is easily predictable.

Irish is also the day-to-day language of Inishmore (Arainn), Inishmaan (Inis Meain), and Inisheer (Inis Oirr), the Aran Island trio cast adrift in Galway Bay. Leaving aside Aran sweaters, the islanders' most outstanding achievement is how they have managed to create minuscule fields from barren rock, a centuries-old endeavor involving seaweed, shelly soil, and animal dung. Cleared stones built the hundreds of miles of gateless walls that prevent the islands' precious soil from being blown away by the Atlantic's buffeting gales.

Farmers and fishermen on the Aran Islands have long been waging battle against the elements. Their stark lifestyle inspired numerous Celtic Revival dramas as well as 1932's classic documentary, *Man of Aran*. Its American director, Robert Flaherty, certainly believed in artistic license: He wanted to show the islanders' continuing dependence on the basking-shark industry, even though it had expired half a century before. And so the fishermen set out to capture a monster of the deep, braving a storm in a fragile hide-coated canoe, shaped like a new moon and known as a *currach*. During the tourist season, the documentary is shown three times a day in Kilronan, Inishmore's main village.

Due to the high cost of transporting building materials, houses on the Aran Islands aren't cheap. Few properties are available for renovation and the IR£65,000 bungalows of Iar Connacht are likely to cost an additional IR£10,000 to IR£15,000 out on the islands. When properties do change hands, they are usually marketed through agents in Galway City. At the time of writing, available properties included a detached bungalow in a scenic position on Inishmaan for IR£78,000, and an eight-bedroom guest-house on Inishmore, the largest of the three islands, for IR£180,000.

Island living won't suit everybody. Winter's storms mean that you can be cut off from the mainland for days at a time, trusting that an army heli-copter will manage to get you to hospital in Galway City if you are ill. Shops are few and the price of day-to-day essentials is eye-watering. And, like your new neighbors, you'll have to stoically suffer the annual influx of anthropologically minded visitors armed with camcorders and highly romantic expectations.

You're not coming here as a starry-eyed tourist so don't make the mis-take of thinking that everything that appears in those lavishly illustrated coffee-table books is gospel fact. Sorry, but Aran women no longer dress in scarlet flannel petticoats, and their menfolk wear jeans rather than home-spun trousers. Their homes are lit by electricity, not lamps filled with oil squeezed from the liver of the poor old basking shark. And as for drowned fishermen being identified through sweaters that carry a unique, personalized pattern, the sad truth is that the story is pure balderdash. This particular item of folklore originated with J.M. Synge's play, *Riders to the Sea*, in which a corpse is recognized by four dropped stitches in a woolen sock.

But Aran sweaters are big business and it would be commercial suicide to let on that high-powered knitting machines now create the vast majority. Aran women only started knitting them in the late 1920s, which rather quashes the notion that the distinctive raised patterns are as ancient as ogham script. Even so, the carefully fostered myth that designs like *Tree of Life*, *Honeycomb*, and *Trinity* have been handed down through the generations as a kind of heirloom is harmless enough—it certainly helps Ireland's export industry!

Galway has a lot more to offer than just its coastal fringe and offshore islands; bargain hunters should definitely check out the eastern parts of the county. Only 45 minutes from Galway city, deep in the countryside's green heart, Ballinasloe is a trim little town of 6 thousand souls drowsing away in the flat limestone pasturelands that mark the county border with Roscommon. Modest cottages in reasonable condition can be had for around IR£30,000, solid Victorian country houses in need of a facelift for IR£50,000 to IR£65,000.

Although you'll not be getting spectacular scenery, what makes Ballinasloe special is that it's the location for the Great October Fair, Ireland's oldest horse fair, which dates back to the 1100s. Fair Week is a

THE CLADDAGH RING

Although Claddagh village is now just another of suburban Galway's housing estates, the fame of this former fishing community lives on in the shape of Claddagh rings. Usually made of gold, these unusual love tokens have a 300-year-old history. Tradition tells of a local boy, Richard Joyce, who was kidnapped by Barbary pirates while traveling to the West Indies. The corsairs sold him to an Algerian master who taught him the secrets of the goldsmithing trade.

When Richard Joyce returned to Galway in the 1690s, he founded his own goldsmith's shop and designed the Claddagh ring. The clasped hands signify friendship, the crown symbolizes loyalty, and—depending on which way you wear it—the heart motif stands for love. If the heart points inward, you are telling the world that your own heart is spoken for. If it points outward, you are available and seeking a new suitor!

snorting, stomping spectacle of horseflesh with around four thousand beasts passing through the town and dealers engaging in the time-honored language of nods, winks, spits, and handshakes. As horse-trading is thirsty work, it's not uncommon for the town's pubs to actually run out of beer!

From dawn until dusk, the Fair Green becomes a heaving sea of hunters, heavy Irish drafts, shaggy-coated Connemaras, tiny Shetland ponies, and eye-catching black and white piebalds. Known in Ireland as "colored horses," piebalds are prized by the traveling people (gypsies) for whom Fair Week is the highlight of the year. In that long-gone era of cavalry troops and horse-drawn carriages, Ballinasloe's Fair Green was Europe's biggest marketplace for horseflesh. It's said that a French officer bought Marengo, Napoleon's magnificent white charger, here in 1801. And although times have moved on, the Great October Fair provides visible proof that Ireland still possesses more horses per head of population than anywhere else in Europe.

Realtor Address Book

Heaslips, 27 Wood Quay, Galway; tel. +353 (0)91 565261

Smith & Co., Newtownsmith, Galway; tel. +353 (0)91 567331

Keane Mahony Smith, 37 Prospect Hill, Galway; tel. +353 (0)91 563744

Matt O'Sullivan, The Square, Clifden, Co. Galway; tel. +353 (0)95 21066. Also with offices at Main St., Oughterard, Co. Galway; tel. +353 (0)91 552503

Paddy Keane & Co., Main St., Ballinasloe, Co. Galway; tel. +353 (0)905 42339

Galway Contacts

Bus Éireann Travel Center, Galway Ceannt Station; tel. +353 (0)91 562000

Connacht Tribune (Galway's local newspaper), Market St., Galway; tel. +353 (0)91 567251

Iarnrod Éireann (rail services), Galway Ceannt Station; tel. +353 (0)91 561444

Tourist Office, Eyre Square, Galway; tel. +353 (0)91 563081

County Mayo

Mayo's island-strewn coastline switchbacks from Killala Bay down to Killary Harbor where it meets up with Galway's Connemara region. Connacht's regional airport, at Knock, provides an easy link to Dublin as well as a number of English cities. You can also take a train to the capital from the Mayo towns of Westport, Claremorris, Ballina, and Castlebar, the county town.

Shaped like a great stone tent, the county's most mesmeric landmark is undoubtedly Croagh Patrick, Ireland's "holy mountain," which has a reputation as a sacred site dating back to at least the time of the pagan Celts. St. Patrick is believed to have spent 40 nights in vigil on its summit in A.D. 441, but whether he performed any snake-charming feats is another matter entirely. Each Garland Sunday, the last Sunday of July, around 50 thousand people go on pilgrimage to a mountaintop oratory, some still making the climb barefoot.

Here, too, are the renowned fishing waters of Lough Conn and Lough Mask. Wealthy anglers often base themselves at Ashford Castle, a fairytale fantasy of a hotel where President and Mrs. Reagan stayed during their Irish visit. A walk through Ashford's woodlands brings you to Cong, a time-stood-still village of crystal rivers, low stone bridges, and a market cross. If it looks strangely familiar, that's probably because much of the filming of *The Quiet Man*, the John Wayne and Maureen O'Hara movie of the early 1950s, was shot here. One of the most historic of Irish villages, Cong also has a ruined abbey, founded in 1134 by Turlough O'Connor, the high king of the time. A stone-built cottage on the outskirts of the village recently changed hands for IR£40,000.

Many foreign buyers elect to buy homes in and around seaside Westport. Laid out in Georgian times, it's an attractive town of wide, tree-lined streets, set-piece squares, and a canal flanked by tall, narrow townhouses, which give one the vague feeling of being in the Low Countries. Then again, that could be all the Dutch accents—Westport is a summer tourism mecca, and a high proportion of visitors come from Holland.

Tourist towns always tend to be fairly expensive places and Westport's housing prices also reflect its status as an employment honey pot. There is no one major employer in the Mayo area, rather a mix of small industries that take in everything from pharmaceuticals to eye-care products, seaweed processors to electrode and paintbrush manufacturers. Within the town, development land fetches IR£100,000 an acre while new luxury homes on half-acre sites sell for around IR140,000.

Regarding the secondhand market, a typical two-bedroom bungalow within Westport town usually achieves a price of between IR£65,000 and IR£75,000. Move inland toward Castlebar and the price drops to nearer IR£55,000. Something larger? A four-bedroom bungalow at Aghagower is priced at IR£70,000. A village with a lake, an ancient round tower, a holy well, and Croagh Patrick views, Aghagower is the midway point on another pilgrim path that meanders between the holy mountain and Ballintubber Abbey.

Within easy reach of Westport, the most sought-after coastal villages are Lecanvey, Murrisk, Newport, and Louisburgh, strung out along the ocean like beads on a rosary. In these communities, the starting price for refurbished cottages with a couple of acres is around IR£60,000, but buyers may have to offer IR£80,000 or more for a particularly good lookout on Clew Bay and its islands. Even a renovation-project cottage can cost IR£50,000 with the right view.

Murrisk is the nearest village to Croagh Patrick and the Garland Sunday pilgrim trail. It's intriguing to discover that the village derives its name from the Muir Iasc, a one-eyed sea serpent that apparently was worshipped by the local inhabitants during Druidic times. It makes one wonder if there was some truth in the legend of St. Patrick banishing the snakes after all!

Folklore is one thing, but a poignant, real-life story is attached to Louisburgh village. It's that of the Doolough tragedy, commemorated every year by a sponsored walk for third-world famine victims. At the height of Ireland's own Great Famine, when the potatoes rotted in the fields, a number of starving families banded together and trudged across the Doolough Pass from Killary Harbor to Louisburgh. There they sought admission to the old Workhouse, but entrance was refused. Almost six hundred people died on the hopeless return journey across the Doolough Mountains, dark and lonely peaks that fully epitomize the brooding savagery of "the scenic West."

THE VILLAGE OF KNOCK

Ireland's spiritual power plant, Knock is one of the world's foremost Marian shrines and a place of continuous prayer. The village draws vast crowds during the May-to-October pilgrimage season; some pilgrims spend their entire summer vacation here, taking part in torchlit rosary processions and all-night vigils. Sundays are particularly hectic, often with around 10 thousand of the faithful patiently waiting to take Communion in the huge Basilica of Our Lady, Queen of Ireland. Holy days are even busier as almost every Catholic parish organizes a coach trip for parishioners.

Knock's fame stems from the evening of August 21, 1879, when 20 villagers claimed to have seen an apparition of three figures near the gabled wall of their church. Bathed in a golden glow, the central figure was recognized as the Virgin Mary. Her unearthly companions were adjudged to be St. Joseph and St. John the Evangelist, holding the Book of Revelation and accompanied by a lamb. Hovering two feet above the ground, the apparition apparently lasted for almost two hours.

Achill, Ireland's largest island, is linked to the mainland by a bridge. Although wintertime weather can be quite squally, Achill encompasses all that's best in Irish scenery: dramatic cliffs and mountains, silvery beaches, and wild moorlands. Here you can find old cottages in need of restoration for IR£28,000, but at the foot of Slievemore Mountain brand-new holiday homes are selling for IR£100,000. Many will be purchased as investment properties: At the time of writing, buyers can take advantage of generous tax concessions if letting out holiday homes to tourists, but tax breaks under the "seaside resort scheme" are due to end in June 1999. A bar/restaurant on the island was recently offered for sale for IR£195,000.

In north Mayo, the area around Ballina, Killala Bay, and the remote Belmullet Peninsula is your best bet for tracking down seaside snips with small coastal bungalows popping up for IR£35,000 to IR£50,000. Or consider the county's agricultural heartland, laid out in a patchwork quilt of emerald-green fields and brown-velvet boglands, all sewn together with gray drystone walls.

Around little farming communities such as Swinford, Foxford, Ballinrobe, and Claremorris, you can still find fix-it-uppers starting at IR£11,000 and small cottage-type properties in good condition for IR£30,000 to IR£45,000. Recent sales in the Ballinrobe district included a pretty traditional cottage for IR£35,000 and an ivy-covered farmhouse in need of some repair for IR£40,000. On the main Galway-to-Sligo road, Claremorris and its satellite villages are even better for bargain properties: Local agent Martin Finn's latest listings carried no less than nine properties for under IR£20,000. Three-bedroom country bungalows can be had for IR£35,000 while IR£52,000 buys a four-bedroom residence on four acres of good agricultural land. A brave soul with a sense of romance and IR£48,000 to spare could even buy the ruins of a 300-year-old castle on three acres near the village of Irishtown.

Why are prices in the Claremorris area substantially cheaper? Well, the first thing that strikes you when strolling around the town is the complete absence of craft stores, gift shops, and other tourist outlets—evidence that coach tours never see the place. House values haven't been artificially inflated by either foreign buyers or city dwellers in the market for holiday homes, undoubtedly because the landscape doesn't offer up the Ireland of loughs and mountains that exists in most people's dreams. There are no major employers in this area, another factor that always sends house prices soaring upward.

With prices for one-bedroom apartments starting at IR£37,500 and four-bedroom bungalows at IR£70,000, Finn also offers a good selection of properties around Knock village, a major pilgrimage site. It's certainly a location to bear in mind if you're considering a self-employment venture such as running a guesthouse. A café/restaurant/bed-and-breakfast business in the village center is priced at IR£180,000.

Realtor Address Book
Collins Estate Agents, Castle St., Castlebar, Co. Mayo; tel. +353 (0)94 22701
Martin Finn, Dalton St., Claremorris, Co. Mayo; tel. +353 (0)94 62216
Philip McComiskey, Church Rd., Ballina, Co. Mayo; tel. +353 (0)96 22433
Vincent O'Malley, Kilbree, Westport, Co. Mayo; tel. +353 (0)98 35109
Brendan Tuohy, North Mall, Westport, Co. Mayo; tel. +353 (0)98 28000

Mayo Contacts
Bus Éireann Travel Center, Ballina, Co. Mayo; tel. +353 (0)96 71800
Rail Services: Ballina (tel. +353 0-96 71818), Castlebar (tel. +353 0-94 21222), Claremorris (tel. +353 0-94 71011), Westport (tel. +353 0-98 25253)
Tourist Information: The Mall, Westport, Co. Mayo; tel. +353 (0)98 25711
Western People (local newspaper), Francis St., Ballina, Co. Mayo; tel. +353 (0)96 21188

County Clare

From the mighty Cliffs of Moher to the starkly beautiful uplands of the moonscaped Burren and the lush green pastures around Lough Derg, Clare packs lots of goodies into a compact area. For me, it encompasses all that's best about western Ireland and although prices have risen, prime coastal properties are nowhere near as expensive as in neighboring Galway. Most Irish people would agree that this is a kind of spiritual home for traditional music and enthusiasts will already know about the legendary music pubs of Doolin, Miltown Malbay, Ennistymon, and Kilfenora.

Yet there's more to this county than first meets the eye. Strolling the streets of Ennis, Clare's county town and commercial center, take a peek at the window displays of bookshops and newsagents. If you're expecting to see the standard fare of books on local history, the Cliffs of Moher, and the wildflowers of the stony Burren region, you'll probably wonder why self-help guides to using computers and the Internet are given such a high profile instead. The reason? Well, sleepy old Ennis recently became Ireland's first Information Age town.

Ennis has a population of just under 16 thousand. By the millennium it's planned that 80 percent of households will have computers and be connected to the Internet. For just IR£200 (a substantial savings on the normal retail price of IR£1,800), every family is entitled to collect a Pentium II personal computer, a bundle of software packages, and Internet access. The only stipulation is that one member of the household shows that he or she can perform five simple tasks: start the computer, open a file and type five lines of script (that they then save), retrieve a document, access the Internet, and post an e-mail message.

Furthermore, any household that's still without a telephone can get a free connection. The project is being funded by Telecom Eireann, the state-owned telecommunications company whose boffins decided that an ordinary west Ireland town would make the perfect testing ground for their new technologies. If you like the idea of living in what is set to become one of the most technologically adept communities in the world, prices for new one- and two-bedroom apartments within the town range from IR£62,500 to IR£90,000. Bungalows in nice residential neighborhoods start at around IR£86,500, but the best value lies out of town in the rural hinterland. Three miles from Ennis an old-fashioned farmhouse in fairly good condition recently sold for IR£45,000.

Achill encompasses all that's best in Irish scenery: dramatic cliffs and mountains, silvery beaches, and wild moorlands.

Clare's coastline will prove a big draw but note that the north of the county is more expensive than the south. In north Clare, right on the shores of Galway Bay, Ballyvaughan is a picturesque harbor village with some excellent pubs and restaurants. Don't miss the seafood at Monk's on the quayside. From here you can explore the traffic-free "Green Roads" of the Burren, old drovers' tracks that lead up into a mysterious world of caves, dolmens, ring forts, and the sad remains of famine villages. Springtime is especially magical for it's then that the Burren's limestone pavements are transformed into a flowery carpet of rare wildflowers: Species include purple-spotted orchids, mountain avens, and vivid blue gentians. Although IR£55,000 buys a two-bedroom cottage in the heart of the Burren, modern bungalow residences along the coast change hands for at least IR£75,000.

Doolin is another desirable coastal village, perfectly positioned between the Burren and the Cliffs of Moher. Those who live here can enjoy traditional music every night and unrivaled views of the Aran Islands. Again,

The Cliffs of Moher

This is one of Ireland's most famous scenic landmarks. You can take an exhilarating eight-kilometer walk along these vertigo-inducing cliffs from the observation point of O'Brien's Tower to Hag's Head. The cliffs tower above crashing Atlantic breakers to a height of almost 200 meters, offering views to take your breath away. Out in Galway Bay, beyond the rocky sea-stacks and natural arches, are the three misty humps of the Aran Islands. To the south you can glimpse the faraway hills of Kerry; look northwest and you'll see the brooding mountains of Connemara. Fringed by a flowery sward of sea pinks, campion, and bird's-foot trefoil, the path to O'Brien's Tower is made of hefty slabs of Liscannor flagstone.

It's easy to escape the crowds as most camera-toting coach-tour visitors simply spend a quick 20 minutes walking from the visitors center to O'Brien's Tower and back again. Head instead to the distant Moher Tower and—apart from the odd backpacker—you can relish the views in complete solitude. The path also forms part of the much longer Burren Way, marked by little arrows on stone markers. As they can sometimes be hard to identify, be careful not to stray too close to the edge. Birds nest all along these cliffs: kittiwakes, guillemots, razorbills, fulmars, and various other species of gulls. You may also spot clown-like puffins and the occasional red-legged chough. Look out for wildflowers such as the white scented flowers of ladies' tresses, dainty pink fairy foxgloves, and cushion-like mossy saxifrage with its abundant clumps of star-shaped flowers blooming among the sea-sprayed rocks between May and August.

it's a brilliant location for botanists and ramblers who enjoy seeking out the remains of historic churches, castles, and prehistoric ruins.

At the lower reaches of North Clare, prices get more affordable around the seaside resorts of Liscannor and Lahinch—one-bedroom apartments start at IR£40,000 and most two-bedroom bungalows cost between IR£62,500 and IR£70,000. Renowned for its unique flagstones with their fossilized surfaces, Liscannor is the more traditional of the two: You can still see black-hulled *currach* boats in the harbor, and the curative powers of St. Brigid's Well continue to attract local people each February 1. Lahinch is more of a golfer's hangout—here the championship links course along the dunes dates back to 1893 and was originally intended for use by officers of the infamous Black Watch regiment.

Most folks in this area go into Ennistymon to do their shopping. Its streets are lined with old-fashioned shop fronts, and market traditions date back to the Napoleonic wars. Come on a Tuesday for the weekly street market, on Friday for the cattle market, at any time to take a scenic walk along the riverbank to the Cascades where you can occasionally see leaping salmon when the waters are in full spate. Heaven alone knows what you would do with 10,000 square feet of an old convent, but the one in Ennistymon came on the market for IR£300,000.

Away from the coast, fixer-uppers can be had for IR£15,000, and ready-to-move-into little cottages are available for around IR£35,000. Some of the most inexpensive properties are to be found on the southeastern edge of the Burren, particularly around the villages of Kilfenora and Corofin.

For one of Clare's prettiest inland locations, make tracks for Killaloe and the shores of Lough Derg. Sheltered by the Slieve Bearnagh hills to the west and the Arra hills to the east, Killaloe is an attractive little place perched on a neck of land where the river Shannon flows out of the lough on its journey toward Limerick. You can walk into county Tipperary by crossing the 13-arched bridge spanning the river. The immediate locality is littered with historic remains: medieval churches, round towers, and those bibles in stone, high Celtic crosses, one of which carries inscriptions both in old-Irish ogham lettering and Norse runic script. Locals claim this was once Ireland's capital—the most famous of the high kings, Brian Boru, is said to have had a palace known as Kincora where the present-day town now stands. Best known as a sailing and water-sports center, today Killaloe does a good summer tourist trade with European visitors who enjoy messing about in boats.

Although Killaloe townhouses can be had for IR£70,000 and small bungalows for IR£62,000, don't expect a waterfront location for this price. Buyers who demand views of the lough will pay at least IR£25,000 for a poky renovation-project cottage. Depending on house size and acreage, quality lake or riverside properties around Killaloe and the nearby communities of Scarriff,

Tuamgraney, and Mountshannon start at IR£90,000. At the lower end of the price scale, right beside the Shannon, a two-story house at O'Briensbridge with stable and paddock was recently available for IR£110,000. Or, for IR£125,000, you could have bought Lough Derg View Cottage. With an unbeatable lookout over the lough, this was a modern home built in the style of a traditional Irish cottage on one-and-a-half acres.

For IR£120,000, another nice buy in the Killaloe district was a four-bedroom residence on a half-acre site overlooking Holy Island. A magical island laden with legends, Holy Island's other name is *Inishcealtra*.

Marked by a high, round tower, here too is a collection of ancient chapels, an anchorite's cell, and early Christian gravestones dating back to the seventh century. Thought to have been founded by St. Colm, the island was an important monastic site until it fell to Viking raiders. Until the 1830s the island's holy well was a popular place of pilgrimage, but the Church discouraged visits after revelries got out of hand. Some local girls were carried off by men intent on what might be described as "inappropriate relationships."

Realtor Address Book
Harry Brann, Killaloe, Co. Clare; tel. +353 (0)61 376380
Costelloes, 5 Abbey St., Ennis, Co. Clare; tel. +353 (0)65 21299
Philip O'Reilly, 22/24 Abbey St., Ennis, Co. Clare; tel. +353 (0)65 29325
McMahons, O'Connell Square, Ennis, Co. Clare; tel. +353 (0)65 28307
Pat Mulcahy, Killaloe, Co. Clare; tel. +353 (0)61 376176
John Vaughan, Parliament St., Ennistymon, Co. Clare; tel. +353 (0)65 71477

Clare Contacts
Bus Éireann, Railway Station, Ennis, Co. Clare; tel. +353 (0)65 24177
Clare Champion (local newspaper), Barrack St., Ennis, Co. Clare; tel. +353 (0)65 28105
Rail Services: to Dublin via Limerick from Ennis; tel. +353 (0)65 40444
Tourist Office, Clare Rd., Ennis, Co. Clare; tel. +353 (0)65 28366

The Southwest

The paintbox villages of the southwest are a favorite hunting ground for foreign home-buyers. Even if you do decide to buy elsewhere, be sure to feast your eyes on some of Ireland's most colorful and spectacular landscapes.

County Kerry

Despite the annual horde of summer visitors, Kerry delivers sheer poetry. Nothing detracts from the bewitching beauty of its landscapes where mountains are reflected in looking-glass loughs and flotillas of islands drift out of a muslin mesh of sea mist. You'll never forget the first time you actually see this enchanted kingdom for yourself: the silver-thread waterfalls spilling down from the Slieve Mish, Derrynasaggart and Macgillyguddy's Reeks mountain ranges, the mirror-bright lakes of Killarney, the rocky Atlantic peninsulas with their basking seals and occasional frolicking dolphin.

For many people, the county is synonymous with the famous Ring of Kerry, the 112-mile circuit around the Iveragh Peninsula, which holds the bulk of the county's scenic goodies. With the national park right on its doorstep, Killarney is where most visitors stay, and the town itself (pop. 13,000) is almost entirely given over to the tourism trade. Although Killarney makes an excellent holiday base, there's not the same sense of intimacy that you'll find in many of the other towns and villages strung around the Iveragh Peninsula. Traveling in a clockwise direction, the litany of lovely coastal towns and villages includes Kenmare, Sneem, Caherdaniel, Waterville, Ballinskelligs, Portmagee, Valentia Island, and Cahirciveen.

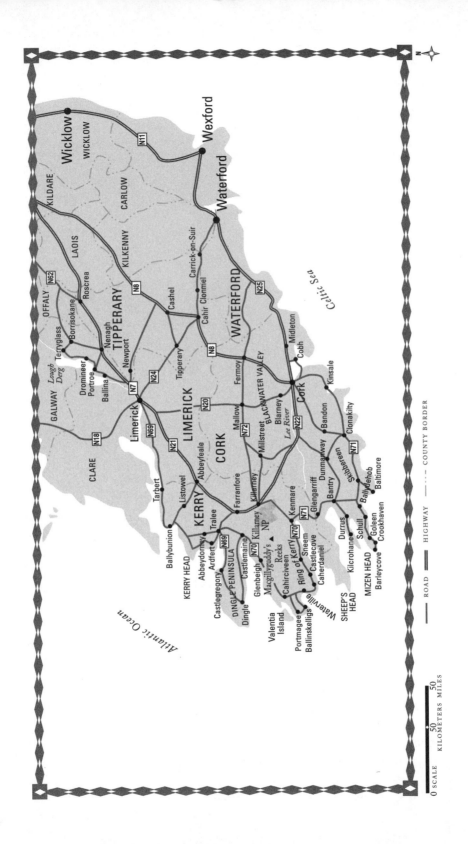

My own favorite Ring of Kerry location is the area bounded by Derrynane, Caherdaniel, and Castlecove. You don't have to choose between mountain and coastal vistas—here you've got the full glory of both and the hauntingly desolate monastic island of Skellig Michael is only a boat ride away. For ramblers, this is one of the way stations on the 135-mile-long Kerry Way, and the surrounding area is an archaeologist's playground of forts, soutterains (underground burial chambers), and standing stones. Those fascinated by the natural world will come across unusual flora such as the Kerry lily, kidney saxifrage, bee orchid, and blue-eyed grass. It's not uncommon to meet up with the local wildlife either—foxes, stoats, hares, seals, and otters abound in this area.

As with all such heavenly places, house prices tend to be stratospheric if you're looking for a modern property. At Castlecove, a pretty two-bedroom house on one acre on the shore with water frontage is priced at IR£200,000. Steep, certainly, but the value is in the priceless view—south over Kenmare Bay toward the peaks of the Beara Peninsula. But that's not to say this part of Kerry is totally unaffordable. Move west to Valentia Island and Knightstown village and for IR£47,000 you could look across to Cahirciveen Harbor from a terrace-style Victorian lighthouse keeper's cottage. Or, near the prehistoric Staigue Fort, an old-style two-bedroom cottage was recently offered for IR£40,000. However, in this location, modest prices usually reflect a need for substantial upgrading rather than just a lick of paint.

In general, the view factor dictates the price of all Kerry properties. Say you're looking for a four-bedroom bungalow that you could turn into a little bed-and-breakfast business. One suitable home, near Farranfore, is priced at IR£70,000. This village is 20 miles from Killarney and well away from the picture-postcard scenery. IR£110,000 buys a similar bungalow within walking distance of Glenbeigh village, on the Ring of Kerry's northern stretch between Lough Caragh and Dingle Bay. Views of the mountains, yes. Seashore lapping at the door, no. For a residence with an ocean panorama, you might have to pay in the region of IR£230,000—the price being sought for a bungalow on a half-acre site at Templenoe Pier, four miles from Kenmare.

With those kinds of prices, you may wonder how local people on low incomes can afford South Kerry properties. Well, town suburbs provide some answers and it's still possible to buy semidetached row houses in Cahirciveen for IR£25,000 and Killarney for IR£50,000. These aren't the kinds of properties that most foreign or holiday-home buyers want, so the market is purely local and not subject to the same ever-upward pressures. Indeed, some urban properties can be reasonably affordable and attractive, too. In the colorful town of Kenmare, a small house near the golf course is priced at IR£40,000. Within the town itself, a perfect gem of a stone-fronted townhouse (three-bedroom) has an asking price of IR£90,000.

If you've got time and enthusiasm, dilapidated cottages in the mountain foothills of the Iveragh Peninsula still sell for under IR£30,000. Realtors describe these sad-eyed hovels as "fixer-uppers," but many are complete wrecks and would seem to be completely beyond redemption.

But don't write off Kerry yet. You *can* buy quality cottages here for between IR£35,000 and IR£42,000. For an affordable slice of the county at a bargain price, the best hunting grounds are to the north, around Listowel and Tralee. With a population of around 20,000, Tralee is Kerry's main town and home to the whimsical Rose of Tralee festival. "Roses" of Irish descent from all over the globe come to take part in what is more of a celebration of Irishness rather than a straightforward beauty contest.

Much of North Kerry is constructed of hilly green fields rather than dramatic mountain scenery, and if this is your first view of the county, you'll wonder what all the fuss has been about. There isn't much to distinguish it from the rural parts of county Limerick, linked to North Kerry by the county border and with much similarity in house prices. The landscape alone explains why you can buy substantial village houses for IR£45,000; three-bedroom country bungalows for IR£50,000; or stone farmhouses, completely refurbished and redecorated for IR£65,000. Small cottages in good structural condition start at around IR£35,000. You're likely to come across such properties in the rural hinterland of villages such as Abbeyfeale, Ardfert, and Abbeydorney. For IR£69,000, an animal-lover looking for a slice of authentic rural Kerry could buy a traditional three-bedroom long farmhouse near Abbeydorney. On just over an acre, the property included four double dog kennels and three loose boxes for stabling horses.

The North Kerry coastline between Tarbert and Fenit is nowhere near as breathtaking as the Iveragh Peninsula, but many Irish families holiday in this area. The most popular resort is Ballybunion where a centuries-old family vendetta resulted in an estimated three thousand eager participants battling it out on the beach in 1834! Interesting buys around this little seaside town include a house with views of Kerry Head that's also within a two-minute stroll of the golf course for IR£50,000, a butcher's shop with overhead living accommodation on Ballybunion's Main Street for IR£75,000, and a seven-bedroom guesthouse for IR£200,000.

North Kerry isn't entirely bereft of gorgeous seascapes and mountain fastnesses—you'll find plenty to enthrall you on the wild Dingle Peninsula. Thirty miles long and with a backbone of mountains, it reaches into the ocean to the west of Tralee and is one of Western Europe's richest sites for monastic beehive huts and other archaeological curiosities. The Dingle Peninsula sees far fewer package tourists than the Iveragh Peninsula, largely because its ribbon-thin roads just weren't designed for coach-tour traffic. With around 1,200 inhabitants, 52 pubs, and some excellent seafood restaurants (try Doyle's), the main settlement is harbor-town Dingle, which has a thriving fishing fleet and does a lucrative trade in taking visitors out to spot Fungie, the famous resident dolphin. The villages scattered west of Dingle town are Irish-speaking, so this is a bilingual region—you'll certainly hear the chatter of Irish in An Café Litearta (the Literary Café), which sells books as well as coffee.

Although unrestored houses on the Dingle Peninsula start at around IR£33,000, you won't have much change left over from IR£60,000 for a modern three-bedroom property or from IR£75,000 for a four-bedroom bungalow. With harbor vistas from the front and mountains to the rear, a three-bedroom house in Dingle town could easily set you back IR£130,000. Want the kind of silver-screen views seen in the movie *Ryan's Daughter*? It was filmed at Inch Beach, a spectacular spot where four-bedroom bungalows have changed hands for IR150,000. However, if you're prepared to live half a mile from the beach, you could buy a three-bedroom bungalow near Castlegregory for IR£60,000. Depending on the views, half-acre sites on the peninsula fetch anything from IR£20,000 to IR£55,000.

Realtor Address Book
Sean Coyne, 2 Main St., Killarney, Co. Kerry; tel. +353 (0)64 31274
Sean Daly, 34 Henry St., Kenmare, Co. Kerry; tel. +353 (0)64 41213
European Auctioneers, 17 The Mall, Tralee, Co. Kerry; tel. +353 (0)66 23144
William Giles, 23 Denny St., Tralee, Co. Kerry, tel. +353 (0)66 21073
Daniel Hannon, 6 Main St., Listowel, Co. Kerry; tel. +353 (0)68 21577
John Moore, Green St., Dingle, Co. Kerry; tel. +353 (0)66 51588
James North, 33 Denny St., Tralee, Co. Kerry, tel. +353 (0)66 22699
Pierse & Fitzgibbon, Property Ireland, 25 Market St., Listowel, Co. Kerry; tel. +353 (0)68 23277

Kerry Contacts
Bus Éireann: to many destinations from Tralee (tel. +353 0-66 23566) and Killarney (tel. +353 0-64 34777)
The Kerryman (local newspaper), Clash Industrial Estate, Tralee, Co. Kerry; tel. +353 (0)66 21666
Rail Services: to Dublin from Tralee (tel. +353 0-66 23522) and Killarney (tel. +353 0-64 31067)
Tourist Information, Ashe Memorial Hall, Denny St., Tralee, Co. Kerry; tel. +353 (0)66 21288

County Cork

Sandwiched between Waterford and Kerry, cosmopolitan Cork is Ireland's largest county. Rich in folklore, music, and wildly seductive landscapes, it's a place that many foreign buyers feel is perfect for raising a young family, starting a new business venture, or simply enjoying their retirement. Like neighboring south Kerry, the scenery is simply dramatic—imagine a hinterland of mountains, loughs, and wooded river valleys, all fringed by a craggy coastline of cliffs, coves, and pristine beaches. That's Cork.

The Gulf-stream climate ensures that winters are mild and cottage gardens rarely see snowfalls. Primroses start blooming in the hedgerows in February and shops stock the new season's vegetables sooner than anywhere else. An added bonus is the county's wide range of sporting activities, which include everything from golf to yachting, hill-walking, fishing, and foxhunting. Outside of Dublin, the southwest coastal region is the country's main tourism mecca so there's plenty of opportunities for anyone considering a business venture.

House values within the county vary enormously and whatever your budget, it shouldn't be too hard to find something suitable. As a rough guide, the dearest locations are villages within easy striking distance of Cork City, high-profile harbor towns such as Kinsale, and the beautiful retreat of balmy Glengarriff, which overlooks Garinish Island and is swooningly expensive. Yes, it's lovely, but anybody who's prepared to pay IR£200,000 for a one-bedroom cottage must have more money than sense!

In contrast, cottages in reasonable repair can be found in the untouristed rural areas around Dunmanway and Bantry for IR£30,000 to IR£40,000. If you're in the market for a renovation project, cottages in rural backwaters start at IR£20,000 and tumbledown farmhouses can sometimes be had for as little as IR£25,000. Even seaside properties aren't all necessarily expensive. At Duneen Strand, a short stroll from the coastal town of Clonakilty in West Cork, two-bedroom holiday cottages start at just IR£39,000.

The biggest problem with county Cork is its sheer size—it can be hard to decide on the best place to begin a house-hunting quest. In general, realtors in Cork City are more likely to deal with properties in the eastern half of the county, between the border with county Waterford and Kinsale, which has its own local agents. If you're more inclined toward West Cork, try Clonakilty, Skibbereen, or Bantry for the widest choice of properties and agents.

Although you probably haven't come to pound the city streets, it's hard to resist spending a day or two in Cork City, wandering the engaging laneways around the river Lee. With a population of around 180 thousand, this is the Republic's second-largest city and has its own university as well as a thriving arts-and-culture scene. Early birds find the best bargains at the flea market on Coal Quay or go to the covered English Market, which at one time was barred to Irish traders. Produce ranges from local cheeses to *drisheen*, a sausage made from sheep's blood. As Cork City is the tourist gateway to the southwest and many visitors spend a night or two here, you may want to check out some guesthouse and B&B properties.

Journeying east to west along the coast road, the first of Cork's old harbor towns is Youghal. Pronounced "Yawl," its town walls date from the thirteenth century and Sir Walter Raleigh was the mayor here in 1588. Next comes Cobh, pronounced "Cove," whose huge natural harbor was the embarkation point for around 2.5 million of last century's emigrants. The Heritage Center chronicles some of their sad stories and also remembers the days when the transatlantic liners, the *Titanic* among them, put into

KILLARNEY'S LAKES

Nestling within the 27,000 acres of Killarney's national park and girdled by mountains are the three magical lakes that conjure up one of Ireland's most quintessential images. The largest is Lough Léin, the "Lake of Learning," which gained its name through the scholars who were rowed over to Inisfallen Island, a renowned center of education in medieval times. Boatmen still take visitors to this tumbledown monastic settlement, originally founded by St. Finian the Leper in the seventh century. As well as being the place where the *Annals of Inisfallen* were written, it's said that Brian Boru, high king of Ireland, studied here during his youth.

Muckross Lake is the middle lake. Stopping points include the ruins of a fifteenth-century abbey that was laid to waste by Cromwell's soldiers in 1652, the Victorian magnificence of Muckross House and gardens, and the Torc waterfall that cascades off the mountains. Following the track around the north shore of the lake brings you to the Old Weir Bridge and the "Meeting of the Waters" where a small river tumbles down from Upper Lake. The entire area is excellent walking and cycling country—hire a bike for IR£5 a day from O'Neills (Plunkett St., Killarney; tel. +353 0-64 31970). If you're traveling by car, a grandstand panorama over Upper Lake toward Purple Mountain can be had from Ladies View where Queen Victoria and her ladies-in-waiting came to picnic.

port here. Under British rule, Cobh's name was Queenstown, and its old nineteenth-century terraces have something of the look of an English seaside town.

On to fashionable Kinsale, which has its own seafaring history. Pubs carry names such as the Spaniard and the Spinnaker, and if you walk along the village's cliff tops to Old Head you can gaze out to where the *Lusitania* went down in 1915 with 1,500 passengers. A center for yachting, fishing, and golf, the town's alleyways are steep and cobbled, houses are painted in a rainbow of pastel colors, and 11 of its 35 restaurants are of the gourmet variety.

With only 2,500 year-round residents, Kinsale really comes to life as a summer port resort; almost half of its properties are sold for investment purposes. New three-bedroom townhouses start at IR£94,000; alternatively, for IR£95,000 you could buy a bijou terraced house at River Meadow with views of the Bandon River and the Marsh bird sanctuary. At the other end of the price scale, Scully House overlooks the flotilla of yachts in Kinsale Harbor and is priced at a massive IR£1.5 million. Once a Georgian gentleman's residence, it presently operates as a top-quality guesthouse and its walled grounds also include a separate guest cottage for self-caterers. If you want to rent a property here, expect to pay around IR£400 per month for a one-bedroom apartment and IR£600 per month for a three-bedroom cottage.

With only 2,500 year-round residents, Kinsale really comes to life as a summer port resort; almost half of its properties are sold for investment purposes.

West of here is color-washed Clonakilty, a pretty heritage town with a magnificent array of traditional hand-painted shop fronts. Its citizens are very proud of the local delicacy—Clonakilty black pudding. If you feel queasy about tucking into pig's-blood sausage, a good place for a pub seafood lunch is An Sugan. Much of Neil Jordan's film *Michael Collins* was filmed hereabouts and it was in Clonakilty that the Free State general went to school. Properties start at IR£39,000 for chalet-type holiday cottages, IR£50,000 for restored country cottages, and IR£70,000 to IR£120,000 for three- and four-bedroom modern bungalows. As always, much depends on the view. IR£120,000 also buys a three-story retail/residential premises within the town limits that has full planning permission for a restaurant.

Protestants founded bustling Skibbereen, but its name became a byword for Catholic suffering and the severe hardships endured by the peasantry during the Famine years. Even though today it's a prosperous farmers' town, memories never fade and visitors are encouraged to follow the Skibbereen Trail around sites associated with the An Gorta Mor, the Great Hunger.

Country cottages for restoration in the Skibbereen area start at around IR£25,000, but at this price we're talking about cottages that need lots and lots of tender loving care. For something more habitable, IR£35,000 is the starting figure. With views of the river Ilen, about IR£40,000 buys an old-fashioned cottage in reasonable repair on a three-quarter-acre plot. However, it's the nearby coastal villages that prove the big draw. Although most village populations in West Cork number less than five hundred year-round residents, they're always swollen with summer visitors and so have a good choice of traditional-music pubs and restaurants.

South of Skibbereen, Baltimore is a lively port and sailing center with a ruined castle that goes by the magical name of Dún na Sead, the Fort of the Jewels. Its former inhabitants, the O'Driscoll clan, enjoyed a million-dollar view over Roaringwater Bay and Carberry's Hundred Islands. Ferries make the journey over to Sherkin Island and Cape Clear Island, a noted birding site lying on one of the migratory-passage routes. One of the strangest events in Baltimore's history occurred in 1631 when 200 of the inhabitants were snatched by Barbary pirates and shipped off to Algiers as slaves. A mile from the village, a traditional blacksmith's forge that has been renovated into a home in excellent repair is priced at IR£100,000.

Other sought-after villages on Roaringwater Bay include Ballydehob and Schull where I saw not one, but *two* farmhouses going as a job lot for IR£65,000. (One had been recently lived in; its neighbor required much more renovation work.) But if you want a quality hideaway with harbor views, expect to pay for it. A three-bedroom bungalow on two and three-quarter acres near Schull has picturesque panoramas and a IR£120,000 price tag to match. Some of West Cork's best beaches are to be found along this stretch of the Mizen Peninsula—the queen of them all is Barleycove, on the road between the villages of Crookhaven and Goleen, where you often see artists trying to capture the beauty of the place on canvas.

With Dunmanus Bay on one side and Bantry Bay on the other, remote Sheep's Head Peninsula takes a 12-mile plunge southwest from Durrus village. It's another splendid spot to get out the easel and paintbrushes, and, located almost at the tip of the peninsula, it's an ideal artist's retreat. Priced at IR£95,000, a restored farmhouse comes with a stone barn already turned into a studio. Halfway along the peninsula, at Kilcrohane, you could buy a completely unrenovated farmhouse on three-quarters of an acre for just

IR£39,000. As it, too, has enticing ocean views, there has to be plenty of investment potential.

If you decide to check out properties away from the coast, avoid county Cork's best-known village: Blarney. Too twee for words, it's a real tourist trap and traffic is simply horrendous. Coach tour after coach tour delivers hordes of would-be stone kissers, all convinced the Blarney Stone has the power to turn them into silver-tongued charmers. Personally, I wouldn't spend IR£3 to bend over backwards from a great and giddy height to slaver over some lump of rock! On the other hand, if you've got a money-spinning idea, it may be just the place—it's a village where tourists are very easily parted from their cash and Blarney Woolen Mills alone manages to sell 900 thousand sweaters to convoys of the credulous every year. Although four-bedroom bungalows in the village are fetching IR£120,000, you can still pick up two-bedroom cottages within the countryside locality for IR£50,000.

Elsewhere, Midleton is a seventeenth-century market town and home to the Jameson whiskey distillery. Townhouses here can be found for IR£35,000 to IR£40,000. Or look to the Blackwater Valley, dotted with castles and ancient sites. Main towns and villages along the valley include Fermoy, Mallow, and Millstreet, which hosts one of Ireland's largest horse shows. On the Bandon River, the countryside surrounding Dunmanway

THE BIG FELLA

Many scenes in Neil Jordan's movie, *Michael Collins*, were shot in the West Cork area. Played in the film by Liam Neeson, Michael Collins was born in 1890 near Clonakilty. Often referred to as "the Big Fella," he was a major figure in Ireland's War of Independence (1919–1921). Using "flying columns" and assassination squads, he organized a ruthless campaign of guerrilla warfare against the British, which eventually resulted in bringing the old enemy to the negotiating table.

Sent to London by Eamon de Valera to negotiate a truce, Collins put his signature to the treaty that partitioned the island of Ireland. In doing so he signed his own death warrant. Southern Ireland split into pro- and anti-treaty factions and former comrades-in-arms were soon spilling their own blood in a bitter civil war. On August 22, 1922, the anti-treaty forces caught up with Collins at Beal-na-Bleath, near the West Cork village of Macroom. His car was ambushed and, rather than fleeing, Collins engaged in a shoot-out that resulted in his death.

and Bandon serves up plenty of habitable properties in the IR£40,000 to IR£60,000 range and is especially good for hunting down bargain cottages for refurbishment.

Realtor Address Book
Hamilton Osborne King, 11 South Mall, Cork City, Co. Cork; tel. +353 (0)21 271371

Irish & European Property, 23 South Mall, Cork City, Co. Cork; tel. +353 (0)21 277606

John Kerr, 17/18 Ashe St., Clonakilty, Co. Cork; tel. +353 (0)23 34944

Key Properties, Bantry, Co. Cork; tel. +353 (0)27 50111

Matt O'Sullivan, Emmet Square, Clonakilty, Co. Cork; tel. +353 (0)23 33367

Sheehy Bros., 10 Short Quay, Kinsale, Co. Cork; tel. +353 (0)21 772338

Cork Contacts
Bus Éireann: to most Irish cities and large towns from Cork; tel. +353 (0)21 508188

The Corkman (local newspaper), 39 Main St., Mallow, Co. Cork; tel. +353 (0)22 42394

The Examiner and *Evening News* (local newspapers), Academy St., Cork; tel. +353 (0)21 272722

Rail Services: direct to Dublin, indirect routes to Waterford and Killarney; tel. +353 (0)21 506766

Tourist Information Office, Aras Fáilte, Grand Parade, Cork; tel. +353 (0)21 273251

County Tipperary

"It's a long way to Tipperary," goes the old First World War marching song. Certainly it's far enough away to have escaped becoming part of the Limerick, Cork, or Waterford City commuter belts. Although this is Ireland's largest inland county, its charms are understated by most tourist guides, and so it still has the air of a well-guarded secret. If peace and tranquillity top your shopping list, take a trip to Tipp and check out its sleepy market towns and even sleepier villages. However, house prices are by no means inexpensive. The county is becoming increasingly popular with affluent Dublin buyers looking to buy weekend homes and take up the traditional rural pursuits of hunting and fishing.

Walled on its southern horizon by the smudgy blue bastions of the Galtee and Comeragh mountain ranges, in the west by the Silvermine Mountains and Lough Derg, Tipperary is essentially farming country. Its central Golden Vale produces prime herds of beef and dairy cattle and local agents often find it hard to keep up with the growing demand for good-quality pasture—40 acres of farmland can easily achieve IR£150,000. As this is also excellent hunting country, any period-type property with a couple of paddocks and outbuildings for stabling generally finds plenty of eager buyers, too.

Any good-condition Georgian "gentleman's house" or rambling old rectory does not come cheap. On 25 acres of parkland and grazing land near Borrisokane village, a few miles east of Lough Derg, Ballylina House was recently advertised with a guideline price of IR£240,000. By Dublin values, this is a steal for a four-bedroom Georgian residence, and it comes with oodles of elegance, too: You can easily imagine a harpsichord tinkling away in the drawing room, a frock-coated master of the house writing up his journal in the study, and ladies in frothy muslin dresses playing croquet on the lawn. Ballylina's grounds also include stabling for horses and a former coach house.

Of course, not everyone wants or can afford a historic property. Away from the grand country-house market, smaller properties are more affordable with numerous rural cottages in the IR£25,000-to-IR£30,000 range and modern two-bedroom bungalows beginning at around IR£39,000. However, those sort of price levels indicate that a property will be very much off the beaten track and you'll pay rather more to gaze over Lough Derg or be within striking distance of the county's prettiest towns: Clonmel, Roscrea, Cahir, Cashel, and Carrick-on-Suir. Just because of its name, you may feel it's worth having a look at Tipperary town, but to be honest, it's rather drab and disappointing. The only real reason to come here would be for the twice-weekly cattle mart or to view a horserace.

Properties are particularly pricey around Cashel, a heritage town that's home to one of Ireland's most splendid historical sights. Once the seat of the Kings of Munster, the Rock of Cashel rises above the Tipperary countryside like the mirage of some Celtic acropolis, crowned with an array of ecclesiastical stonework dating back to medieval times: a round tower, intricately carved high crosses, a ruined cathedral, and a castle tower house. It was from this lofty aerie that St. Patrick reputedly plucked a shamrock to illustrate the doctrine of the Holy Trinity.

But as Cashel is the one Tipperary town to which tourists flock in any great numbers, it may prove a good location for anyone seeking a guesthouse opportunity. At the upper end of the market, a seven-bedroom home that operates as a B&B recently came up for auction carrying a guideline price of IR£165,000. On the county's southeastern border, surrounded by cider apple orchards, is Carrick-on-Suir (pop. 5,500), which sees far fewer visitors. A riverside market town, its history goes back to the Middle Ages when it was an important center for the wool trade. Here you can buy pretty bungalows from IR£59,000. An old-fashioned two-story quayside house in the town center is priced at IR£88,000.

South Tipperary's main town for work, shopping, restaurants, and realtors is Clonmel: with around 20,000 inhabitants this is as close as the county gets to big-city lights. Ten miles west of Carrick-on-Suir, it's another riverbank town of atmospheric backstreets and quayside mills surrounded by good hill-walking territory. Overlooked by Slievenamon Mountain, a two-story cottage with all the necessary facilities was recently on sale for IR£28,000. On the other hand, spankingly modern three- and four-bedroom villa-type bungalows sell for IR£70,000 and up.

There's still a quaintly old-fashioned air to Clonmel and it gives a good inkling of what a Georgian coaching town must have been like. Down from the turrets of the West Gate, Hearns hotel was once the home and headquarters of Charles Bianconi who came over from Lombardy in

THE AGE OF WONDERS

Great ones for lists and catalogs, the long-bearded sages of the Middle Ages weren't content with just seven wonders of the world. Two miles east of Roscrea town is a place that used to be known as the Thirty-first Wonder of the World: a sacred Celtic isle called Monaincha or Insula Viventium, the "Island of the Living." Reputed to hold the secret of everlasting life, its only hint of past glories is a little ruined church, and sadly the site has long been dispossessed of its island status by drainage schemes.

In previous centuries only the wealthy could afford the services of a doctor, and the Irish peasantry were more concerned with having a pain-free life than traveling to remote islands in a quest for immortality. The High Crosses of Ahenny and one of the Crosses at Kilkieran are crowned with removable capstones, sometimes known as *mitre* stones or bishop's hats. Tipperary lore suggests that headache sufferers sought to relieve their pain by placing these capstones upon their own pates. It seems a curious notion. There you are with a throbbing migraine and you want to balance a *boulder* on your head? Should the aspirins run out, you may be better off seeking relief from the waters of St. Kieran's Well, beside Kilkieran churchyard. It, too, reputedly cures headaches.

Italy to found Ireland's first coach service in 1815. "The Bian" was a horse-drawn two-wheeler that carried both the mail and up to six passengers who sat back-to-back facing the roadside.

North Tipperary's chief town is Nenagh. Although not a particularly picturesque town, its realtors generally have a good supply of inexpensive cottages in the rural hinterland where narrow forested roads climb up from Newport into the Silvermines Mountains. As their name suggests, this was once a center for silver mining though the term "mountains" is something of an exaggeration. The highest point, Keeper Hill, tops out at a rather underwhelming 676 meters. The range links up with an intriguing-sounding plateau called the Devil's Bit, and most local kids can reel off the story about how this gap in the hills came by its strange name. Long ago, the Devil himself flew over Tipperary and, just for the hell of it, decided to bite a chunk out of the mountains. Finding that it wasn't the most palatable of snack foods, he spat it out and that's how the Rock of Cashel was formed. Or so the legend goes.

In this part of north Tipperary, ready-to-move-into cottages on a typical half-acre patch of land start at IR£28,000. Some really tempting homes are available if you're willing to pay fractionally more. At the time of writing, IR£37,500 and IR£55,000 bought pretty whitewashed three- and four-bedroom cottages at Templederry and Rathcullen. At the other end of the price scale, offers of around IR£325,000 were sought for Glencullo Lodge. On 13 acres, this beautiful eighteenth-century residence sits at the foot of Keeper Hill, two and a half miles from Silvermines village.

West of Nenagh and the Silvermines is the Tipperary shore of Lough Derg, part of the famous river Shannon navigation scheme. Always busy in summertime with boating visitors, the shore is strung with little marinas and attractive lakeside villages such as Terryglass, Dromineer, Garrykennedy, Portroe, and Ballina, the latter linked to Killaloe in county Clare by an arched stone bridge. The two counties and their lakeshore villages are in friendly competition to win the tourism battle so there's no shortage of good restaurants, curio shops, traditional-music pubs, and summer festivals. House prices are similar to the Clare side of the shore: upwards of IR£90,000 for luxury bungalows with doorstep panoramas of the lough.

Realtor Address Book

Barry Walsh Estates, 91 Main St., Carrick-on-Suir, Co. Tipperary; tel. +353 (0)51 640528

John Lee & Son, Main St., Newport, Co. Tipperary; tel. +353 (0)61 378121

Shee & Hawe, 62 Main St., Carrick-on-Suir, Co. Tipperary; tel. +353 (0)51 640041

William Talbot, 52 Keynon St., Nenagh, Co. Tipperary; tel. +353 (0)67 31496

Tom Pollard & Co., Emmet St., Clonmel, Co. Tipperary; tel. +353 (0)52 22755

Tipperary Contacts

Bus Éireann: between most Tipperary towns and Dublin, Cork, and Limerick; hub of operations is Carrick-on-Suir (tel. +353 0-51 79000)

Nenagh Guardian (local newspaper), 13 Summerhill, Nenagh, Co. Tipperary; tel. +353 (0)67 31214

Rail Services: from Clonmel to Cork, Limerick, and Rosslare with connections to Dublin from Limerick Junction (tel. +353 0-52 21982); trains also call at Nenagh and Carrick-on-Suir (but not Cashel); for routings ring Thurles Station (tel. +353 0-504 21733)

Tourist Information, Sarsfield St., Clonmel, Co. Tipperary; tel. +353 (0)52 22960

The Sunny Southeast

When I think of the southeast, I see gorgeous green meadows, ancient abbey ruins, pretty villages and horses galloping along sandy beaches. Despite the savage Viking and Norman past, this is Ireland at its most gentle. Even the weather here usually decides to be kind!

County Kilkenny

Don't ignore Kilkenny just because it doesn't possess a coastal fringe. Its verdant landscape is pastoral perfection, dotted here and there with picture-book villages, shady woodland copses, ramblers' tracks, and winding rivers banked by lacy white clouds of cow parsley. Lost in the fields are some hauntingly beautiful monastic settlements, and you'll also stumble across a wealth of high crosses, round towers, and castles dating from Norman times. An added bonus is Kilkenny town, the country's best-preserved example of a medieval city.

Sometimes called the Marble City, Kilkenny town is the place to head for first. Although wandering around its castle, abbeys, and maze of crooked laneways can make you feel as if you're trapped in a time warp, the modern world is always there when you need it. Kilkenny has good train and bus services to Dublin, or, if you're driving, it's 70 miles from the capital by road—distant enough to deter the commuter crowds. With around 20 thousand inhabitants, this is a large town by Irish standards and thus laden with all the essentials: excellent shops, health services, restaurants, the Watergate theater, and three annual arts festivals. And you'll find 68 pubs and St. Francis' Abbey, now the headquarters of the Smithwicks Brewery.

Rather than demolish their ancient buildings, Kilkennians simply give them a new lease on life. The tourist office is located in the Shee Alms House on Rose Inn Street, built as a paupers hospital in 1582 and used as such until 1830. Dating back to 1284, the home of the infamous Witch of Kilkenny on St. Kieran's Street is now a popular pub and restaurant. On Parliament Street, Kilkenny's Archaeological Society and the genealogical county records have found a home in the Rothe House, built by a wealthy merchant for his young bride in 1594. One of the town's more recent architectural ventures was the construction of the castle's new coach houses and stables in 1760. Set in a flower-filled courtyard, these buildings are now used by local craftspeople and the Kilkenny Design Center.

Although Kilkenny's old black marble pavements were lifted in 1929, much more remains to distract you from your house-hunting plans: pleasant riverside walks below the castle, St. Canice's Cathedral, the Black Abbey, and the Tholsel, where medieval villains were publicly burned at the stake. No one really knows how long people have been walking through the dark passageway of the Butterslip, but records show that in 1616 market traders were using it. Nowadays people buy their dairy produce in supermarkets, but older residents can still recite a traditional rhyme about the Butterslip:

If you ever go to Kilkenny,
Look for the hole in the wall.
Where you get twenty-four eggs for a penny
And butter for nothing at all.

Unfortunately, houses within Kilkenny town don't sell for "nothing at all" kinds of prices. It's an affluent community with people employed in the service industries, brewing, and food production—Avonmore Foods employs hundreds of workers at its Kilkenny plant on the road to Ballyragget. Prices vary considerably and, as always, much depends on location and the type of home sought. One of the town's most sought-after residential addresses is Sion Road, which tracks the broad, bosky vale of the River Nore. Here an elegant five-bedroom residence on an elevated site changed hands for IR£250,000. At the other end of the price scale, IR£65,000 still buys little terraced houses in the suburbs. Four-bedroom bungalows within walking distance of the town center are fetching around IR£130,000, but you would probably have to pay IR£180,000 for a three-story townhouse in quite poor repair in the heart of the medieval quarter. Pubs in prime locations are shockingly expensive. Near the twelfth-century castle, on Rose Inn Street (a town-center street that's as pretty as its name), Andy's Tavern came up for auction carrying a guideline price of IR£600,000.

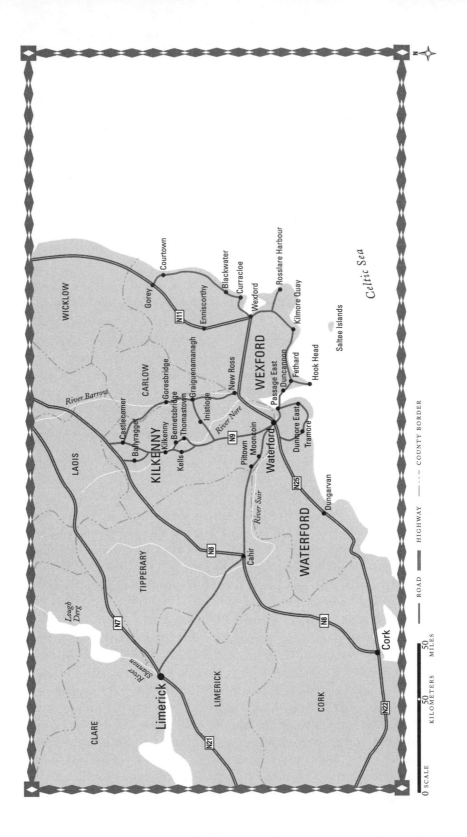

South Kilkenny's countryside brims with more affordable enticements, particularly if you concentrate on the small towns and villages beside the banks of the Barrow, Nore, Munster, and Suir Rivers, which are all excellent fly-fishing rivers. If your new neighbors aren't involved in farming, chances are they'll be doing something arty with clay, crystal, wool, gemstones, wood, or leather—this part of the country has a very high concentration of craftspeople. There's always room for new blood and new ideas, and just because you've never done anything remotely crafty in your life doesn't mean it's too late to start. The Crafts Council of Ireland runs courses in jewelry making, pottery, and design skills from its training center in the Castle Yard in Kilkenny town. Whether you're a craftsperson looking for a new market or are interested in taking a course, you can contact them there or by phone (tel. +353 0-56 61804).

Along with ancient Thomastown, Kilkenny's main craft clusters are the villages of Goresbridge, Graiguenamanagh, Stoneyford, and Bennetsbridge. As an example of typical prices in the surrounding area, IR£27,500 is being sought for a smallish, boxy bungalow while IR£70,000 is the price of an immaculately renovated turn-of-the-century cottage. River-view properties command a premium and a three-bedroom modern property with an acre of well-tended gardens overlooking the Nore valley near Thomastown is priced at IR£83,000. Even so, it's a grand location with all the history you ever wanted within walking distance. Thomastown takes its name from Thomas Fitzanthony, a Welsh-Norman knight who founded this place of time-toppled medieval walls and castles in 1197. Less than two miles down the road, Jerpoint Abbey silhouettes the skyline. Today its towers and cloisters are in ruins, but this was once one of the finest Cistercian abbeys in Ireland.

The medieval monks couldn't get enough of county Kilkenny's real estate. Five miles west of Stoneyford, they took over Kells Priory, a former Norman castle with seven gray towers and massively thick curtain walls that perches above the King's River, a tributary of the Nore. Now abandoned to time and the elements, Kells is made even more atmospheric by the fact that the government seems to have forgotten its existence—there's no ticket office, no guided tours, no designated visiting hours. Just you, the sheep, and maybe a ghost or two. Due south of here is the little village of Knocktopher, where an old-fashioned residential shop sold for IR£89,000 and renovation projects start at around IR£10,000.

Nor did the holy men neglect to colonize the banks of the river Barrow. With the thirteenth-century Cistercian splendor of Duiske Abbey on the doorstep, Graiguenamanagh's name actually means "the grange of the monks." Here, on 12.5 emerald acres, a restored five-bedroom farmhouse with a range of outside offices in the yard and six newly constructed loose boxes (for stabling horses) is available for IR£300,000. Buy this and you'll also be getting 670 yards of game- and course-fishing rights on the adjoining river.

Not all farmhouses are that expensive, and obviously a lot depends on location, state of repair, and the amount of land being sold with the property. If you're seeking a renovation project, IR£25,000 buys a stone farmhouse for renovation at Kilmanagh, 10 miles west of Kilkenny town. IR£32,000 buys a two-story farmhouse on one acre of land at Piltown, in the south of the county near the Kilkieran high crosses and the river Suir. Note, though, that it also requires extensive repairs. Five miles down the road, at Mooncoin, a pretty pink-painted farmhouse with the same amount of land indicates the value that these types of properties can achieve once restoration has taken place. The vendors are seeking IR£80,000.

What if you want an ordinary little village house? Again, look around Piltown where small terrace-type cottages in good condition start at

---

If your new neighbors in South Kilkenny aren't involved in farming, chances are they'll be doing something arty with clay, crystal, wool, gemstones, wood, or leather.

IR£25,000 and detached two-story village houses at IR£45,000. In Mooncoin, a six-bedroom guesthouse sold for IR£83,000. As this locality is so close to the county border, note that Carrick-on-Suir (county Tipperary) agents tend to handle properties hereabouts.

Many foreign buyers are attracted to Kilkenny's Georgian country houses and estates, and you can pay as much as IR£550,000 for a residence like Ballyragget's Grange Manor, an ivy-clad mansion with room for dozens of visiting grandchildren and a river gurgling through its 25-acre grounds. Yet not all historic properties cost a fortune, and any Georgian house is likely to prove a good investment in the long run. Built in simple classic style, these types of residences will never go out of fashion—after all, nobody is making them any more!

Priced at IR£150,000 and needing full internal renovation, Tinford House is a four-bedroom Georgian home beside the eighteenth-century 10-arched bridge in Inistioge village. Pronounced "Inishteeg," this adorable little village is backdropped by dark, goblin woods on the banks of the river Nore below Thomastown. Around the grassy square, lined with a shady canopy of lime trees, most pubs and shops have kept their original facades. It's not all that surprising to discover that Inistioge has been featured in a number of recent movies—one was the romantic weepy *Circle of Friends*, adapted from a novel of the same name by Irish writer Maeve Binchy. If you're looking for a more up-to-date residence in Inistioge, IR£125,500 is the price of a three-bedroom bungalow—expensive, but the price includes stables and 13 acres of land.

Realtor Address Book

Ganly Walters Boyd, 5 William St., Kilkenny (tel. +353 0-56 64833); and Lowe St., Thomastown (tel. +353 0-56 24600)

Fitzgeralds, 24 Patrick St., Kilkenny; tel. +353 (0)56 70888

M.F. Grace, Callan, Co. Kilkenny; tel. +353 (0)56 25163

J. David Hughes, 20 Parliament St., Kilkenny (tel. +353 0-56 63437); and Main St., Graiguenamanagh (tel. +353 0-503 24437)

Walter Walsh, Mill St., Thomastown, Co. Kilkenny; tel. +353 (0)56 24485

Kilkenny Contacts

Bus Éireann: to Dublin, Cork, and Waterford (tel. +353 0-56 64933); from the Parade, Kavanagh's runs buses to Cashel in Tipperary via Kells and Fethard; also to Carlow, Thurles, and Portlaoise (tel. +353 0-56 31106)

Rail Services: to Dublin and Waterford; tel. +353 (0)56 22024

Tourist Information, Shee Alms House, Rose Inn St., Kilkenny; tel. +353 (0)56 51500

County Wexford

Filling Ireland's southeast corner, maritime Wexford has a strong agricultural base and has been inhabited since prehistoric times. Although Wexford was converted to Christianity by St. Ibar in the fifth century, its name comes from the Norse word *Waesfjord*, meaning sandy harbor or harbor of mud flats. The Viking invaders who settled here were followed by the Normans in 1169 for whom Wexford was their first Irish port of call. Then, as now, the county's main settlement was Wexford town. Unfortunately, relatively few traces of the distant past remain—for that you can thank Cromwell, who attacked the town in 1649, putting an estimated three quarters of its two thousand citizens and all of its Franciscan friars to the sword.

Today, around 16 thousand people live in the Wexford town area with smaller numbers concentrated in Gorey, Enniscorthy, New Ross, and Rosslare Harbour, the main ferry port to South Wales in Britain. Over a quarter of the population is aged between 25 and 44 and employment is

The Witch of Kilkenny

Born in Kilkenny in 1280, Alice Kyteler was the daughter of a wealthy Norman banker who had established a money-lending venture in the town. The business eventually passed into Alice's hands through inheritance, but the ecclesiastical authorities of the day were staunchly opposed to women being in trade and she made many enemies. As in many other witchcraft cases, money may have been the reason behind her eventual downfall. Seemingly a woman of healthy appetites, Alice worked her way through four husbands, all of whom mysteriously expired for no apparent reason. Some townsfolk believed that she had poisoned the lot of them, others whispered that it was the work of the Devil.

At her trial in 1324, she was accused by the Bishop of Ossory of heresy and of trafficking with his Satanic Majesty. Witnesses swore that they had seen Alice and her maidservant slaughtering cockerels and sweeping dust from the town's streets to the house of William Outlawe, Alice's son. In the murky world of medieval magicking, this was a form of transference whereby dust represented gold and Kilkenny's wealth would all fall to William. In other words, witchcraft.

The court found the defendants guilty. Alice and her servant Petronella were sentenced to burn at the stake, William to be hanged. However, Alice managed to engineer an escape and fled to England while William bought his pardon by funding the reroofing of the choir stalls in St. Canice's Cathedral. Only the poor servant girl paid the ultimate penalty. Petronella was burned at the Tholsel, outside Kilkenny's City Hall, along with many of her mistress's possessions. The house on St. Kieran's Street where Alice and Petronella lived now goes by the name of Kyteler's Inn.

found in a diversity of both multinational and indigenous enterprises; everything from food production to data processing and light engineering, to the manufacture of pharmaceutical products and car components. In addition, Wexford has benefited from the government's decentralization program. A number of State departments have relocated here—they include the Environmental Protection Agency and Teagasc, the State's agricultural research center.

Despite the economic boom times, young local couples haven't been priced out of the market and, unlike in Dublin, it's still possible for them to get onto the housing ladder. One-bedroom starter apartments in Wexford town can still be had for IR£47,500, and workaday suburban semis go for IR£50,000 to IR£60,000. However, larger showpiece apartments in top locations around the harbor and quays can cost over IR£100,000.

Although Wexford town is no longer a commercial port (the Slaney estuary is too silted up with centuries of river mud), it still has the feel of a seafarers' hangout. One of its most famous sons was John Barry, who emigrated to America and founded the United States Navy. Its ribbon-thin streets can get very roisterous during the summer Viking Festival, though for classier entertainment you should come for October's Opera Festival.

Golden sandy beaches are county Wexford's star attraction and many have been awarded the European blue flag for excellence. Near Gorey, in the north of the county, you'll find beautiful strands beside the villages of Ballymoney and Courtown; the endless golden chain then continues through Morriscastle, Kilmuckbridge, Blackwater, and Curracloe, which was featured in the recent Tom Hanks movie, *Saving Private Ryan*. South of Wexford town lies Rosslare Strand and Carne; round the corner to the south coast proper and you'll come across Kilmore Quay, Fethard, Hook Head, and Duncannon.

As nowhere within the county is more than a two-hour drive from Dublin, Wexford is a favorite location for holiday home–buyers. Consequently prices are fairly buoyant and the typical three- or four-bedroom bungalow-type property with sea views falls somewhere into the IR£80,000-to-IR£180,000 category. For example, new three-bedroom houses at Raven's Point, at the southern end of Curracloe's seven miles of sandy heaven, are selling for IR£92,500. Along with miles of forest walks and sand dunes, there are excellent marina facilities here. In addition, buyers will be right beside one of Europe's most renowned nature reserves: the North Sloblands. During the winter months, the Slobs provide a feeding ground for around 10,000 migratory Greenland white-fronted geese, more than half the world's entire population.

That's not to say less-expensive properties can't still be found. A 10-minute drive from Wexford town, near Murnstown village and Johnstown Castle, a three-bedroom bungalow is available for just IR£62,000. And although this is an inland location, if you look due south you can see the ocean and the distant smudge of the Saltee Islands whose surrounding treacherous waters gave rise to the nickname "the graveyard of a thousand ships." If you prefer to buy a plot of land within sight of the coast and build a home, half-acre sites with planning permission start at IR£17,500.

Coastal cottages also fall into a wide price range. At Mauritiustown, near Rosslare strand, a traditional two-bedroom cottage just changed hands for IR£39,500. Once thatched, now slated, the cottage had a 200-year-old history and, though pretty enough from the outside, required quite a lot of refurbishment and upgrading. As an example of what you might have to pay for a restored gem, Muck Lodge is being offered at IR£135,000. At Kilmuckbridge, near Gorey, this beautiful Old-world house stands on a three-quarter-acre plot of landscaped gardens.

If your heart is set on a thatched property, the area around the fishing village of Kilmore Quay is your best bet. Lining the main street, almost all the local houses are pictures of whitewashed, thatched perfection. Like every visitor who turns up for July's seafood festival, you too will probably want to own one. All well and good if you have deep pockets, but are you prepared to part with IR£185,500? That's the price tag for a large thatched house at Neamston on a one-third-acre site with views of the ocean, the Saltee Islands, St. Patrick's Bridge, and Kilmore Quay harbor.

Those who can afford a property around Kilmore Quay won't flinch at paying IR£200,000 for Duncannon's Martello tower, a circular stone tower built in 1815 as a vantage point and defense post against French invasions. Now converted into a two-bedroom home, it offers panoramic coastal views and you can impress your friends by telling them your kitchen was once an army gunpowder room! South of Duncannon, some lovely walks crisscross the largely deserted Hook Peninsula, which points into the ocean like a witch's bony finger. The lighthouse on the headland dates back to the twelfth century, and the peninsula itself is dotted with crumbling castles, forts, and abbeys.

This area has another and very curious historical claim to fame. Ever heard the phrase "by hook or by crook" and wondered how it originated? Cromwell coined it during his campaign to capture Waterford City, which lies a few miles west across the county border. What he was referring to was two possible landing points: Hook in Wexford and Crooke in county Waterford. The city would fall to his army by Hook or by Crooke.

Although the Wexford coastline seems to hold all the aces, don't ignore the hinterland. Fixer-uppers can still be found for under IR£30,000, and countryside areas deliver a good choice of attractive cottages and small houses at reasonable price levels. You'll come across many in "move-in-tomorrow". condition for between IR£40,000 and IR£60,000. At Bridgetown, 10 miles from Wexford town, a two-story double-fronted cottage with three bedrooms requires only minor upgrading and is priced at IR£33,500. At Ballywilliam village near the town of New Ross, IR£59,500 buys a two-bedroom traditional house with whitewashed walls, plenty of stone outbuildings, and a grassy paddock. No work needs to be done on the property at all.

Earlier this year, a two-story farmhouse with one acre of land on a secluded laneway near Killnick was snapped up for just IR£49,750. For a residence only five miles from the coast and 10 miles from Wexford town, this was exceptionally cheap. The reason for the low price was the farmhouse hadn't been occupied for four years and so was in need of upgrading and interior modernization. However, a good slated roof had preserved the property's basic structure, and if you come across something similar on your travels, go for it—it will be a great investment.

At the other end of the price scale, IR£215,000 buys a nine-bedroom guesthouse property at Ferrycarrig, three miles from Wexford town on the Enniscorthy Road. The village attracts plenty of visitors, for this is the site of the Irish National Heritage Park, a kind of outdoor historical theme park with re-creations of everything from neolithic burial tombs to a replica Viking shipyard complete with a replica Viking long ship.

Carry on northward along the road through the heart of strawberry-growing countryside and you'll come to Enniscorthy, a little town on the banks of the river Slaney. A 20-minute drive from the beaches and back-dropped by the Blackstairs Mountains, this busy little town has plenty of waterfront inns, brightly painted shop fronts, a thirteenth-century castle, and an annual summer strawberry festival. "It's the biggest small town in the world," claims one enthusiastic local realtor, "a town that's rocketing from nowhere."

Spanking-new riverbank apartments start at IR£67,500, though if you're not fussy about a view, you can buy one-bedroom apartments within the town for IR£30,000. More mainstream residential properties in the suburbs are generally sold for somewhere between IR£40,000 and IR£85,000. In the immediate surrounding countryside, IR£45,000 is a typical price for a renovated cottage. One of the nicest villages is Ferns with yet another collection of castle and abbey ruins. This was once the base of the Kings of Leinster, whose number included the notorious Dermot MacMurrough who invited the Normans over to Ireland and thus brought about centuries of English rule. House prices around Ferns range from IR£33,000 for a *very* small cottage to IR£120,000 for a modern four-bedroom detached residence with landscaped gardens.

A Night at the Opera

Even non–opera goers have probably heard of Bizet's *Carmen* and Strauss' *Die Fledermaus*. But have you ever had the chance to enjoy *Fosca, I Cavalieri di Ekebu* or *Sarlatan*, the tragicomic tale of a quack doctor who falls in love with a beautiful hypochondriac? If you'd visited 1998's Wexford Festival, an 18-day October extravaganza of opera and much else besides, you could have seen all of the above-mentioned operas.

Along with its Nordic setting, the hammers, fire, and alcoholic Lutheran pastor of *I Cavalieri di Ekebu* had given this particular opera something of a cult status in Sweden. But the Wexford performance of *Sarlatan* was the first on stage since its last outing 60 years ago, at Brno in Czechoslovakia. The career of its Czech composer, Pavel Haas, was brutally cut short when he went to his death in the gas chambers of Auschwitz in 1944.

Since Wexford's Opera Festival began in 1951, the focus has been on bringing to light obscure operas that for one reason or another have been unjustly neglected or forgotten. It attracts an international crowd of opera lovers. Wexford town itself takes on a carnival atmosphere with storekeepers competing for the kudos of having the best festive window display, and artists and audiences alike thronging the cafés and bars along Main Street and the Quays. No other small-town Irish festival offers such a perfect excuse for revelers to get out their evening dresses and dinner jackets!

Tickets for the three showpiece operas aren't cheap: Last year's prices were pitched at between IR£40 and IR£50 for each performance. Daytime and late-night events are more affordable, costing between IR£6 and IR£12. For booking and information about this year's October Festival, contact the Wexford Festival Opera Box Office, Theater Royal, High Street, Wexford town, Co. Wexford; tel. +353 (0)53 22144.

Realtor Address Book

Corish's, Custom House Quay, Wexford town, Co. Wexford; tel. +353 (0)53 22288

Haythornewaite Auctioneers, Selskar, Co. Wexford; tel. +353 (0)53 46046

Simon Kavanagh, Templeshannon, Enniscorthy, Co. Wexford; tel. +353 (0)54 35335

Kehoe & Associates, Commercial Quay, Wexford town, Co. Wexford; tel. +353 (0)53 44393

Michael O'Leary, The Bullring, Wexford town, Co. Wexford (tel. +353 0-53 24611); and at Slaney Pl., Enniscorthy, Co. Wexford (tel. +353 0-54 35061)

Warren Estates, Main St., Gorey, Co. Wexford; tel. +353 (0)55 21211

Wexford Contacts

Bus Éireann: to Dublin, Rosslare Harbour, Gorey, Limerick, and Killarney in Kerry (tel. +353 0-53 22522); private buses to Enniscorthy and Co. Carlow with **Kavanagh's** (tel. +353 0-53 43081)

The Guardian (local newspaper), Thomas St., Gorey, Co. Wexford; tel. +353 (0)55 21423

Rail Services: to Dublin, Rosslare Harbour, Enniscorthy, and Wicklow (tel. +353 0-53 22522)

Tourist Office, Crescent Quay, Wexford town, Co. Wexford; tel. +353 (0)53 23111

County Waterford

Waterford is the Crystal County, renowned throughout the world as the home of the exquisitely crafted crystal that shares its name. With around 44 thousand people, Waterford City is the county's main population center and also the Southeast's biggest commercial port, always busy with freighters and container ships. Although much of Waterford's outskirts are a featureless sprawl of industrial development, it's proud of its reputation as a working city. Thanks to its strategic location on the river Suir estuary, this is a true trading settlement and has been for over a millennium. While you probably wouldn't want to live within the city confines, do pay a visit, for at its heart lies a fascinating kernel of historical heritage. Surrounded by the remnants of medieval walls, its streets and laneways track back through the centuries to the time of the Victorians, the Georgians, and even the Anglo-Normans, who wrested the settlement of *Vadrafjord* from the Vikings in 1170 during a three-day siege.

The city's most famous Norman landmark is Reginald's Tower, a stone replacement for the original wooden watchtower built by Reginald the

Dane in 1003 where guard could be kept over the long ships in the harbor. The Tower has witnessed an incredible amount of history: The all-conquering Norman lord Strongbow and the Irish princess Aoife held their wedding feast here above the rubble and ashes of the fallen Viking city; it has served as a royal guesthouse, a military arsenal, a mint, and a gaol (jail). And although the motto on the city's coat of arms is *Urbs intacta manet Waterfordia* (Waterford remains unconquered), the besieged townsfolk did eventually surrender to Cromwellian forces in 1650.

To give you an idea of house prices within Waterford City, many three-bedroom homes in semidetached suburbia are fetching between IR£45,000 and IR£65,000 depending on location; four-bedroom semis in good residential neighborhoods are going for IR£85,000. Small Victorian terraced houses can be had for IR£62,000, with larger townhouses around the Cathedral Square area fetching IR£130,000.

With county Cork to the west and county Wexford to the east, Waterford's coastline has sandy coves, cliff-top walks, and some particularly attractive harbor towns and fishing villages. Coastal property prices tend to be fairly high as everywhere is within easy commuting distance of both Waterford City and Cork City. If you want to be near Waterford City, the most affordable area is inland, tracking westward along the Suir River valley. Look around villages like Portlaw and you'll find refurbished terraced cottages for IR£21,000 and detached cottages with river views for IR£38,000.

In the southeast of the county, five miles from Waterford City, the oddly-named Kill St. Nicholas is a speck of hamlet within strolling distance of the toy-town harbor of Passage East and Woodstown Beach. Here IR£90,000 buys a three-bedroom detached bungalow with a wildflower-meadow garden. The neighboring village is Dunmore East, a lovely fishing village and holiday retreat with plenty of thatched cottages and a busy harbor that entices many oceangoing yachts from Europe. The village seems to have the lot: a twelfth-century castle, a nineteenth-century lighthouse, some good inns and restaurants, cliff-top and woodland walks, and great beaches. Ladies' Cove is right in the village, while a short stroll south brings you to Counsellor's Strand, a beach that flies the much-coveted EU blue flag, which is awarded for cleanliness and safety. Although no thatched cottages were for sale at the time of writing, new three-bedroom houses around Dunmore East can be had for between IR£99,000 and IR£110,000. Alternatively, consider a home with an income—Alpine Cottage currently operates as a small B&B establishment and is on the market for IR£155,000.

Traveling west, the next place you'll come to is Tramore, but unless you have kids in tow, you'll probably pass straight through. A traditional blue-collar seaside resort, its safe golden beach is perfect for the bucket-and-spade brigade to build elaborate castles and bury snoozing dads in the sand. The huge Trabolgan "holiday village" is here, and when it rains the crowds descend on Splashworld, an indoor leisure center with swimming pools, water slides, and chutes. Fine for a family day out, but do you really want to live in a town of penny arcades and burger joints? If so, the two-bedroom bungalows around the town sell for IR£65,000 to IR£70,000.

Leave Tramore behind, drive across Great Newtown Head, and you're back in the world of deserted coves and sleepy-hollow fishing villages. Anywhere around Annestown, Bonmahon, Stradbally, Clonea, or Ballinacourty makes an idyllic retreat, but the location factor means you may have to pay IR£100,000 for even a three-bedroom bungalow with sea views. Move a short distance inland, however, and you can still find old-style cottages in decent repair for IR£30,000. Just three miles from Bonmahon and the beach, Cusack's agency (see Realtor Address Book, later in this chapter) was recently selling a cottage for this price in the hamlet of Georgetown Kill. For those looking to build a property, a typical one-acre site with planning permission for a residence and views of the sea is likely to cost around IR£70,000.

Next stop along the coast is Dungarvan, the administrative center for county Waterford. It's a good base for making property forays into east Cork, the West Waterford hinterland, and around the Comeragh Mountains that straddle the county's northern border with Tipperary. One- and two-bedroom apartments overlooking Dungarvan Harbor start at IR£52,000 to buy; IR£400 per month to rent. Want to rent a fully furnished house beside the sea? IR£550 is the monthly rent for the Old Schoolhouse at Annestown, a large refurbished cottage.

Not far from Dungarvan, one of the most desirable West Waterford properties to be marketed this year was Valentina Cottage. Carrying a guideline price of IR£350,000, and with a lookout over the Bride River valley, this immaculately-restored cottage had the requisite thatched roof and exposed timber-beam ceilings that foreign buyers dream about. An added selling point was that the nine acres of grounds included a productive vineyard. The mild Gulf-stream weather in this part of the world means that it's quite possible to grow certain varieties of grapes, and you shouldn't be surprised if you see palm trees growing in south-coast gardens.

Thankfully not all rural properties are so pricey, and small habitable cottages in the Nire Valley area still surface for around IR£35,000. One IR£40,000 gem I liked the look of was a two-bedroom traditional stone cottage that had already been renovated. Sitting on just over an acre, it had a new pitched slate roof and a fitted pine kitchen. Near the county Tipperary border, the Nire Valley qualifies as a "secret place," perfect for anybody wanting to live off the beaten track. I took a walking holiday in

The Crystal Connection

As an object of desire, Waterford crystal is just about unsurpassable. It rings sweet as a bell and gleams with an almost magical silvery brilliance—the great mystery is how something so beautiful can be created from such mundane mineral products as red lead, silica sand, and potash. Producing this luxury crystalware demands great skill, and it takes between 8 and 10 years for the glass-blowers, cutters, and engravers to fully learn their art.

Waterford's connection with crystal-making dates back more than two hundred years, to 1783 to be precise, when George and William Penrose founded the Waterford Glass House on the city quayside. The new crystal business quickly flourished and went on to win a number of gold medals at the Great Exhibition in London. Unfortunately for the Penrose family and their workers, the company went out of business in 1851, mainly through the British government's imposition of a crippling import tax on the raw minerals that are needed to produce this heavy crystalware.

With Irish independence came the urge to breathe new life back into old crafts and Waterford Crystal was reborn in 1947, relaunching its wares on the world market four years later. So successful was the revival that the company had to move to larger premises on the Cork Road. Today the factory employs around 1,600 people and visitors can take a workshop tour and do serious damage to their credit cards in the Crystal Gallery. Even a tiny crystal napkin-holder will cost you at least IR£20.

this unspoiled area last fall, staying in Ballymacarbry village and hiking the lavender ridge-tops of the Comeraghs, gentle mountains that only rise to 800 meters maximum. Steeped in legend, dark, jewel-like loughs lie deep in corries (cirques) in the mountains' rocky flanks, and local lore whispers of fairy cattle emerging from the waters on moonlit nights. Although part of county Waterford, the Nire Valley's nearest town is Clonmel in Tipperary. Check out agents there for local properties.

Realtor Address Book

Phil Cusack, Main St., Kilmacthomas, Co. Waterford; tel. +353 (0)51 294364

Edmund Spratt & Son, Grattan house, Dungarvan, Co. Waterford; tel. +353 (0)58 42211

Lawrence McDonald, 15 Parnell St., Waterford City, Co. Waterford; tel. +353 (0)51 853199

O'Shea & O'Toole, 11 Gladstone St., Waterford City, Co. Waterford; tel. +353 (0)51 876757

Waterford Contacts

Bus Éireann: to Dublin, Cork, Limerick, Galway, Kilkenny, and Rosslare; tel. +353 (0)51 879000

Rail Services: to Dublin, Kilkenny, Limerick, and Rosslare; tel. +353 (0)51 873401

Tourist Information Office, Merchant Quay, Waterford City, Co. Waterford; tel. +353 (0)51 875788

Waterford News (local newspaper), 25 Michael St., Waterford City, Co. Waterford; tel. +353 (0)51 874951

The Northwest and Lakelands

F ar from the well-worn tourist trails, the underrated counties of Ireland's Northwest and Lakelands are an ideal choice for getting away from the usual stresses of modern life. More so than anywhere else, it's here that bargain hunters will find some of the country's most affordable properties.

County Sligo

A land of literature and legend, Sligo is synonymous with the poet William Butler Yeats who spent many childhood summers here. Tagged "Yeats Country," its most distinctive landmark is Benbulben, a flat-topped table mountain famed in Irish mythology as the site where the hero Diarmuid met a sticky end on the tusks of a magic boar.

Many places throughout the county resonate with eerie magic: the Lake Isle of Innisfree, shimmering Lough Arrow and Lough Gill, the bluebell glades of Slish Wood, and the dolmens and stone circles of Carrowmore—a mysterious necropolis whose secrets date back to the Bronze Age. Here too is Knocknarea, traditionally held to be a hollow hill and one of the strongholds of the *Sidhe* (the fairies). Crowned by a cairn, Knocknarea is also reputed to be the final resting place of Maeve, a tempestuous goddess-queen who waged battle against Ulster's warriors for possession of the Brown Bull of Cooley.

With 19 thousand citizens, the county's only sizable settlement is

Sligo town. On the quality-of-life scale it has all the right ingredients: a good general hospital and services, train links to Dublin, and a vibrant array of cultural activities. It also has a wonderfully authentic center retaining much of the character of times past. Visit a time-warp pub like Hargadon's on O'Connell Street and it feels as if you've been transported back to the last century, especially during winter when a potbellied stove blazes in the main bar.

On the banks of the Garavogue River, Sligo's shopping streets are always busy, drawing people from Leitrim, Roscommon, and south Donegal whose own little towns aren't quite so well stocked. Cinemas, restaurants, and the Hawk's Well theater give the town a year-round bustle; regular summertime events include the Arts Festival and the Yeats' Summer School, attended by scholars from all over the world.

Within Sligo town's environs, the average three-bedroom home fetches IR£60,000; four-bedroom houses within a five-mile radius are generally priced between IR£75,000 and IR£95,000. It's a good place to find rental properties—the town's estate agents enjoy a lively lettings market, thanks to sizable numbers of hospital staff and students from the Regional Technical College seeking accommodation. Depending on size and location, quality country properties can be had for between IR£350 and IR£400 a month. Apartments within town generally let for between IR£250 and IR£300 a month.

In more remote corners of the county, two-bedroom bungalows hover around the IR£40,000 price mark. Like cottages, their price usually depends on proximity to town or coastline. In rural backwaters you'll find plenty of traditional-style cottages in various states of repair selling for between IR£9,500 and IR£30,000. However, move the exact same cottage to the coast and there's every likelihood its price will have doubled.

Attractive north Sligo villages for living the country lifestyle include Carney, Cliffoney, and Grange, where IR£50,000 buys a three-bedroom bungalow. At Drumcliffe, W.B. Yeats is buried in the Protestant churchyard—his great-grandfather was once rector here. Under the shadow of Ben Bulben, the gravestone bears an epitaph Yeats penned himself: "Cast a cold eye on life, on death Horseman, pass by!"

The south of the county has more of an unexplored feel. At Achonry, IR£30,000 buys a five-room cottage on a three-quarter-acre plot, but the "garden" is in need of some loving care and attention. In these parts it's rare to come across the kinds of gardens filled with the hollyhocks, sweet peas, and old-fashioned damask roses that the word "cottage" always conjures up!

A bit more off the beaten track, Coolaney nestles beneath the Ox Mountains—here a small shop with overhead living accommodation

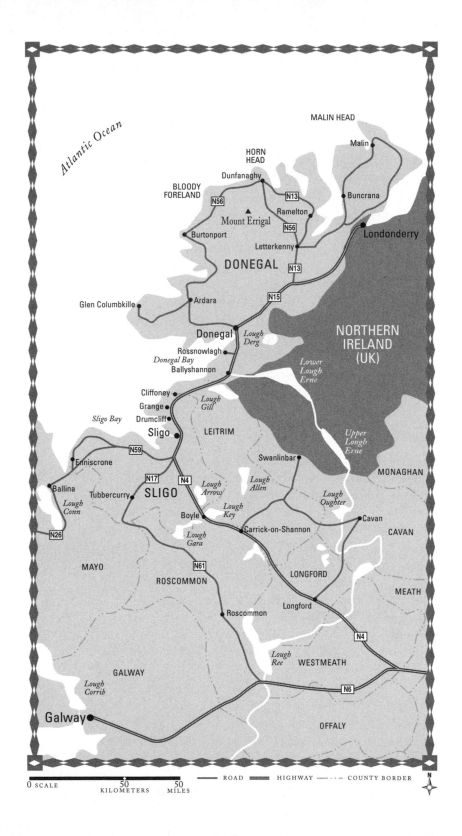

recently sold for just IR£40,000. Another good place in south Sligo to find inexpensive bucolic bolt-holes is in the countryside around Tubbercurry village: Two-bedroom cottages in good condition start at IR£25,000, and renovation projects begin at IR£10,000. Priced at IR£30,000, Knocknashee Cottage takes its name from the distant hill of Knocknashee, which translates as "Hill of the Fairies" and is the site of an ancient ring fort. Four miles from Tubbercurry, IR£39,000 is the price of a bijou cottage with just three rooms. Basically this is a real hermit's cottage and what you're paying for is the accompanying site: 19 acres of eight-year-old forest, which should be ready for thinning in another six years. Although electricity is nearby and thus easily connected, any prospective buyer would have to make do with water from a stream until they bored a well for domestic use. Now, didn't you always yearn for the simple life?

The two main seaside villages in the north of the county are Rosses Point (site of an 18-hole golf course that holds regular tournament events) and Strandhill, which is popular with surfers. At low tide you can walk across from Cummeen Strand to Coney Island and look out to sea from the Wishing Chair in which St. Patrick reputedly sat. This, I hasten to add, is not the Coney Island in New York! A small, refurbished cottage close to Strandhill's shops, school, and beaches has a guideline price of IR£45,000 but modern bungalows fetch IR£80,000 and up. Period properties hereabouts can cost anywhere from IR£200,000 to IR£500,000.

Further south, Enniscrone is trimmed by a five-mile stretch of golden sands and is another stop for golfers on the western links trail. Believers in the powers of thalassotherapy come to immerse themselves in the village's curious seaweed baths, here since Edwardian times. If you're looking for something large enough to run as a B&B business, four-bedroom bungalows sell for IR£70,000 and up. A three-bedroom country house, a 20-minute stroll from the beach, could be yours for IR£50,000.

Realtor Address Book
Des Butler, Quay St., Sligo; tel. +353 (0)71 45923
IPM Estates, Stephen St., Sligo; tel. +353 (0)71 43710
Matt Mulholland, Markievicz Rd., Sligo; tel. +353 (0)71 42845
McCarrick & Sons, Tubbercurry, Co. Sligo; tel. +353 (0)71 85050
Schiller & Schiller, Ardtarmon Castle, Ballinfull, Co. Sligo; tel. +353 (0)71
   63284

Sligo Contacts
Bus Éireann: to Dublin, Galway, Ballina, and Derry in Northern Ireland
   (Macdiarmada Station, Sligo; tel. +353 0-71 60066)

The Fairy Folk

Sligo's folk heritage chronicles countless strange stories about apparitions of the land. In his *Fairy and Folk Tales of the Irish Peasantry* (Dover, 1992), W.B. Yeats concluded that when the pagan gods of the Celts were no longer worshipped, they diminished in the popular imagination until eventually they turned into "the good people," or fairies. During the nineteenth century it was also reputed that fairies were fallen angels or, alternatively, the heathen dead. Barred from heaven, they weren't wicked enough to deserve a place in hell and so had to live out a shadowy existence in secret places: caves, hollow hills, burial mounds, and the ancient earthen forts known as *raths*.

Superstition warned that it was important to treat these ancestral spirits with respect. Fairies held the power to bring wealth to a farm or to give fishermen a good catch. When neglected or badly treated, they could turn spiteful. Thanks to *pishogues* (fairy spells), hens stopped laying eggs, milk turned sour, and livestock fell sick. But naturally every spell had its counterspell and the four-leafed shamrock, a motif of good luck, was thought to guard against otherworldly bewitchments.

The best-known character in folklore is the leprechaun, or fairy shoemaker. Legend claims that if you catch one he'll lead you to a crock of gold. However, if you take your eyes off him for just one second, he'll disappear. A more menacing figure is the Banshee, for it's said that the sound of her eldritch wail outside a house signifies a death in the family. In some tales the banshee appears as a beautiful young woman wearing fine clothes; in others she is described as a wizened old crone draped in a shroud. Sighting the *bean nídhe*, the fairy washerwoman, is also a premonition of disaster. In heroic myths, warriors doomed to fall in battle often see her beside water. She is wailing and washing out bloodstained clothing—theirs.

Rail Services: to Dublin, stopping at Longford, Mullingar, and a number
  of other stations (Macdiarmada Station, Sligo; tel. +353 0-71 69888)
Sligo Champion (local newspaper), Wine St., Sligo; tel. +353 (0)71 69222
Tourist Office, Temple St., Sligo; tel. +353 (0)71 61201

County Donegal

The distance from Dublin to Donegal's heartland is barely 150 miles, but it
really can feel like traveling to the opposite ends of the earth. Best known for
its tweeds, Donegal's name means "Fort of the Foreigner" (*Dún na nGall*), a
reference to the ninth-century Viking invaders who established forts here.
Geographically part of Ulster Province, this is the Republic's northernmost
county, a place of blue, windswept mountains, heathery moorlands, and small
communities where the welcome is warm and generous. The Irish language
remains in daily use along its western fringe, particularly around Gweedore
(*Gaoth Dobhair*), and it's still fairly common to hear handweavers' looms clat-
tering away in many a little cottage.

Ramblers soon discover that Donegal is a walker's paradise with more
than 400 miles of jigsaw-puzzle coastline. Toy-town fishing ports give way to
long, pristine beaches punctuated by cliffs, caves, and rocky promontories
that absolutely teem with birdlife. Scenic splendors include the Bloody
Foreland, Horn Head, and the giddy heights of Slieve League, whose sea
cliffs (1,972 feet) are the highest in Europe. At the center of the county is
quartz-tipped Mount Errigal and Glenveagh National Park—25,000 acres of
blanket bogs and forested mountains with roaming herds of red deer.

The map shows that Donegal shares a border with Northern Ireland.
How close you are to what is euphemistically termed as "the other tradition" is evidenced by the Twelfth of July celebrations in Rossnowlagh, a
seaside village just north of Ballyshannon town. Rossnowlagh is home to
the Republic's only Orange Order Parade, an event in which Protestant
men wearing bowler hats and orange sashes march through the village to
pay tribute to King Billy—William of Orange. He defeated the Catholic
King James II at the Battle of the Boyne in 1690.

For many years "the Troubles" kept timid travelers away from these
parts and also ensured house prices remained at bargain-basement levels.
According to one local realtor, the east of the county still offers Ireland's
best-value properties with village houses starting at around IR£40,000 and
large detached bungalows from IR£60,000. Having suffered from decades
of severe economic hardship and population decline, properties in border
villages are even less expensive. However, too many villages along
Donegal's eastern edge have a gloomy, run-down feel. Fishing, clothing
manufacture, and tweed production are the county's major industries and

they're all sited away from the border. The Celtic Tiger is still to pay a visit to communities like Pettigo where only 30 percent of the working-age population is employed.

In the more scenic west, and especially on the coast, properties sell faster and for a lot more money, and you may have to go up to IR£100,000 for a large residential property. This is holiday-home territory and you'll be in competition for prize properties with city buyers from Dublin, Belfast, and many other places. The good news is that most second-home buyers are seeking modern properties in sight of the sea and they tend to ignore the habitable little cottages in the folds of the hills that can still be unearthed for less than IR£25,000. And, if your dream is to own a tavern, recent sightings of pubs for sale include one on Ballyshannon's Main Street for IR£125,000 and another in Mountcharles village for IR£140,000.

Donegal's remoteness is another factor that has helped keep the cap on the property market. Trains don't come this far north and most local bus services can only be described as infrequent. But while the county's sense of separateness has an undoubted charm, prospective new residents ought to weigh all the pros and cons of buying a property here, particularly if planning to live in Ireland all year round. Yes, summers can be glorious, but the gray gloom of winter is another proposition entirely. You're in for a dose of Ulster weather—mist rolls in, rain drizzles down, and you may come to feel that your little home feels rather like a prison. Donegal isn't the ideal location for anyone suffering from SAD (seasonal affective disorder).

Even so, Donegal is undoubtedly popular with Dutch and German buyers who seem to like the idea of living in a place where sheep outnumber people. The best places to begin a house-hunt are in the county's main towns: Letterkenny, Buncrana, Ballyshannon, Donegal town, and the seaside resort of Bundoran. All have a good choice of realtors with properties spread over the county.

In the southern half of Donegal one interesting buy was Kearney's Cottage near Mountcharles, a fully refurbished three-bedroom dormer cottage dating back to the 1900s. Offered at IR£60,000, this represented good value as the shopping, social, and recreational facilities of Donegal town are less than three miles away from the village. "Dormer" is a word you'll come across fairly often in relation to cottages and houses. If you're puzzled by the term, what it generally refers to is an original single-story dwelling that now has a loft conversion, whereby extra rooms have been built into the roof space.

Also in south Donegal, IR£45,000 seems exceptional value for a three-story terraced townhouse in the West Port area of Ballyshannon, a lively town of steep, characterful streets that hosts a big folk festival over the August bank holiday. Of course, the main drawback with buying older-type properties is that they often require you to spend quite a lot on maintenance. Priced at IR£80,000 and a short walk from the seaside resort town of Bundoran, a modern three-bedroom bungalow beside the salmon-rich Drowes River typifies what is the ideal home for most Irish buyers. Within the town itself, IR£55,000 is the price of Woodbine Cottage, one of those single-story urban cottages dating from the turn of the century.

Donegal covers a huge area (this is the second-largest county after Cork) and it can take hours to get from the commercial fishing port of Killybegs to the county's northernmost tip, Malin Head. Its footloose flocks of sheep, its Irish-language signposts, and its extremely narrow roads laced with scary hairpin bends make for extremely slow driving times, so don't go thinking that you'll be able to inspect any more than a handful of homes in a day or two.

Once you hit the house-hunting trail, one western Donegal village where you might want to look for properties is Glencolumbcille, an Irish-speaking community of whitewashed cottages on the sheltered side of the Slieve League peninsula. Credited with converting Scotland to Christianity, St. Columbcille (a.k.a. St. Columba) lived here during the sixth century and the hilly neighborhood is studded with holy sites and prehistoric curiosities. On the saint's Pattern Day, June 9, villagers take part in an evening pilgrimage around the sacred places. Summers can be quite lively with tourists coming to check out the village's traditional-music pubs and wandering around the open-air folk museum for a glimpse into the rural past. A two-bedroom cottage here sold for IR£22,000.

> *Donegal is a walker's paradise with more than 400 miles of jigsaw-puzzle coastline.*

Facing Arranmore Island where two-bedroom holiday cottages can be had for IR£27,000, Burtonport village recently offered up an interesting buy in the shape of Atlantis House. With two acres of land and priced at IR£160,000, this seven-bedroom Victorian residence with "servants' quarters" at the rear seemed the ideal kind of property to convert into a small country house hotel or guesthouse. You would pay at least IR£500,000 for such a property on Ireland's east coast, and even then you wouldn't be able to sample the terrific seafood in local Burtonport haunts like the Lobster Pot and Kelly's Bar. A little further on is the Bloody Foreland, so called because the setting sun paints the peninsula a fiery crimson.

On Sheephaven Bay, Dunfanaghy village is a captivating stop on the magical seven-mile-long Atlantic Drive that links Rosguill Peninsula to the giddy heights of Horn Head. To help attract visitors to this remote corner, local people have transformed Dunfanaghy's former Workhouse into a heritage center that chronicles the hardships of the Famine years of 1845 to 1847. Those who enjoy outdoor pleasures will find an 18-hole golf course here along with wonderful walks around Killahoey Beach, Ards Forest Park, and out to crumbling Doe Castle, built in the sixteenth century by Scottish mercenaries. It's a much sought-after location and, at the time of writing, new three-bedroom holiday cottages were fetching IR£68,500.

Across the Bay, Downings is another engaging little hamlet where fishing boats land catches of salmon, lobster, and crab. In this part of the county the price of a two-bedroom modern bungalow or a similar-sized cottage in good condition tends to fall into the IR£45,000-to-IR£50,000 range. At remote Kerrykeel, overlooking Mulroy Bay, IR£60,000 seemed a positive snip for a four-bedroom bungalow, though it's probably too far off the beaten track to be a lucrative B&B proposition.

The next spit of land is the Fanad Peninsula, separated from the Inishowen Peninsula by Lough Swilly. The lough has many myths associated with it: one is that its name comes from *Suileach*, a four hundred–eyed water monster that was slain by the local hero, St. Colmcille. To cross from one peninsula to the other first entails a southerly journey back through Ramelton (sometimes spelled "Rathmelton") to Letterkenny. More a village than a town, Ramelton dates back to the seventeenth century and was the setting for *The Hanging Gale*, a major 1995 TV drama that commemorated the onset of the Great Famine. Townhouses here can still be had for IR£40,000, and the Reynolds agency was selling an old-fashioned thatched cottage for IR£35,000. If you're passing by this way, look out for the hamlet of Ray Bridge, which overlooks the Swilly estuary. Here IR£150,000 is the price of Ray Cottage, a residential business that is currently trading as a pottery studio.

My own favorite Donegal village is Ardara, a stone's throw from the wild Atlantic shores of southwest Donegal. If you've a yen for huge deserted beaches and mysterious sea caves right on the doorstep, then this is one of the most perfect locations in the whole of the Northwest. Ardara itself is protected from the sea breezes by steep, heather-clad hills, its cluster of pink, white, and teal-blue dwellings nestling in their valley like some secret forgotten settlement. Long renowned as a center for tweeds and knitwear, it's a place where spinning wheels aren't regarded as museum-piece objects. Each June the village hosts an old-fashioned weavers' fair with displays of spinning, carding, and loom-weaving. The hub of village social life is Nancy's, a historic inn whose labyrinthine passageways lead to tiny rooms where traditional musicians gather around open fires. Here it costs IR£65,000 and up for bungalows with enough rooms to maintain a bed-and-breakfast, but you can add on another IR£20,000 for any property with a sea view.

Realtor Address Book

Anderson Auctioneers, Main St., Donegal Town, Co. Donegal; tel. +353 (0)73 22888

McElhinney & Son, Main St., Bundoran, Co. Donegal; tel. +353 (0)72 41261

Sean Meehan, Main St., Bundoran, Co. Donegal; tel. +353 (0)72 41351

Paul Reynolds & Co., 10 Lr Main St., Letterkenny, Co. Donegal; tel. +353 (0)74 22399

Porter Properties, 12 Main St. Lr, Buncrana, Co. Donegal; tel. +353 (0)77 61083

Rainey Estate Agents, Market Square, Letterkenny, Co. Donegal; tel. +353 (0)74 22211

Donegal Contacts

Bus Éireann: to Dublin, Cork, Galway, and points in between; to Northern Ireland; and a number of local routes including Killybegs and Bundoran; offices at Ballyshannon (tel. +353 0-72 51101), Donegal Town (tel. +353 0-73 21101), and Letterkenny (tel. +353 0-74 21309)

Donegal Democrat (local newspaper), Donegal Rd., Ballyshannon, Co. Donegal; tel. +353 (0)72 51201

Tourist Information Office, Derry Rd., Letterkenny, Co. Donegal; tel. +353 (0)74 21160

The Lakelands: Counties Cavan, Leitrim, and Roscommon

Sparsely populated and with very little in the way of tourist sights, the low-key lakelands are worth considering if you yearn for an Ireland where you can get even further away from it all. Apart from anglers and boating enthusiasts, these counties see few foreign visitors, probably because the scenery is serene rather than spectacular. Along with dozens of little loughs, the border county of Cavan has an undulating landscape of drumlin hills, shaped for all the world like upturned egg cartons. Leitrim is another border county of forested glens and rushy wetlands where smart white cruisers lazily drift along the Shannon River and its tributaries into Lough Ree and the more pastoral landscape of Roscommon.

This really is small-town Ireland, steeped in old-fashioned ways and provincial pastimes. One of the biggest centers of population in the lakeland region is Roscommon town—at the last census count, home to just 3,600

St. Patrick's Purgatory

Fancy the idea of a three-day break on an island marooned in the middle of a remote lake for just IR£13? Of course you do, so let's set sail with Mr. Snow the ferryman to Station Island and a retreat wryly described by past visitors as "Ireland's holy health farm." Six miles north of Pettigo, the island with its cluster of grim buildings known as St. Patrick's Purgatory is the location for the toughest pilgrimage in Christendom: Lough Derg.

Donegal's Lough Derg isn't to be confused with the lake of the same name in Clare. This isn't a place where you find cozy pubs, pleasure crafts, and water sports—what you get instead is a chance to quite literally renounce the world, the flesh, and the Devil. The three-day course in pain and suffering is almost shockingly medieval and would undoubtedly test the ascetic resolve of a Trappist monk. On arriving on the island, the first thing that happens is that you are deprived of your footwear—socks and shoes aren't given back until you leave the island. Your bare and bloody feet spend the next three days stumbling over the jagged remains of beehive cells where Celtic monks lived out their days in lonely isolation.

Chanting long patterns of prayer, pilgrims also take part in a vigil, which effectively means being deprived of sleep for 36 hours. Nor can they take any comfort in the pleasures of the table—there's only one meal a day served at St. Patrick's Purgatory and it consists of dry toast and black tea. First chronicled back in the 1100s, the Lough Derg pilgrimage used to be even tougher than it is today—pilgrims once spent the vigil inside a cave instead of the Basilica. Having suffered Lough Derg's agonies myself, I can promise you that the pilgrimage is an experience you'll never forget.

Pilgrimages take place between June 1 and August 15. Contact the Prior, St. Patrick's Purgatory, Lough Derg, Pettigo, Co. Donegal; tel. +353 (0)72 61518.

people. Most other towns number around two thousand residents, so you soon get to know local names and faces. Go into a remote country pub and conversations will be revolving slowly around the weather, local politics, and the price that sheep are fetching at Tulsk and Drumshanbo markets. You often see locals playing the 25-card game, an unfathomable combination of whist and brag where winners compete for fierce prizes that sometimes take the form of livestock. Don't get involved unless you want to go home with a heifer!

Individuals who buy properties here tend to have renounced the consumer-driven world and exchanged the rat race for drowsy tranquillity and a very simple lifestyle. Unless you are perfectly happy with a dearth of good restaurants, theaters, and fashion stores, it may be too laid-back for your tastes. However, this is a part of the country where many properties have remained at amazingly affordable levels. Ten years ago I bought a little mint-condition cottage on an acre of land overlooking Lough Key in county Roscommon for just IR£10,000. And though you will have to pay at least IR£30,000 for a similar cottage nowadays (two bedrooms, kitchen, sitting room, and bathroom), it's good value when you realize that it would cost around IR£40,000 to build one new.

Laced with bluebell woods and studded with islands, the Lough Key area is increasingly popular with Dubliners seeking holiday hideaways, so properties aren't quite as inexpensive as in more remote parts of the lakelands. For example, a pretty four-room, whitewashed country cottage that you could move into immediately is priced at IR£48,000. If you like the idea of growing your own vegetables, the price includes four acres of land and stone-built outbuildings that could be converted into a workshop or studio. And even if you're without transport it's easy enough to reach: Trains run south to Dublin and north to Sligo from the nearby town of Boyle, which has a reasonable selection of stores for day-to-day shopping and its own summer arts festival.

Yet even today, the IR£10,000 country cottage still exists. But don't get excited—nowadays you're only likely to find it in the middle of nowhere and it will undoubtedly require a lifetime's work to refurbish it to anything resembling modern requirements. At the time of writing you could have bought cottages for this price near the border village of Swanlinbar in county Cavan and at Loughlynn in the unscenic western half of county Roscommon. But (and it's a big but) you only get what you pay for. IR£10,000 is unlikely to buy even a scrap of basic home comfort.

What exactly do you get for IR£10,000? Alas, not a lot—probably a corrugated iron roof covering a poky sitting room, a kitchen with an old-fashioned cooking range, and one bedroom. Perhaps best described as "something to suit a desperate man," cottages such as these were built in the days when farm laborers weren't concerned with bathroom facilities and were happy to use an outhouse toilet or the fields.

With IR£15,000 to IR£20,000 to spend, it's not unreasonable to expect something small and habitable with an electricity connection and plumbing facilities. IR£25,000 certainly buys good-condition two-bedroom cottages around Belturbet and Virginia in Cavan. The prices of Cavan properties are astonishing. For example, IR£30,000 would have bought a seven-bedroom former doctor's residence in Blacklion. Well, perhaps it's not *that* astonishing: Blacklion is a border-crossing point into Northern Ireland. Even so, if peace lasts, property values here will soar.

Hunt around and you may even get an inexpensive waterfront location. On an acre of land with private lake frontage, IR£20,000 buys a four-room semidetached cottage overlooking Lough Rynn in north county Leitrim. The Lough Rynn estate's most notorious owner was William Clements, the third Earl of Leitrim who treated his nineteenth-century tenant farmers as little better than slaves and allegedly exercised the *droit de seigneur* on local brides-to-be. A little north of here, at Mohill, you could buy a three-bedroom residence within walking distance of the town for IR£45,000.

The Arigna Hills in north county Roscommon are also good bargain-hunting territory—here IR£19,750 buys a traditional cottage near the Miner's Way walking trail down into Keadue village. Every August the village hosts a harp festival in honor of the last of the great Irish bards Turlough O'Carolan, a blind eighteenth-century harpist. His grave lies a mile from Keadue, at Kilronan, where pilgrims still visit St. Lazair's holy well. The sacred spring reputedly holds the cure for backache, and you can walk through shadowy woods beside Lough Meelagh where an ancient court cairn evokes the mysteries of the Celtic past.

The lakeland region does have one little pocket of affluence: Carrick-on-Shannon. The county town of Leitrim, its marina is one of the biggest on the Shannon and provides a base for boat rental companies. The area has become even more popular with the recent opening of the Ballyconnell Canal, which links the Shannon with the river Erne in county Fermanagh. Unlike a decade ago, holidaymakers can now continue their boating odyssey upriver through Leitrim's countryside into Northern Ireland. Naturally enough, many break their journey to stock up on supplies and discover Carrick's waterfront pubs, so the town is always full of good-natured bustle.

French and German visitors adore their boating holidays and quite a few return to buy homes in the area. Riverside properties always find eager buyers from both home and abroad so vendors take full advantage and the premium can be as high as 25 percent for a Shannonside residence. Another factor which has pushed up house values around Carrick has been the opening of a wood-pulp plant that employs around five hundred people downriver at Drumsna. New one-bedroom apartments in Carrick start at IR£40,000 and three-bedroom townhouses at IR£63,000. The average price of a two-bedroom modern bungalow in the immediate area is IR£50,000. Country cottages around Carrick's satellite river villages also fetch more than in remoter corners of the lakelands. For example, a three-bedroom stone-built cottage at Rooskey is priced at IR£40,000.

Something different? Up in the lonely Leitrim hills around Lough Allen and the Cavan border, IR£100,000 buys Creevelea Manse, a former presbytery with an adjoining cut-stone chapel. Built in 1860 to serve families of Scottish descent, the church and its presbytery stand on four and a half acres with views down a bosky valley toward the lough. Throughout the Republic a number of Protestant churches and their manses have been deconsecrated and sold into private ownership, but they usually command far higher prices: At the other end of the country, in county Cork, the asking price for a similar property was IR£250,000. The present owners plan to turn Creevelea into a youth hostel, but such a property could possibly be transformed into a small restaurant, too.

An equally unusual property that comes with full planning permission for a restaurant is a nineteenth-century stone-built stationhouse at Knockcroghery, county Roscommon. Trains haven't passed through the village since 1963 and the building has been converted into a modern home with living space on two levels: five bedrooms, open-plan kitchen/living room, lobby, and bathroom. The guideline price is IR£250,000. Should the purchaser go ahead with restaurant plans, it would be sited in a renovated stone outbuilding further along the old station platform. Here, too, you're not far away from water: Knockcroghery is on the west bank of Lough Ree, another of the Shannon loughs. It's a place where it may pay to carry a camera—old folktales whisper of the Lough Ree Monster, a humpbacked creature that seems to be a cousin of the equally shy and elusive monster in Scotland's Loch Ness!

Realtor Address Book

Robert Clarke, Holborn Hill, Belturbet, Co. Cavan; tel. +353 (0)49 22294

James Cleary, Main St., Castlerea, Co. Roscommon; tel. +353 (0)907 20011

Vincent Egan, Elphin St., Boyle, Co. Roscommon; tel. +353 (0)79 62464

William Farrell, Main St., Carrick-on-Shannon, Co. Leitrim; tel. +353 (0)78 20976

Foley & Harrison, Main St., Virginia, Co. Cavan; tel. +353 (0)49 47249

O'Reilly, Taylor & Tweedy, Main St., Cavan town, Co. Cavan; tel. +353 (0)49 31599

Lakeland Contacts

Busaras, Store St., Dublin; tel. +353 (0)1 836 6111

Bus Éireann, Sligo; tel. +353 (0)71 60066

Leitrim Observer (local newspaper), St. Georges Terrace, Carrick-on-Shannon, Co. Leitrim; tel. +353 (0)78 20025

Roscommon Herald (local newspaper), Patrick St., Boyle, Co. Roscommon; tel. +353 (0)79 62004

Tourist Information: on Roscommon and Leitrim contact Bord Fáilte's Sligo office at Temple St. (tel. +353 0-71 61201); on Cavan contact the Dublin office at Baggot St. Bridge (local tel. 1850 230 330)

Train Services: to Dublin from Boyle (tel. +353 0-79 62027), Castlerea (tel. +353 0-907 20031), and Roscommon town (tel. +353 0-903 26201) in county Roscommon; from Carrick-on-Shannon (tel. +353 0-78 20036) in county Leitrim

Planning Your Fact-Finding Trip

If the Emerald Isle is new to you, don't over-egg the pudding by trying to cram too much in. Independent travelers often think they'll be able to see everything in less than a week. Yes, Ireland is a small country, but clocking up the distances takes much longer than almost every first-time visitor imagines.

It's easy to look at a map and plan a weeklong trip with overnight stays in Dublin, Cork, Kerry, Clare, Galway, Mayo, and Sligo. But such an itinerary would be utterly senseless. Where's the joy in spending most of your precious holiday time on the road, seeing nothing but snapshot views and fleeing like hunted refugees from one overnight stop to another? Yes, you'll have the kudos of bragging to friends that you covered the entire west of Ireland but you could have saved your money and bought a video. A jaunt like that is strictly for the demented and won't even give you an inkling of what makes Ireland so special.

How are you going to make time to feel the pulse of a strange town or absorb any local history and folklore? Or to walk along a silver strand to a little fishing village and watch the nets and lobster pots being mended? There certainly won't be any chance to go exploring off the beaten track, along narrow byways and pilgrim paths where the distractions range from tumbledown medieval tower houses to holy wells dedicated to obscure saints. And where will you find opportunities to visit realtors' offices and pick up property listings?

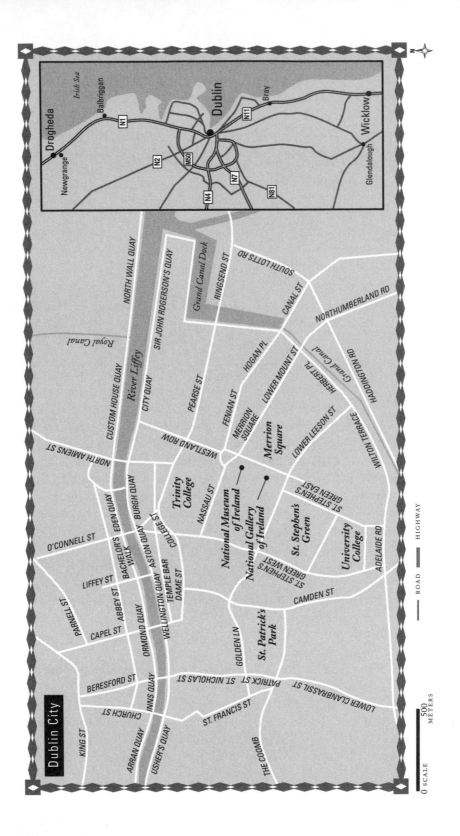

Dublin City

N

Irish Sea

Drogheda
Newgrange
Balbriggan
N1
Dublin
N2
M50
N4
N7
N81
Bray
N11
Wicklow
Glendalough

North Wall Quay
Royal Canal
River Liffey
Sir John Rogerson's Quay
Grand Canal Dock
Ringsend St
South Lotts Rd
Canal St
Northumberland Rd
Custom House Quay
City Quay
Pearse St
Hogan Pl
Lower Mount St
Grand Canal
Haddington Rd
North Amiens St
Westland Row
Fenian St
Merrion Square
Merrion Square
Herbert Pl
Lower Leeson St
Wilton Terrace
O'Connell St
Eden Quay
Bachelor's Walk
Burgh Quay
Aston Quay
College St
Nassau St
Trinity College
National Museum of Ireland
National Gallery of Ireland
St. Stephen's Green
St Stephen's Green East
University College
Adelaide Rd
Liffey St
Abbey St
Wellington Quay
Temple Bar
Dame St
St Stephen's Green West
Camden St
Parnell St
Capel St
Ormond Quay
Golden Ln
St. Patrick's Park
Beresford St
Inns Quay
St. Nicholas St
Patrick St
Lower Clanbrassil St
King St
Church St
Arran Quay
Usher's Quay
St. Francis St
The Coomb

ROAD
HIGHWAY

0 SCALE
500 METERS

"But I haven't time for a lengthy trip," you may be saying. "Not this year." Maybe you haven't, but that doesn't mean that you have to tick off *every* major tourist destination mentioned in the guidebooks. Take your time and get to know one or two areas really well—everything else will still be here on your next trip.

Forget those plans to leave Cork City after breakfast, have the Ring of Kerry done by teatime, and be in Dingle by nightfall. You'll be left with no time at all to discover the endless pleasures of West Cork: harbor town Kinsale with its cliff-top fortresses and higgledy-piggledy laneways where the shops and restaurants are bright as paint and laden with flower-filled window boxes; the color-washed cottages and old-fashioned shopfronts of Clonakilty; Roaringwater Bay and Carberry's Hundred Islands; the beautiful coves and cliff-top walks that stud Cork's coast all the way to Mizen Head. Do you really want to forgo all those delights just for the sake of following the same breakneck itinerary as the tour buses?

The first thing to determine is what exactly you hope to get from an Irish vacation. What's enticing you across the Atlantic in the first place? Ireland's scenery and historical heritage? The quirky pubs, colorful festivals, and traditional-music culture? Maybe it's even the chance to trace your roots and get to know local people in the area your ancestors came from. With a bit of preliminary planning, it won't be difficult to devise an itinerary to cover your own particular interests. And even if your partner has a different holiday agenda, that shouldn't present problems. Wherever you travel in Ireland, golf fiends and fishing addicts are well catered for!

Package-tour Versus Solo Travel

To be honest with you, for me there's no contest—I'd opt for solo travel every time. On most coach-tour holidays you'll be entirely in the company of people of your own nationality—that's fine if you like your compatriots, not so great if you're hoping to meet ordinary Irish people.

By and large, the tour companies travel the same routes, stay in similar hotels, and offer the same kinds of options: a whistle-stop tour around the postcard destinations interspersed with endless opportunities for stocking up on gifts and souvenirs. Kissing the Blarney Stone, attending some pseudo-medieval banquet, and shopping for leprechaun soap-on-a-rope at Bunratty Folk Park doesn't mean you'll have touched base with the real Ireland. I recently spoke with an American visitor who told me about a trip to Howth's Abbey Tavern near Dublin, a place that specializes in catering for coach parties. He was enjoying himself until something suddenly clicked. Apart from the waiting staff and singers, every last person there was a foreign tourist.

The trouble with high-profile tourist areas is the great preponderance of other tourists—not just Americans, but crowds of Brits, Italians, Japanese, and just about any other nationality you care to mention. Like it or not, when you visit Killarney and Bunratty you're destined to be just another faceless unit on the great tourism conveyor belt. That said, a packaged coach tour allows you to see a fair bit of the country if time is very limited and you don't want to hire a car.

Of course, there's a world of difference if you choose a small tour company catering for specialist interests. Like-minded fellow travelers usually make for good company, especially if you're single. If you enjoy history and culture, it's hard to imagine anything worse than being on a non-specialized tour and finding your traveling companion is determined to witter on about shopping opportunities. Thankfully any archaeology tour (or indeed a golf or fishing tour) isn't going to be constantly halting to deliver its participants to the doors of Blarney Woolen Mills, Avoca Handweavers, and various crystal outlets. A browse through travel sections of major newspapers will give you an idea of what U.S. tour companies offer in the way of specialized Ireland trips.

Going It Alone

Depending on time available, my recommendation is to first spend a couple of days getting acquainted with **Dublin**. From the Liffey Quays to its elegant Georgian squares, the city is compact enough to explore on foot and there's more than those legendary pubs to keep you busy: Visit Trinity College and see the Book of Kells, spend some time in the art galleries and museums, plunge into the stores around Grafton Street, and wander the cobbled laneways of bohemian Temple Bar with its numerous bars and restaurants.

One side-trip from the capital that is not to be missed is to the prehistoric passage tombs at **Newgrange** and **Knowth** in county Meath. Built over five thousand years ago by neolithic farmers, these mysterious tombs are older than both the pyramids and Stonehenge. On a loop of the river Boyne, Newgrange is famous throughout the world for its connection with the winter solstice when a shaft of sunlight penetrates the pitch-black central chamber at dawn each December 21. If you don't have a hire (rental) car, **Bus Éireann** offer a Boyne Valley and Newgrange tour from Dublin for IR£15. You can book direct from the Busaras office on Store Street: tel. +353 (0)1 836 6111.

Another fascinating excursion from Dublin is into the Garden County: **Wicklow**. If you're traveling through the Wicklow Mountains, two places that definitely merit visits are the magnificent formal gardens of

Powerscourt and the ancient monastic site of **Glendalough**. You could combine both with **Mary Gibbons Coach Tours**, which offers a number of day trips from the capital. The above-mentioned trip costs IR£16 with pick-ups from many main hotels. Contact the company at 12 St. Catherine's Court, Newgrove Avenue, Sandymount, Dublin 4; tel. +353 (0)1 283 9973.

Dublin isn't short on hotels, guesthouses, and bed-and-breakfast establishments. If you arrive without accommodation, tourist offices at the airport and on O'Connell Street offer an accommodation-booking service for a fee of IR£2. If you want to treat yourself to a five-star hotel, the **Westbury** (tel. +353 0-1 679 1122) on Grafton Street is handily placed for shops and theaters. Rates per night are from IR£75 per person (sharing), and include a full Irish breakfast.

In the heart of Georgian Dublin, the three-star **Mont Clare** hotel (tel. +353 0-1 661 5663) on Merrion Square offers a special weekend rate of IR£115 (two nights, including breakfast). If you want to sample guesthouse accommodations, the Victorian **Tavistock House** (64 Ranelagh Rd.; tel. +353 0-1 496 7377) is only a 10-minute walk from St. Stephen's Green and Grafton Street. Weekend rates (two nights, including breakfast) are IR£65; a three-night midweek stay costs IR£90.

Follow your trip to the capital with a stay in one or two areas that particularly appeal. Rather than constantly changing your accommodations,

---

SIGHTSEEING SAVINGS

It won't cost a penny to visit **Dublin's National Museum** where you can marvel at the wonderful stash of Celtic gold artifacts. If you're interested in art, another free treat awaits at the **National Gallery** on Dublin's Merrion Square: It has good collections by renowned Irish artists such as Jack B. Yeats and Paul Henry, as well as works by Rembrandt, El Greco, Goya, and Picasso.

Of course, not everything is free. If you intend to visit lots of Irish castles and monasteries it can be quite costly. Anyone planning a serious assault on Ireland's historical trail should pick up an IR£15 **Heritage Card** that can be used for an entire year. This allows unlimited access to numerous historical sites under the care of Dúchas, Ireland's Office of Public Works. Contact the Heritage Service, Dúchas, 51 St. Stephen's Green, Dublin 2; tel. +353 (0)1 661 3111.

base yourself in a central location and then explore the surrounding area on day trips. Car hire gives more freedom but daily coach excursions are readily available during summer from main tourist centers. Look at what you could do on days out from a base in **Galway City**:

• Head west toward **Clifden** and explore the landscapes of **Connemara** and its coastal villages.

• Take the ferry to one of the **Aran Islands**, rocky bastions of Gaelic civilization where Irish is the day-to-day language.

• Walk part of the **Burren Way** in Clare, looking for rare wildflowers and plotting a course past neolithic stone settlements and abandoned famine villages. After a lunchtime picnic, move on to the **Cliffs of Moher** then call in for refreshments at **Doolin** village, renowned for traditional music.

• Sample oysters and seafood at Moran's of the Weir, a quaint thatched pub and restaurant near the oyster village of **Clarinbridge**. Then continue to **Kinvara**, a pretty fishing village in south county Galway.

• Take a pleasure cruise up island-studded **Lough Corrib** to fairytale Ashford Castle in county Mayo. Then walk through the castle's woods to **Cong** village with its ruined abbey, market cross, and stone bridges.

Five minutes by taxi from Galway city center, one of the best places to stay is the five-star **Glenlo Abbey Hotel** (tel. +353 0-91 526666). A charmingly restored eighteenth-century manor house at Bushy Park, it has its own golf course beside Lough Corrib and an excellent restaurant. Special weekend rates (two nights, breakfast included, and one dinner) are IR£189.75 per person, sharing.

If you prefer city bustle, Eyre Square is only a short stroll from the countless stores, pubs, and restaurants around Shop and Quay Streets. Looking over Eyre Square, the **Great Southern** hotel (tel. +353 0-91 564041) offers a raft of special deals: three-night midweek breaks from IR£135 PPS (per person shared), five-night midweek breaks from IR£229 pps, and weekend breaks from IR£72 pps.

Mostly charging between IR£18 and IR£20 per person per night, there's a plethora of B&B establishments in Galway's seaside suburb, Salthill. It's only a 10-minute bus ride to the heart of the city and you can watch the sun going down over Galway Bay. Try Mrs. Monaghan at **Montrose** (3 Monksfield, Salthill, Galway; tel +353 0-91 525673) or Mrs. Wrynn at **Fenagh House** (11 Rockbarton Green, Salthill, Galway; tel +353 0-91 522835).

For something a little different, stay in a two-bedroom luxury apartment in a converted old grain mill beside the river Corrib in Galway city center. Apartments sleep four and cost IR£250 per week in the low season, rising to IR£480 per week during July and August. Sometimes (though not in high summer) there may be one available for a two-night weekend stay

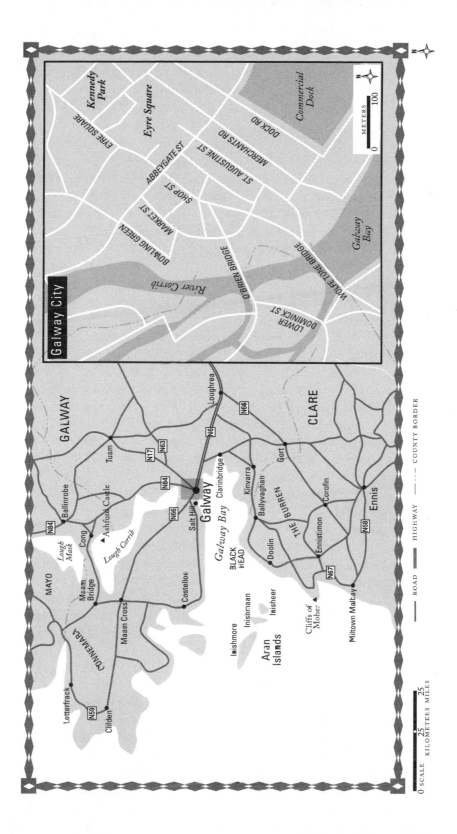

in which case the cost is IR£160. Contact **Granary Hall**, 58 Dominick Sreet, Galway; tel. +353 (0)91 564581.

Explore West Cork and Kerry

Spare at least four or five days for this spectacularly scenic region, drifting slowly westwards from **Kinsale** to **Clonakilty** and the pretty harbor villages of **Glandore, Baltimore**, and **Schull**. There's no shortage of restaurants and good music pubs in any of these places, but when it comes to gourmet cuisine, Kinsale offers the widest choice of top-notch restaurants. Distractions include taking a boat trip across Roaringwater Bay to **Cape Clear Island**, or hiking along shady lanes and discovering the mysterious Druidic stone circle at **Drombeg**. And though they're a bleak and emotionally upsetting reminder of Ireland's troubled past, the famine sites around Skibbereen shouldn't be missed.

For one of West Cork's best beaches, continue west from Schull along the Mizen Peninsula and watch for signs for **Barleycove**. If the sea temperature is warm enough, it's safe to bathe at this sheltered spot and the light turns the ocean into an entrancing swirl of sapphire, jade, and turquoise. During summer, the colors of the West Cork coast are simply delectable: purple heather blanketing the mountains, gardens overflowing with pink and blue hydrangea bushes, and hedgerows ablaze with blood-red fuchsias, orange montbretias, lacy white cow parsley, and the mauve spires of foxgloves.

From **Bantry**, head north through the Caha Mountains of the Beara Peninsula that is shared by counties Cork and Kerry. The winding road dips down into the garden village of **Glengarriff** before continuing to **Kenmare**, a stopping point on the famous **Ring of Kerry**. A bustling town of brightly painted houses, many of which date back to the seventeenth century, Kenmare's name in Irish is Neidín (the little nest). One of its best known crafts is lace-making, a business originally set up by the nuns of the Poor Clare Convent to create employment after the great famine of 1845.

Whizzing around the 112-mile length of the Ring of Kerry takes a minimum of six hours, and that's only allowing for cursory stops at the main highlights. Summer traffic over the mountain passes which link Kenmare to the main tourism hub, **Killarney town**, moves at the speed of molasses—you've been warned! Around the Ring of Kerry itself, the distractions are almost endless: pleasure cruises on the **Lakes of Killarney**, walking the old coach roads and nature trails of **Killarney National Park**, a boat trip out to the remote pinnacle of **Skellig Michael** where anchorite monks once lived out a lonely, storm-tossed existence.

If you've a penchant for archaeological sites, Kerry's Irish-speaking

Dingle Peninsula has more than two thousand—everything from monastic beehive huts to prehistoric forts. A drive around the peninsula delivers up magical views across to the deserted **Blasket Islands,** and the silver strand at **Inch** is one of the country's best. **Dingle town**'s music pubs provide lively entertainment and many serve evening meals for between IR£5 and IR£6. Served with fries and fresh vegetables, a piece of freshly caught sole the size of a dinner plate cost me IR£5.95 in Murphy's, one of a string of cozy inns along Strand Street near the harbor. Anglers here supplement their income by taking visitors on sea-fishing excursions and trips to see Fungie, the Dingle Dolphin. Dolphin trips cost IR£6; if he fails to show, you'll get your money back.

Bed-and-breakfast accommodations are an excellent value. Why pay for expensive hotel rooms when you'll be spending most of your time seeing the sights? And there's no need to worry about advance booking. Any tourist office in this area can book you accommodations in another part of the southwest for a IR£2 fee, no matter how many phone calls it

GRATUITIES

When eating out, it's customary to leave around 10 percent of the bill, though this doesn't apply in fast-food places or eateries with counter service where patrons help themselves. Some restaurants add the tip as a service charge to your bill, so check it carefully. It's not necessary to tip again, and if you've received bad service, stand up for your rights and refuse to pay the service charge.

Don't tip bartenders unless drinks are brought to a table. As few establishments offer table service anyway, it's not something you'll encounter much. However, if you get into conversation with a friendly bartender, you may want to ask him or her to join you in a drink.

It's not obligatory to tip porters, but most people give a 50p or IR£1 coin to avoid feeling uncomfortable. Nor is it obligatory to tip taxi drivers, but few enjoy being deprived of their expected 10 percent—some Dublin cabbies aren't slow in treating ungrateful customers to rather colorful language. As regards hairdressers, it's customary for women to tip around 10 percent. Barbershops and unisex salons don't really expect a man to leave anything. On coach-tour vacations it's usual to tip both the guide and driver around IR£10 apiece. Your holiday company will explain whether this is already included in the package price.

Top Tips

- Passport in order? You'll need it to enter Ireland. Just in case there's an accident, ensure it's valid for longer than your intended stay. U.S. citizens don't need visas.
- If you take vital medication, carry a doctor's letter detailing why you need it and any generic brand that could be substituted.
- Take advantage of duty-free shopping. Current allowances let you import 200 cigarettes, one liter of spirits, two liters of wine, 60 milliliters of perfume, 250 milliliters of eau de toilette, and dutiable goods to the value of IR£73.
- Try planning your visit outside of July and August. Transatlantic fares are lower and driving around Ireland will be much more leisurely.
- Change currency and traveler's checks in banks, normally open weekdays between 10 a.m. and 3 p.m. Hotels, bureaux de change, and post offices offer less favorable rates.
- When buying gifts, watch for stores displaying "Tax Free Shopping" signs. Non-EU citizens can claim back VAT (sales tax) on purchases. You'll be given a voucher that can be cashed at Dublin or Shannon Airport.
- Don't forget comfy walking shoes and raingear. And leave room in the suitcase for those bulky Aran sweaters you'll be taking back.
- Guard against pickpockets, particularly at Dublin's bus and railway stations.
- Don't barge to the front of the queue at taxi ranks. It's not appreciated!

takes. I walked into the tourist office in Kenmare in county Kerry at four-thirty in the afternoon and they booked me a B&B in Bantry in county Cork for that same August night. Three B&Bs I can recommend for a tour of the southwest are:

• **Mrs. Sheila O'Regan, Riverside B&B**, 5 Millgrove, Fernhill Road, Clonakilty, Co. Cork; tel +353 (0)23 35221. A 10-minute walk from the town center, all rooms are en-suite with their own TV and tea/coffee making facilities. The full Irish breakfast includes the famous (or infamous) Clonakilty black pudding. A nice touch is tea and homemade cakes in the kitchen on arrival. Price per person: IR£18.

• **Mrs. Sheila Brennan, Elsloo B&B**, Newtown, Bantry, Co. Cork; tel +353 (0)27 50471. A 15-minute walk from town on the Glengarriff Road, you can't miss it—this ivy-covered bungalow has the prettiest garden in Bantry and is directly opposite the G.A.A. grounds. The owners are friendly, and though not all rooms are en-suite (shared bathroom), tea-making facilities are provided. Price per person: IR£15.

• **Mrs. Mary Sheehy, Sheehy's B&B**, Milltown, Dingle, Co. Kerry; tel +353 (0)66 51453. Opposite St. Brendan's Creek and a wildflower meadow, this pink-painted B&B is a 15-minute stroll from Dingle town center. Rooms are en-suite, there's a comfy guest lounge, and the chatty owners let you borrow walking and cycling maps. Price per person is IR£17.

If you intend to treat yourself to a top-class hotel, do it in Killarney and contemplate the splendor of the lakes from your window. The pampered luxury offered by **Hotel Europe** (Lakeshore Road, Killarney; tel. +353 0-64 31900) is just heaven—guests can go boating on the lake, horseback-riding, or work off any excess energies in the leisure center, which includes a gym, saunas, and an indoor swimming pool. The price of a "summer special" (two nights, breakfast included, and one dinner) is IR£129 per person.

Special Interest Vacations

If you want to do more than tour and explore, it's easy to put together your own special interest vacation. Many Irish hotels and guesthouses arrange activity breaks at reasonable prices. The below costs were for the summer of 1998 and are per person. For more ideas, call into any Bord Fáilte office for the latest "Holiday Breaks" brochure.

Golf: Dingle Skellig Hotel, Dingle, Co. Kerry; tel. +353 (0)66 51144. Three-star hotel on Dingle Bay with links golf at Ceann Sibeal, Dingle's par 72 championship course. Non-golfing partners could go horseback-riding, angling, dolphin-watching, or take a boat trip to the Blasket Islands. Weekend (two nights, including breakfast, plus one dinner) plus one round of golf: IR£135.

Painting, bog craft, or fly-fishing: Pontoon Bridge Hotel, Pontoon, Co. Mayo; tel. +353 (0)94 56120. Best known as a fishing hotel, the Pontoon Bridge also teaches you to paint landscapes in oils and watercolors, on location or in studio. Bog-craft courses include field trips collecting mosses, lichens, and other materials to create models or scenes from the bog landscape. Special breaks (two nights, including breakfast, plus one gourmet dinner) and two-day activity course: IR£150 low season, IR£165 high season.

Walking: Hanora's Cottage Guesthouse, Nire Valley, Ballymacarberry, Co. Waterford; tel. +353 (0)52 36134. The hosts provide packed lunches, maps, walking sticks, and—if needed—a guide for walking trips in the Comeragh Mountains. When you come down from the hills, Jacuzzi baths and tempting dinners await: The chef trained at the famous Ballymaloe cookery school. Three nights midweek (including breakfasts and two dinners) and two days walking: IR£130. Guides cost extra.

Romance: Tinakilly Country House Hotel, Rathnew, Co. Wicklow; tel. +353 (0)404 69274. Go on, spoil yourself. Victorian Tinakilly is a four-star luxury hotel not far from Dublin. If you've a taste for champagne breakfasts in bed, log fires, and candlelit dinners, this is heaven. Weekend (two nights, breakfasts included, plus one dinner): IR£180.

Island Hopping: Brian Hughes, Connemara Safaris, Sky Road, Clifden, Co. Galway; tel. +353 (0)95 21071. Low-level walks exploring the archaeology and botany of rarely visited western isles like Inishbofin, Clare, Turk, and Shark. The IR£349 price includes four nights accommodation, dinners, breakfasts, picnics, guides, luggage transfers, and—if needed—rain gear.

Appendix

E ver wondered what the Irish name Áine means? Or how many millimeters there are in an inch? And where you can find a tour operator offering trips to Ireland? Like an attic, an appendix is useful for storing all those bits and bobs that you can't find room for elsewhere.

Emergency Phone Numbers

For ambulance; police; fire service; or coastal, mountain, and cave rescue, dial either **999** or **112** and ask the operator for the emergency service you want. Calls are free.

For non-emergency medical concerns, contact the appropriate regional health board for information on local doctors and dentists. You'll find numbers in the golden pages of the telephone directory under Health Boards. If you're not sure which authority to contact, ring this toll-free number from anywhere within the Republic: 1800 520520.

Other Useful Phone Numbers and Addresses

Embassy of the United States in Ireland: 42 Elgin Road, Dublin 4; tel. +353 (0)1 668 8777

Embassy of Ireland: 2234 Massachusetts Ave. NW, Washington, D.C. 20008; 202/462-3939. There is also diplomatic representation at consulate offices in Boston (617/267-9330), New York (212/462-3939), Chicago (312/337-1868), and San Francisco (415/392-4214).

Irish Business Organization of New York: FDR Station, P.O. Box 6214, New York, NY 10154; 212/750-8118. Another resource for networking within the Irish and American-Irish business communities.

Revenue Commissioners (Indirect Taxes), Stamping Bldg., Dublin Castle, Dublin 2; tel. +353 (0)1 679 2777. Information about Value Added Tax (VAT).

Tourism Information: Bord Fáilte, 345 Park Ave., New York, NY 10154; 212/418-0800. Also at this address are the offices of the **Irish Trade Board** (212/371-3600) and Ireland's **Industrial Development Agency** (212/750-4300), whose mission is to attract foreign business to Ireland.

Ireland Provinces and Counties

The Republic of Ireland

Leinster Province: counties Carlow, Dublin, Kildare, Kilkenny, Laois, Longford, Louth, Meath, Offaly, Westmeath, Wexford, Wicklow

Munster Province: counties Clare, Cork, Kerry, Limerick, Tipperary, Waterford

Connacht Province: counties Galway, Leitrim, Mayo, Roscommon, Sligo

Ulster Province: counties Cavan, Donegal, Monaghan

Northern Ireland

Ulster Province: counties Antrim, Armagh, Derry (Londonderry), Down, Fermanagh, Tyrone.

Public Holidays

New Year's Day January 1
St. Patrick's Day March 17
Good Friday
Easter Monday
May Holiday, first Monday in May
June Bank Holiday, first Monday in June
August Bank Holiday, first Monday in August
October Bank Holiday, last Monday in October
Christmas Day December 25
St. Stephen's Day December 26

Tour Operators

Although some package trips to Ireland (for example, with Trafalgar Tours) are only bookable through travel agents, you could also check out the brochures from these operators:

• **Crystal Travel & Tours**, 8 Chestnut Hill Ave., Brighton, MA 02135; 800/327-3780

• **Round Tower Travel**, 18 Central St., Norwood, MA 02062; 888/762-9090

• **Ireland Vacations**, 5644 Westheimer #280, Houston, TX 77056; 281/469-9120

• **IL Discovery Tours**, Agora South, 1050 SE Fifth Ave., Suite 100, Delray Beach, FL 33483; 561/243-6276

• **Brian Moore International Tours**, 1208 VFW Pkwy., Suite 202, Boston, MA 02132; 800/982-2299

• **Irish Festival Tours**, P.O. Box 169, Warminster, PA 18974; 215/675-3117
• **Classic Golf Tours**, 3045 South Parker Rd., Suite 201, Aurora, CO 80014; 303/751-7200
• **Celtica Tours**, 430 Franklin Village Dr. #143, Franklin, MA 02038; 800/299-CELT
• **Mystical Journeys**, PO Box 777, Alpharetta, GA 30239; 770/664-6014
• **TWA Getaway Vacations**, 1415 Olive St., St. Louis, MO 63103; 800/892-4141.

Table of Metric Conversion

Weight

Imperial	Metric
1 ounce (oz.)	28.3 grams (g)
1 pound (lb.)	454 grams
2.2 pounds	1 kilogram (kg)
1 stone (14 lb.)	6.36 kilograms

Length

Imperial	Metric
1 inch (in.)	25.4 millimeters (mm)
1 foot (ft.)	30.5 centimeters (cm)
1 yard (yd.)	.914 meters (m)
1 mile (mi.)	1.61 kilometers (km)
.39 inches	1 centimeter
3.28 feet	1 meter
.62 miles	1 kilometer

Volume

Imperial	Metric
1 pint (pt.)	568 milliliters (ml)
1 gallon (gal.)	4.55 liters (l)
1.76 pints	1 liter

(An imperial gallon is larger than the U.S. gallon of 3.79 liters.)

Area

Imperial	Metric
1 square foot (sq. ft.)	929 square centimeters (cm²)
1 square yard (sq. yd.)	.836 square meters (m²)
1 acre	.405 hectares (ha)

1 square mile (sq. mi.)	259 hectares
10.8 square feet	1 square meter
2.47 acres	1 hectare
247 acres	1 square kilometer (km²)

Speed

Imperial	Metric
1 mile per hour (MPH)	1.61 kilometers per hour (km/h)
.621 mile per hour	1 kilometer per hour

Temperature

Centigrade to Fahrenheit: multiply by 1.8 then add 32
Fahrenheit to Centigrade: subtract 32 then multiply by 5/9

Time Difference

Ireland sets its clocks by Greenwich mean time. Without taking into account daylight savings, when it's seven in the morning in New York, it's noon in Ireland. In mid-March the clocks go forward by one hour; at the end of October they are put back an hour (spring forward, fall back). Midsummer evenings the light doesn't fade until around 11 o'clock in the west.

Recommended Reading

Angela's Ashes, by Frank McCourt. Scribner, 1996.

Celtic Sacred Landscapes, by Nigel Campbell Pennick. Thames & Hudson, 1996.

Fairy & Folk Tales of Ireland, by W.B. Yeats (editor). Simon & Schuster, 1998.

The Great Hunger: Ireland 1845–1849, by C.B.F. Woodham Smith. Penguin USA, 1995.

Mythic Ireland, by Michael Dames. Thames & Hudson, 1996.

Oxford Illustrated History of Ireland, by R.F. Foster (editor). Oxford University Press, 1991.

The Peoples of Ireland: From Prehistory to Modern Times, by Liam de Paor. University of Notre Dame Press, 1990.

The Tain, translated from the Irish epic, *Tain Bo Cuailnge*, by Thomas Kinsella. Oxford University Press, 1983.

To School Through the Fields: An Irish Country Childhood, by Alice Taylor. St. Martin's Press, 1994.

Tracing Your Irish Ancestors, by John Grenham. Genealogical Publishing Company, 1993.

Writer's Ireland: Landscape in Literature, by William Trevor. Thames & Hudson, 1986.

If you're on-line you can order these books through www.amazon.com. Otherwise one of the best places to source Irish-related books is Irish Books and Media, Franklin Business Center, 1433 East Franklin Ave., Minneapolis, MN; 612/871-3505 or 800/229-3505.

Some Irish Names and Their Meanings

Girls
Áine: radiance or splendor (Anne)
Aisling: dreamer (Ashling)
Aoife: beautiful, pleasant (Eva)
Bríd: High One (Bridget)
Deírdru: sorrowful (Deirdre)
Étaín: jealousy (Edwina)
Gráinne: she who strikes fear (Grace)
Medb: she who intoxicates (Maeve)
Niamh: brightness (Neeve)
Sorcha: radiance (Sara)

Boys
Aodhán: fire (Aidan)
Aonghas: young god (Angus)
Cathal: strong in battle (Charles)
Coilín: whelp, young pup (Colin)
Eoghan: yew-born (Owen)
Fionnbhar: fair-haired (Finbar)
Lughaidh: Lugh the god (Louis)
Muiris: sea-strength (Maurice)
Ruairi: red king (Rory)
Tadgh: poet (Todd)

Clothing and Shoe Sizes

Clothing and shoe sizes may initially seem a bit confusing. My advice is try before you buy. U.S. women's-wear sizes are smaller than Irish/UK sizes so don't buy straight from the rack. Both men's and women's shoes are often imported from Germany and Italy and usually sized in European numbers.

Women's Clothing

American	8	10	12	14	16	18	20
Irish/UK	10	12	14	16	18	20	22
European	36	38	40	42	44	46	48

Men's Suits and Jackets

American	34	36	38	40	42	44	46
Irish/UK	34	36	38	40	42	44	46
European	44	46	48	50	52	54	56

Shirt Collar Sizes

American	14	14.5	15	15.5	16	16.5	17
Irish/UK	14	14.5	15	15.5	16	16.6	17
European	36	37	38	39	40	41	42

Women's Shoes

American	6	6.5	7	7.5	8	8.5	9
Irish/UK	4.5	5	5.5	6	6.5	7	7.5
European	36	37	38	38	38	39	40

Men's Shoes

American	6.5	7.5	8.5	9.5	10.5	11.5	12.5
Irish/UK	6	7	8	9	10	11	12
European	40	41	42	43	44	45	46

Useful Web Sites

www.hookemacdonald.ie

If you're looking for a house or apartment to rent in the Dublin area, check out Hooke & MacDonald's "Let on the Net" site. When I looked these realtors had a good range of available properties including a furnished one-bedroom apartment in the Rathmines area for IR £550 per month.

www.wow.ie

WOW means What's on Where. If you want nationwide listings for films, music, theater and gallery openings throughout Ireland, this site should fit the bill.

www.jesuit.ie

Need some spiritual guidance? Although not everyone will want to pray in front of a computer screen, Ireland's Jesuit priests are now online. Their Web site includes a "Sacred Space" with a daily prayer.

www.nationalarchives.ie

Ireland's National Archives now has a searchable database. It includes the Ireland—Australia transportation index, complete with names, trial dates, and crime descriptions. I discovered numerous Harvey namesakes who made the journey down under on convict ships. In 1838 an unfortunate 22-year-old named Thomas Harvey from Louth was sentenced to seven years transportation for stealing a plate.

www.rte.ie

Up to date Irish news, radio programs plus daily TV and radio listings from RTE, the state-owned broadcaster.

http://foxleap.fortunecity.com/irishlyrics

Who will plow the fields all day and who will thresh the corn? That's the first line of "The Bantry Girl's Lament." Or maybe you want to know the words to "The Wild Colonial Boy"? You'll find the lyrics to more than 100 traditional Irish folk songs on the Web.

www.iha.ie

Irish racehorses—an investment or a gamble? Run by the Irish Horseracing Authority, this is an informative site for those who want to buy a thoroughbred or simply check out the fixture list calendar for race meetings.

www.golfclubireland.com

Golf enthusiasts will want to experience the rub of the Irish green. This site includes pars for various Irish golf courses, green fees, club memberships and much more besides.

www.ostlan.com

Go to Ostlan for a guide to pubs and restaurants. The site includes a review section—you can write your own review or see what previous happy (and disgruntled) diners have said about Irish establishments.

www.millennium-ireland.com

Ireland knows how to throw a party and many of the country's famous festivals are promised to be extra special during the millennium year. To whet your appetite, check out this Web site devoted to all things Y2K.

Realtor Information

Here is contact information to select realtors for various counties in Ireland.

County Cavan

Foley & Harrison, Main St., Virginia, Co. Cavan; tel. +353 (0)49 47249
Robert Clarke, Holborn Hill, Belturbet, Co. Cavan; tel. +353 (0)49 22294
O'Reilly, Taylor & Tweedy, Main St., Cavan town, Co. Cavan; tel +353 (0)49 31599

County Clare

Philip O'Reilly, 22/24 Abbey St, Ennis, Co. Clare; tel. +353 (0)65 29325
Costelloes, 5 Abbey St, Ennis, Co. Clare; tel. +353 (0)65 21299
McMahons, O'Connell Square, Ennis, Co. Clare; tel. +353 (0)65 28307
John Vaughan, Parliament St., Ennistymon, Co. Clare; tel. +353 (0) 65 71477
Harry Brann, Killaloe, Co. Clare; tel. +353 (0)61 376380
Pat Mulcahy, Killaloe, Co. Clare; tel. +353 (0)61 376176

County Cork

John Kerr, 17/18 Ashe St, Clonakilty, Co. Cork; tel. +353 (0)23 34944
Matt O'Sullivan, Emmet Square, Clonakilty, Co. Cork; tel. +353 (0)23 33367
Sheehy Bros., 10 Short Quay, Kinsale, Co. Cork; tel. +353 (0)21 772338
Key Properties, Bantry, Co. Cork; tel. +353 (0)27 50111

Hamilton Osborne King, 11 South Mall, Cork City, Co. Cork; tel. +353 (0)21 271371

Irish & European Property, 23 South Mall, Cork City, Co. Cork; tel. +353 (0)21 277606

County Donegal

Rainey Estate Agents, Market Square, Letterkenny, Co. Donegal; tel +353 (0)74 22211

Paul Reynolds & Co., 10 Lr. Main St., Letterkenny, Co. Donegal; tel. +353 (0)74 22399

Anderson Auctioneers, Main St., Donegal Town, Co. Donegal; tel. +353 (0)73 22888

Porter Properties, 12 Main St. Lr., Buncrana, Co. Donegal; tel. +353 (0)77 61083

Sean Meehan, Main St., Bundoran, Co. Donegal; tel. +353 (0)72 41351

McElhinney & Son, Main St., Bundoran, Co. Donegal; tel. +353 (0)72 41261

County Galway

Heaslips, 27 Wood Quay, Galway; tel. +353 (0)91 565261

Smith & Co, Newtownsmith, Galway; tel. +353 (0)91 567331

Keane Mahony Smith, 37 Prospect Hill, Galway; tel. +353 (0)91 563744

Matt O'Sullivan, The Square, Clifden, Co. Galway; tel. +353 (0)95 21066. Also with offices at Main St., Oughterard, Co. Galway; tel. +353 (0)91 552503

Paddy Keane & Co., Main St., Ballinasloe, Co. Galway; tel. +353 (0)905 42339

County Kerry

Daniel Hannon, 6 Main St., Listowel, Co. Kerry; tel. +353 (0)68 21577

Pierse & Fitzgibbon, Property Ireland, 25 Market St., Listowel, Co. Kerry; tel. +353 (0)68 23277

Sean Daly, 34 Henry St., Kenmare, Co. Kerry; tel. +353(0)64 41213

Sean Coyne, 2 Main St., Killarney, Co. Kerry; tel. +353 (0)64 31274

European Auctioneers, 17 The Mall, Tralee, Co. Kerry; tel. +353 (0)66 23144

Wm. Giles, 23 Denny St., Tralee, Co. Kerry, tel +353 (0)66 21073

James North, 33 Denny St., Tralee, Co. Kerry, tel +353 (0)66 22699

John Moore, Green St., Dingle, Co. Kerry; tel. +353 (0)66 51588

County Kilkenny

J. David Hughes, 20 Parliament St., Kilkenny; tel. +353 (0)56 63437 and

Main St., Graiguenamanagh; tel. +353 (0)503 24437
Fitzgeralds, 24 Patrick St., Kilkenny; tel.+353 (0)56 70888
M.F. Grace, Callan, Co. Kilkenny; tel. +353 (0)56 25163
Walter Walsh, Mill St, Thomastown, Co. Kilkenny; tel. +353 (0)56 24485
Ganly Walters Boyd, 5 William St., Kilkenny; tel. +353 (0)56 64833 and
Lowe St., Thomastown; tel. +353 (0)56 24600.

County Leitrim
Wm. Farrell, Main St., Carrick-on-Shannon, Co. Leitrim; tel. +353 (0)78
20976

County Mayo
Martin Finn, Dalton St., Claremorris, Co. Mayo; tel. +353 (0)94 62216
Brendan Tuohy, North Mall, Westport, Co. Mayo; tel. +353 (0)98 28000
Vincent O'Malley, Kilbree, Westport, Co. Mayo; tel. +353 (0)98 35109
Philip McComiskey, Church Rd., Ballina, Co. Mayo; tel. +353 (0)96
22433
Collins Estate Agents, Castle St., Castlebar, Co. Mayo; tel. +353 (0)94
22701

County Roscommon
James Cleary, Main St., Castlerea, Co. Roscommon; tel. +353 (0)907
20011
Vincent Egan, Elphin St., Boyle, Co. Roscommon; tel. +353 (0)79 62464

County Sligo
Schiller & Schiller, Ardtarmon Castle, Ballinfull, Co. Sligo; tel. +353 (0)71
63284
Des Butler, Quay St, Sligo; tel. +353 (0)71 45923
IPM Estates, Stephen St., Sligo; tel. +353 (0)71 43710
Matt Mulholland, Markievicz Rd., Sligo; tel. +353 (0)71 42845
McCarrick & Sons, Tubbercurry, Co. Sligo; tel. +353 (0)71 85050

County Tipperary
John Lee & Son, Main St., Newport, Co. Tipperary; tel. +353 (0)61
378121
William Talbot, 52 Keynon St., Nenagh, Co. Tipperary; tel. +353 (0)67
31496
Shee & Hawe, 62 Main St., Carrick-on-Suir, Co. Tipperary; tel. +353
(0)51 640041
Barry Walsh Estates, 91 Main St., Carrick-on-Suir, Co. Tipperary; tel.
+353 (0)51 640528

Tom Pollard & Co., Emmet St., Clonmel, Co. Tipperary; tel. +353 (0)52 22755

County Waterford

O'Shea & O'Toole, 11 Gladstone St., Waterford City, Co. Waterford; tel. +353 (0)51 876757

Lawrence McDonald, 15 Parnell St., Waterford City, Co. Waterford; tel. +353 (0)51 853199

Phil Cusack, Main St., Kilmacthomas, Co. Waterford; tel. +353 (0)51 294364

Edmund Spratt & Son, Grattan house, Dungarvan, Co. Waterford; tel. +353 (0)58 42211

County Wexford

Corish's, Custom House Quay, Wexford town, Co. Wexford; tel. +353 (0)53 22288

Kehoe & Associates, Commercial Quay, Wexford town, Co. Wexford; tel. +353 (0)53 44393

Michael O'Leary, The Bullring, Wexford town, Co. Wexford; tel. +353 (0)53 24611. Also with an office at Slaney Pl., Enniscorthy, Co. Wexford; tel. +353 (0)54 35061

Simon Kavanagh, Templeshannon, Enniscorthy, Co. Wexford; tel. +353 (0)54 35335

Warren Estates, Main St., Gorey, Co. Wexford; tel. +353 (0)55 21211

Haythornewaite Auctioneers, Selskar, Co. Wexford; tel. +353 (0)53 46046

Index

Map Index

Cater to Your Interests on Your Next Vacation

**The 100 Best Small Art Towns in America
3rd edition**
Discover Creative Communities, Fresh Air, and
Affordable Living
U.S. $16.95, Canada $24.95

**The Big Book of Adventure Travel
2nd edition**
Profiles more than 400 great escapes to all corners
of the world
U.S. $17.95, Canada $25.50

Cross-Country Ski Vacations
A Guide to the Best Resorts, Lodges, and Groomed
Trails in North America
U.S. $15.95, Canada $22.50

Gene Kilgore's Ranch Vacations, 5th edition
The Complete Guide to Guest Resorts, Fly-Fishing,
and Cross-Country Skiing Ranches
U.S. $22.95, Canada $35.50

Indian America, 4th edition
A traveler's companion to more than 300 Indian
tribes in the United States
U.S. $18.95, Canada $26.75

Saddle Up!
A Guide to Planning the Perfect Horseback
Vacation
U.S. $14.95, Canada $20.95

Watch It Made in the U.S.A., 2nd edition
A Visitor's Guide to the Companies That Make Your
Favorite Products
U.S. $17.95, Canada $25.50

The World Awaits
A Comprehensive Guide to Extended Backpack
Travel
U.S. $16.95, Canada $23.95

**JMP travel guides are available
at your favorite bookstores.
For a FREE catalog or to place a
mail order, call: 800-888-7504.**

John Muir Publications ◆ P.O. Box 613 ◆ Santa Fe, NM 87504

About the Author

Steenie Harvey lives in county Roscommon in the west of Ireland. Born in the United Kingdom of Latvian and English parents, she moved to Ireland in 1988 with her Scottish husband Michael and their daughter Magdalen. After renting a house for a year, Steenie and her family decided to buy their own Irish property—a hilltop cottage overlooking the magical waters of Lough Key.

A freelance writer, Steenie writes about travel, folklore, and real estate for publications both at home and abroad. Her U.S. magazine credits include *The World of Hibernia*, *The World & I*, and *International Living*; she was *IL*'s "Travel Writer of the Year" in 1997. Recent travels have taken her to the Greek islands, the jungles of Malaysian Borneo, and eastern Germany.

Along with delving into Ireland's Celtic heritage, Steenie also enjoys opera, organic gardening, and countryside hikes. *Live Well in Ireland* is her first book.